Praise for *A Leadership Guide for Today's Disabi*
Overcoming Challenges and Making Cha

M000096656

"A comprehensive and detailed how-to guide for positive organizational change...designed to bridge the considerable gap between exhortations to adopt evidence-based practice and the processes and procedures of actually implementing this approach."

—**Roger J. Stancliffe, Ph.D., FIASDID, FAAIDD**
Professor of Intellectual Disability, Faculty of Health Sciences, The University of Sydney

"A timely and important resource to inform and enable organization leaders to support people with intellectual and developmental disabilities in ways that are consistent with changing paradigms of disability and support systems."

—**Michael L. Wehmeyer Ph.D.**
Professor, Department of Special Education; Director, Kansas University Center on Developmental Disabilities; Senior Scientist, Beach Center on Disability, University of Kansas

"Challenging, thoughtful, practical, and readable....This book should be read and then practiced by everyone seeking to improve organization and policies in the field of intellectual and developmental disabilities."

—**Roy I. Brown Ph.D., Dip Psych, FIASSID**
Emeritus Professor, University of Calgary, Canada, and Flinders University, Australia

"An important step forward in dealing with the complex matter of quality....The very modern and practical ideas of system, synthesis, and alignment assures us that we can manage the complex matter of quality in a simple way. You can't do without [this book]."

—**Patty van Belle-Kusse, MSc,**
Raad van Bestuur, Stichting Arduin, CEO (the Netherlands)

"Long awaited...serves as both a testimony and guidebook to the continuing vital role of disability organizations and the need to ensure their continued growth and sustainability as values-based, high-impact entities navigated by professionally groomed and motivated leaders."

—**Rick Rader, M.D., FAAIDD**
Director, Morton J. Kent Habilitation Center, Orange Grove Center, Chattanooga, Tennessee

"The premier text for the design and implementation of highly effective change strategies. This is must reading for all leadership personnel in community service and rehabilitation programs."

—**Paul Wehman, Ph.D.**
Professor, Physical Medicine and Rehabilitation, Virginia Commonwealth University

"The authors have clearly outlined practical strategies that will assist support organizations to respond effectively to the imperatives of person-centered planning and the delivery of individualized supports in a time of severe economic restraints."

—**Trevor R. Parmenter, Ph.D.**
Professor Emeritus, The University of Sydney

A Leadership Guide for Today's Disabilities Organizations

A Leadership Guide for Today's Disabilities Organizations

Overcoming Challenges and Making Change Happen

by

Robert L. Schalock, Ph.D.
Hastings College, Nebraska

and

Miguel Ángel Verdugo Alonso, Ph.D.
University of Salamanca, Spain

with invited contributors

·PAUL·H·
BROOKES
PUBLISHING CO. ®

Baltimore • London • Sydney

Paul H. Brookes Publishing Co., Inc.
Post Office Box 10624
Baltimore, Maryland 21285-0624
USA

www.brookespublishing.com

Typeset by BLPS Content Connections, Chilton, Wisconsin.
Manufactured in the United States of America by
Sheridan Books, Inc., Chelsea, Michigan.

Library of Congress Cataloging-in-Publication Data

Schalock, Robert L.
A leadership guide for today's disabilities organizations : overcoming challenges and making change happen /
by Robert L. Schalock and Miguel Ángel Verdugo Alonso ; with invited contributors.
      p.   cm.
Includes bibliographical references and index.
    ISBN 978-1-59857-181-3 (perfect)
    ISBN 1-59857-181-8 (perfect)
    1. People with disabilities—Services for—United States.   2. People with disabilities—Rehabilitation—United States.   3. Developmentally disabled—United States.   I. Verdugo, Miguel Ángel. II. Title.

HV1553.S25 2012
362.4068'4—dc23   2012000285

British Library Cataloguing in Publication data are available from the British Library.

2016   2015   2014   2013   2012

10   9   8   7   6   5   4   3   2   1

Contents

About the Authors

Robert L. Schalock, Ph.D., is Professor Emeritus at Hastings College in Nebraska and Adjunct Research Professor at the University of Kansas (Beach Center on Disabilities), University of Salamanca in Spain, Ghent University in Belgium, and Chongqing University in China. His national and international work has focused on the conceptualization, measurement, and application of the concept of quality of life and the supports paradigm. He has worked with organizations, systems, and national governments in the development and evaluation of community-based programs for people with intellectual and closely related developmental disabilities. He has published widely in the areas of program development and evaluation, quality of life, systems of supports, and evidence-based practices. (rschalock@ultraplix.com)

Miguel Ángel Verdugo Alonso, Ph.D., is Professor of Psychology of Disability and Director of the Institute on Community Integration (INICO) at the University of Salamanca in Spain, and Director of the Information Service on Disability of the Ministry of Health, Social Services, and Equality in Spain. He has been Director of the Master's in Integration of People with Disabilities: Quality-of-Life program and Director of the Master's in Integration of People with Disabilities: LatinoAmerican program at the University of Salamanca since 1990. He is also editor of the journal *Siglo Cero.* (verdugo@usal.es)

About the Contributors

Andrea S. Aznar, M.S., is coordinator, along with Dr. Diego Gonzalez Castanon, of ITINERIS Foundation. ITINERIS is an Argentinean organization that has provided training and research consultation in 10 countries throughout Latin America since 1999. Its two coordinators and a team of 12 collaborators (university professionals, family members, and self-advocates) have trained staff within 113 organizations on applying the concepts of quality of life, rights, self-determination, inclusion, and supports. (itineris@fibertel.com.ar)

Gordon Scott Bonham, Ph.D., is president of Bonham Research and has been the researcher for the Maryland Ask Me! Project since its beginning in 1997. He earned his Ph.D. in sociology from the University of Michigan and conducted research at the National Center for Health Statistics, University of Louisville, and Towson University prior to starting his applied human services research business. (gbonham@bonhamresearch.com)

Valerie J. Bradley, M.A., has been the president of Human Services Research Institute since it inception in 1976. She has directed numerous state and federal policy evaluations that have contributed to the expansion, enhancement, and responsiveness of services and supports to people with disabilities and their families. She is the principal investigator of a national technical assistance initiative in quality assurance and codirects a national 30-state initiative on performance measurement known as The National Core Indicators. Val is a recent past president of the President's Committee on Persons with Intellectual Disabilities and American Association on Intellectual and Developmental Disabilities. (vbradley@hsri.org)

Brian R. Bryant, Ph.D., is a researcher with the Meadows Center for Preventing Educational Risk, College of Education, University of Texas at Austin (UT-Austin). He also teaches courses in special education at UT-Austin and at Texas State University. His primary research interests are in mathematics and reading learning disabilities, support needs for individuals with intellectual and developmental disabilities, and assistive technology applications across the life span. (brianrbryant@aol.com)

John Butterworth, Ph.D., is a senior research fellow and Coordinator of Employment Systems Change and Evaluation at the Institute for Community Inclusion, University of Massachusetts in Boston. He directs projects on employment support, organization change, state systems change, and employment policy. (john.butterworth@umb.edu)

Claudia Claes, Ph.D., is a lecturer at the Faculty of Social Work and Welfare Studies of University College Ghent and a researcher at the department of orthopedagogics, Ghent University in Belgium. Her research interests include quality of life, person-centered planning, and individualized supports. (Claudia.claes@hogent.be)

Diego Gonzalez Castanon, M.D., is a medical practitioner in Buenos Aires and codirector of ITINERIS. ITINERIS is an Argentinean organization that has provided training and research consultation in 10 countries throughout Latin America since 1999. Its two coordinators and a team of 12 collaborators (university professionals, family members, and self-advocates) have

◇◇◇

trained staff within 113 organizations on applying the concepts of quality of life, rights, self-determination, inclusion, and supports. (itineris@fibertel.com.ar)

Txema Franco, M.B.A., has a law degree from the University of Deusto, a master's degree in human resources management from the Basque Country University, and an M.B.A. from Deusto Business School. He has been Managing Director at Lantegi Batuak since 2004. Lantegi Batuak serves more than 2,000 people with intellectual and developmental disabilities. (tf@lantegi.com)

Jim Gardner, Ph.D., has served as President and CEO of CQL/The Council on Quality and Leadership. He has worked as a unit director in a large public institution, an executive director of a regional education collaborative, a vice president of a university center on excellence in intellectual and developmental disabilities, and a director of an educational center at a private psychiatric health care system. He has served on numerous local and national nonprofit boards and advisory councils. He has also held faculty positions at John Hopkins University and the University of Maryland–College Park. (jfgardner@thecouncil.org)

Chun-Shin Lee, M.Div., is Chairman of the Taiwan Community Living Consortium and director of the Vocational Training Center for people with intellectual and developmental disabilities. He has worked with adults with disabilities for more than 30 years, especially in the development of a nationwide vocational training and placement system. His focus is on developing a model for community-based living for people with intellectual and developmental disabilities in Taiwan and bringing both the vocational and community living models to mainland China. (chunshin.lee@vtcidd.org)

Ruth Luckasson, J.D., is a Distinguished Professor of Special Education and Chair of the Department of Educational Specialties in the College of Education at the University of New Mexico. She is a past president of American Association on Intellectual and Developmental Disabilities and currently serves on The Arc-U.S. Legal Advisory and Human Rights Subcommittee. She previously served on the President's Committee on Mental Retardation (now PCPIDD) and as Chair of the American Bar Association's Commission on Mental and Physical Disability Law. (ruthl@unm.edu)

Sean McDermott, M.A., is currently the CEO of the Edmonton Region Community Board, Persons with Developmental Disabilities Program. He has worked for more than 30 years in human services, focusing on strategic planning and evaluation. (sean.mcdermott@gov.ab.ca)

Remco Mostert, B.A., is a member of the quality staff at Arduin (a community-based organization in the Netherlands) and a master trainer of the Personal Outcomes Scale. He interviews on a daily basis a large variety of clients about their quality of life. As chairman of the Arduin Support Team he is also responsible for the introduction and implementation of the Individual Support Plan. (rmostert@arduin.nl)

Lester Parker, M.B.A., has been the executive director of the Adirondack Arc since 1987. The Adirondack Arc, which is an award winning chapter of the New York State Chapter of The Arc (NYSARC), supports people with disabilities and their families in Franklin and Hamilton Counties in New York state. (arcmtnman@mac.com)

Joanna Pierson, Ph.D., has served as the executive director of the Arc of Frederick County, Maryland, since 1979. During that period she has helped the organization grow from one staff person to a statewide provider of service coordination for more than 10,000 people with intellectual and developmental disabilities. She has also seen the spin-off of that service to enable the Arc to provide employment and residential supports as a local provider agency. She is an adjunct associate professor at the University of Maryland School of Social Work and is a past president of American Association on Intellectual and Developmental Disabilities. (jpierson@arcfc.org)

Martha E. Snell, Ph.D., is a professor of education in the Curry School of Education at the University of Virginia, where she directs the graduate program in severe disabilities. Her research interests include positive behavior supports, inclusion in general education, teacher collaboration, and early communication. (snell@virginia.edu)

Kees Swart, B.A., has been an information technology employee at Arduin since 2000. He is closely involved in the computerization of individual support plans. He has expertise in developing web-based data systems and in data processing, analysis, and retrieval/reporting. (kswart@live.nl)

Javier Tamarit, M.A., is a psychologist and a consultant in organization development. He is also visiting lecturer at the University of Salamanca (INICO). Since 2001 he has been FEAPS quality manager and has been supporting people with autism and intellectual and developmental disabilities and their families for more than 30 years. (calidad@feaps.org)

Jos van Loon, Ph.D., works at Arduin, a service and supports provider in the Netherlands, as both a psychologist/manager and as a researcher in the process of deinstitutionalization. He has an appointment in the Department of Special Education at Ghent University and works collaboratively with the University and Arduin and conducts research on quality of life, inclusion, self-determination, and individualized supports. (jloon@arduin.nl)

Stijn Vandevelde, Ph.D., is a lecturer and researcher at the Faculty of Social Work and Welfare Studies of University College Ghent and a visiting professor at the Department of Orthopedagogics, Ghent University in Belgium. His research interests include quality of life, substance abuse in people with intellectual and developmental disabilities, and the relationship between forensic issues and intellectual disabilities. (Stijn.vandevelde@hogent.be)

Foreword

Across the United States, state and local service delivery systems for people with intellectual and developmental disabilities (ID/DD) are struggling to close the persistent gap between service demand and service availability. This chasm, reflected in the all-too-common phenomenon of multiyear waiting lists, existed before the current deep economic recession began. But, recession-induced federal and state budget cuts have exacerbated the situation and increased the urgency of employing new strategies.

For a number of years, it has been evident to astute observers of the ID/DD service sector that a linear expansion of existing services will not solve the chronic shortfall in service capacity. Instead, outdated service modalities need to be abandoned in favor of new, person-centered policies and practices. Early generations of community services were based on a set of premises that have proven to be invalid—namely that congregation and specialization are essential elements of any cost-effective approach to supporting people with lifelong disabilities. Yet, discredited program models—congregate living facilities, sheltered workshops, and day activity programs—remain prominent features of service delivery systems in many states. Clearly, one of the major challenges facing the disability field today is to institute a workable process of making the transition to a system of flexible, person-centered, cost-efficient home and community supports—and to do so in a way that respects the interests of all individuals with disabilities as well as other affected parties.

The authors of this book lay out a set of proven system change strategies which ID/DD organizations can use to illuminate the path toward a more effective, efficient, and sustainable service delivery process. The book begins with a brief review of factors that are forcing ID/DD organizations to alter their traditional approaches to organizing, financing, and delivering services, including dwindling resources, burgeoning service demand, and the shift toward individualized support, self-determination, evidence-based practices, and personal outcome measures. The authors offer eight change strategies that have been employed successfully by ID/DD organizations in transitioning to community support—in contrast to community service—agencies. The proposed change process begins with efforts to instill 21st century values throughout the organization and operate on the basis of such values. It emphasizes leadership as the irreplaceable catalyst of organizational change and the related importance of using technology wisely and empowering people with disabilities, their family members, and the organization's staff to become active participants in the change process.

Each subsequent chapter of the book deals, in depth, with one of the change strategies recommended by the authors. Easy-to-complete self-assessment tools are included to help readers evaluate the status of changes underway within their own organizations and pinpoint weaknesses which need to be addressed. The remaining sections of each chapter elaborate on the strategies to be used—whether the goal is to build high performing teams, introduce and use personal outcome measures, foster innovation, institute a performance-based management system, or overcome resistance to change. In addition to their own extensive experience in advising ID/DD organizations here and abroad, the authors draw upon the current management and organizational change literature; however, the book is written in straightforward, easy-to-understand language that avoids impenetrable academic jargon. Better yet, the book is replete with examples of ID/DD organizations that have successfully used the proposed eight strategies to institute and manage various components of the organizational change process. The authors have assembled 20 contributors who offer real life examples of how various system change strategies can be effectively employed.

Leading economists tell us that, unlike most economic downturns which have occurred since World War II, the current recession could last for several more years. Faced with spiraling health care costs, an aging population, a persistent level of structural unemployment, and a ballooning debt burden, public policy makers at all levels of government will be forced to make wrenching changes in social welfare programs over the next few years. Given its high level of dependence on public funding—especially funding through such major social entitlement programs as Medicaid, Social Security, and Supplemental Security—organizations serving people with intellectual and developmental disabilities will be placed in a particularly vulnerable position. Survival will depend on visionary leadership, agility, and a willingness to adapt. Readers of this book will be better positioned to navigate the shoals of the new, less forgiving social welfare environment if they are prepared to embrace the authors' recommended system change strategies.

Robert M. Gettings
Former Executive Director of the National Association
of State Directors of Developmental Disabilities Services

Preface

We have written this book to assist leaders and managers of organizations and systems serving individuals with intellectual and developmental disabilities (ID/DD) to successfully meet the challenges they currently face regarding dwindling resources in a time of increasing needs, work force shortages, service fragmentation, quality issues, structural changes, the emergence of public–private service provision entities, and expectations for increased transparency and accountability. As a leadership guide, we show how ID/DD organizations can devise and employ eight change strategies whose purpose is to enhance the organization's effectiveness in terms of personal outcomes and efficiency in terms of organization outputs. These eight change strategies relate to using 21st century thinking styles, measuring and using personal outcomes and organization outputs, developing high-performance teams, employing a systems of supports, using evidence-based practices, implementing a performance-based evaluation and management system, creating value through innovation, and overcoming resistance to change. In the process of employing these strategies, ID/DD organizations become increasingly more creative in how they deploy human, technical, and financial resources and thereby redefine themselves and become more sustainable.

The eight change strategies we present in the book are also responsive to the changing landscape of ID/DD service delivery organizations and systems. This landscape reflects the significant impact of four major paradigm shifts in the field: the quality-of-life concept, the ecological model of disability, a system of supports, and the reform movement. More specifically, over the last 30 years we have seen a significant movement from 1) public services for people with ID/DD that are easy to identify and describe to highly complex networks comprised of widely varying levels and types of providers, settings, and structures; 2) traditional standards and methods associated with compliance and documentation to a focus on assessing personal outcomes and organization outputs; 3) external monitoring and evaluation to internally based performance monitoring and quality improvement; 4) facility-based services to community-based individualized support systems; 5) a quality-of-care focus to a quality-of-life emphasis; and 6) government as a provider of services to government as a contractor, monitor, and standards setter for individualized services and supports.

Over the last 30+ years we have worked nationally and internationally with ID/DD organizations and systems that have adapted to this changing landscape. Our involvement with organizations has been multifaceted and has included consultation in the evaluation of support needs, program development, program evaluation, outcomes research, and continuous quality improvement. We have also worked with larger ID/DD systems in policy development, systems analysis, and systems change. We have used what we have learned from these experiences as well as current management and organization change literature to formulate the change strategies and our suggestions for implementing them. We have also reached out to a number of our colleagues who have applied these strategies in their organizations or research endeavors. Each of the real-life examples shared by the 20 contributors demonstrates that change can occur, especially when organizations create value through innovation, are led by individuals with vision, clarity, and conviction, involve personnel in the change process, and seek the wisdom of clients who play an active role in the redefining process.

Throughout the text, we have worked hard to communicate clearly and with a minimum of academic verbiage. We also recognize that change is hard, and because knowledge is cumulative we offer our best guidance about the benefits and potential pitfalls regarding the strategies we discuss. In addition, we have

- Approached issues from the perspective of being proactive, focusing on the future, and using best practices that emanate from current models of human functioning, individualized supports, and the concept of quality of life

- Explained the challenges of an inclusive society and the complexity and changes in current ID/DD programs and organizations as they address the need to be effective and efficient and use evidence-based practices

- Focused on inclusion, empowerment, the multidimensionality of human behavior, and outcomes evaluation as the basis for continuous quality improvement

As psychologists we have worked over the last 30 years with three types of leaders: those who make things happen, those who resist making things happen, and those who wonder what has happened. Similarly, we have worked with individuals who say, "Why now?...Let's wait"—an attitude that is consistent with St. Augustine's admonition, "Lord, let me be chaste...but not yet." It is our strong belief that ID/DD leaders currently need to make things happen and redefine how ID/DD organizations approach their clientele and structure the services and supports provided to them. Indeed, it is time to implement change strategies that enhance an organization's effectiveness, efficiency, and sustainability.

In the end, a leadership guide to today's disability organizations will be read only if the reader finds its contents relevant and the suggested change strategies realistic and attainable. This has been our intent throughout our endeavor. Our work has been assisted greatly by Ms. Rebecca Lazo, Senior Acquisitions Editor at Brookes Publishing, who throughout our 2-year effort provided invaluable insight, guidance, suggestions, and support. We are indebted to Rebecca and to Ms. Darlene Buschow, who provided much needed technical support and expertise. And finally, we are grateful to the following doctoral students who helped us in the literature searches: Laura E. Gómez, Patricia Navas, Alba Ibáñez, Ester Navallas, Verónica Guillén, Eva Vicente, and Juan A. Gonzalez.

To our valued colleagues who strive on a daily basis to improve people's lives.

May this book facilitate that process.

1

Understanding and Meeting the Challenges Faced by Intellectual Disability/ Developmental Disability Organizations

What You Can Expect in This Chapter

➤ A discussion of the 10 challenges currently faced by organizations that provide services and supports to people with intellectual and developmental disabilities and a way to evaluate your organization's status regarding these challenges

➤ An overview of eight change strategies that allow an organization to successfully meet these challenges

➤ A discussion of **change catalysts** that are required for organization change and redefinition: **values**, leadership, **empowerment**, and **technology**

➤ A listing of the characteristics of a redefined organization providing services and supports to people with intellectual and developmental disabilities

Organizations providing services and **supports** to people with **intellectual** and **developmental disabilities (ID/DD)** are currently facing in the second decade of the 21st century a number of challenges that impact their **effectiveness, efficiency,** and **sustainability.** As these organizations embrace the future, they must accept two facts. First, their standard practices are not working as well as many would like, and second, it is necessary to think seriously about how to redefine ID/DD organizations so that they can meet the ever-increasing need to more effectively produce enhanced **personal outcomes** and more efficiently generate **organization outputs** that reflect good returns on investment. Do not overlook the importance of meeting the challenges discussed in this chapter, and note how successfully addressing them can contribute to an organization's sustainability. Their impact is increasingly being seen in licensing requirements, accreditation standards, performance **monitoring**, and consumer expectations.

The purpose of this book is to describe how ID/DD organizations can successfully implement eight **change strategies** that will help them redefine themselves and, in the process, become more effective, efficient, and sustainable. This first chapter begins that call to action by describing the specific challenges faced nationally and internationally by ID/DD organizations, summarizing the key aspects of eight change strategies that address these challenges, discussing critical catalysts that bring change about, and listing the essential characteristics of a **redefined ID/DD organization.** The chapter concludes with a discussion of action steps that your organization can take now to meet today's challenges.

UNDERSTANDING THE CHALLENGES YOUR ORGANIZATION FACES

Think for a moment about your organization or state ID/DD system and the challenges you face on a daily basis. At a general level, these challenges involve dwindling resources with an increasing need for services and supports, structural changes from top-down hierarchies built along vertical lines of authority to organizations built along horizontal lines of action, and increased social and political expectations and requirements for ID/DD organizations and systems to demonstrate effective outcomes, ensure efficient **resource allocation**, and maintain **evidence-based practices.**

These challenges can be more successfully addressed by understanding the powerful forces that are driving them and the context or "landscape" within which they are occurring. Three powerful forces are driving the need for organization redefinition: economic, political, and professional. Economically, all levels of government are experiencing dwindling resources concurrent with an increased demand for services and supports. This condition is leading policymakers to reconsider how resources are allocated and increasing the emphasis on natural supports. Social-politically, there is an emphasis on the personal and social benefits derived from the involvement of people with **disabilities** in education or rehabilitation programs, combined with the expectation that ID/DD organizations be more effective and efficient. Professionally, there is a shift from general services to individualized supports, an emphasis on self-determination and self-direction, and an expressed need for evidence-based practices.

These three forces are operating within a changing landscape for ID/DD organizations. This landscape is characterized by a significant movement from

Easily identifiable and describable public services for people with ID/DD	→	Highly complex networks that comprise widely varying levels and types of providers, settings, and structures
Traditional standards and methods associated with compliance and documentation	→	A focus on assessing personal outcomes and organization outputs
External monitoring and **evaluation**	→	Internally based performance monitoring and quality improvement
Facility-based services	→	Community-based, individualized support systems
A quality of care focus	→	A **quality-of-life** emphasis
Government as a provider of services	→	Government as a contractor, monitor, and standards setter for individualized services and supports

Table 1.1. Significant challenges currently faced by organizations providing services and supports to people with intellectual and developmental disabilities

> Dwindling resources
> Increased demand for services and supports
> Movement from vertical to horizontal structure
> Shift from general services to individualized supports
> Emphasis on self-determination and self-direction
> Focus on personal outcomes
> Resource allocation based on assessed support needs
> Use of natural resources
> Emphasis on evidence-based practices
> Calls for increased effectiveness and efficiency

These three forces (economic, social-political, and professional) and the characteristics of the changing landscape of ID/DD organizations have coalesced into 10 significant challenges faced internationally by ID/DD organizations. These are listed in Table 1.1.

> ### Tool for Application
Organization Self-Assessment 1.1 (p. 14) allows you to evaluate your current status on the 10 challenges listed in Table 1.1. The challenges listed in the self-assessment should be well known to all readers; if not, specific examples of each can be found in Chapters 4 (horizontal versus vertical structure), 5 (supports), and 6 (evidence-based practices). The glossary contains definitions of *effectiveness* and *efficiency*.

So, how did your organization do on the self-assessment? If you have lots of 1s, reading this chapter (and book) is essential. If your have mainly 2s and 3s, the eight change strategies described in Chapters 2–9 will be most beneficial. If you have mainly 4s, use the material found in the book to further your work and cross-validate what you have done. If your total score exceeds 35, you should share your work with others. Our experience as we have worked with ID/DD organizations and systems nationally and internationally during the late 20th century and early 21st century is that the ratings of most organizations and systems will range from 2 to 3 on each of the challenges.

The issue before the ID/DD field generally—and your organization specifically—is whether to continue providing services and supports as we have done in the past or whether we should, instead, successfully overcome these challenges through **redefining** how organizations do business and implementing those eight change strategies that form the basis of this book. Our premise in writing this book is that organizations and systems have the potential to grow and develop over time (i.e., change) and thus increase their effectiveness and efficiency. Frequently, all they need is a good road map to do so. The change strategies introduced next can provide that road map. Throughout the book, our road map is clarified and enhanced through the inclusion of real-life case studies, examples, checklists, exercises, and tools. These are provided by both the authors and a group of 20 national and international collaborators.

MEETING THE CHALLENGES: EIGHT CHANGE STRATEGIES

The eight suggested change strategies presented in this book did not just happen. Rather, they have emerged from three major sources. The first source is our 30+ years of national and international work with ID/DD organizations that, to various degrees, have successfully implemented one or more of the proposed change strategies. Second, the strategies represent **best practices** in both public and private businesses that are increasingly focused

on personal outcomes and organization outputs. Third, the strategies have empirical support regarding their ability to enhance an organization or system's effectiveness and efficiency. The distinction between personal outcomes and organization outputs is important.

- Personal outcomes such as increased self-determination and self-help skills are
  the benefits derived by program recipients that are the result, directly or indirectly, of program activities, services, and supports.

- Organization outputs are the organization-referenced products that result from the
  resources a program uses to achieve its goals and from the actions implemented by
  an organization to produce these outputs. Examples include aggregated personal
  outcomes, effort and efficiency indicators, program options, and network indicators.

Figure 1.1 presents a schematic of the eight change strategies discussed in Chapters 2–9.
To help prepare you for Organization Self-Assessment 1.2 (p. 15), critical aspects of each
strategy are described in Table 1.2 (p. 5).

➤ Tool for Application

By studying Table 1.2, you will have a better understanding of the focus of each of the
eight change strategies proposed in this book. Consider how familiar personnel within your
organization are with them, and the degree to which each of the eight strategies is implemented. Completing Organization Self-Assessment 1.2 will provide that information. The
eight change strategies are listed in the left column of the self-assessment.

   Your familiarity and use profiles from the above assessment can be used for multiple
purposes. First, they reflect how much you have already thought about these or similar organization change strategies. The profile and total score indicate a baseline that can be used for
your strategic planning activities, and the desired scores can be used to establish **benchmarks**
against which you can evaluate progress. The profiles will suggest resources you will need
to either develop or reallocate, and thereby clearly identify, your technical assistance needs.

Figure 1.1.   Change strategies involved in redefining organizations that provide services and supports to people with intellectual and developmental disabilities.

Table 1.2. The focus and description of successful change strategies

Focus of strategy	Brief description
Thinking styles (Chapter 2)	Systems thinking: 1) multiple systems (macro, micro, meso) that affect human behavior, and 2) organizations that describe their input, throughput, and output dimensions
	Synthesis: integrating information from multiple sources
	Alignment: placing or bringing into line critical organization functions
Personal outcomes and organization outputs (Chapter 3)	Personal outcomes that include behavior change indicators, symptom reduction indicators, and **quality-of-life indicators**
	Organization outputs include number of people served; unit costs; and number of people placed into more independent, productive, and community-integrated environments
High-performance teams (Chapter 4)	Characteristics include teamwork, synergy, raising the performance bar, focusing on "us" accountability, and promoting a learning culture
A **system of supports** (Chapter 5)	A standardized assessment of the pattern and intensity of support needs and the implementation of individualized support strategies
Evidence-based practices (Chapter 6)	Practices that are based on current best evidence and used as a basis for clinical, managerial, and policy decisions
Performance-based evaluation and management system (Chapter 7)	The availability and analysis of client- and organization-referenced data sets that can be used for **reporting**, monitoring, evaluation, and quality improvement
Creating value through innovation (Chapter 8)	Increasing an organization/system's sustainability through social capital, networking, **consortia**, knowledge production, horizontal and vertical alignment, and values-based business
Overcoming resistance to change (Chapter 9)	Strategies include pacing change, recognizing that people need a vision of the future, showing the benefits of change, and empowering line staff and consumers to effect change

Finally, your profiles will identify the chapters of this book that will be most useful in successfully implementing each change strategy.

CATALYSTS THAT BRING ABOUT CHANGE AND REDEFINITION

A catalyst is something that brings about change but is not used up in the process. Throughout each chapter, we incorporate principles from four major change catalysts: values, leadership, empowerment, and technology. Redefining ID/DD organizations through the eight proposed change strategies will not occur without these catalysts. Although we discuss them here to underscore their importance and role in understanding and meeting today's challenges, their impact on redefining ID/DD organizations will be evident in the material and examples found in each of the subsequent chapters. For ease of reading, key aspects of each catalyst are summarized in Table 1.3 (p. 6).

Values

Values are critical in organization change because they provide the framework for best practices. The values we express throughout the book are those reflected at the individual, professional, and organization levels. At the individual level, the values of dignity, equality, empowerment, self-determination, nondiscrimination, and inclusion provide the framework and criteria for best practices. At the professional level, ethical best practices are characterized by focusing on justice (treating all people equally), beneficence (doing good), and autonomy (respecting the authority of every person to control actions that primarily affect himself or herself). At the organization level, redefined organizations are based on the values of respect,

Table 1.3. Key aspects of the four change catalysts

Catalyst	Key aspects
Values	Values are the properties of an entity or phenomenon that are desirable, important, and of worth.
	Important values in the intellectual and developmental disabilities field include dignity, equality, empowerment, self-determination, nondiscrimination, and inclusion.
	Values provide the framework for best practices at the professional and organization levels.
Leadership	Leadership is about change.
	Essential leadership roles are mentoring and directing, coaching and instructing, inspiring and empowering, and collaborating and partnering.
Empowerment	Empowerment entails supporting and enabling people to gain a sense of competence, relatedness, and autonomy.
	Empowerment leads to more positive self-concept, increased motivation, and heightened reliance on personal resource base.
Technology	Technology includes instruments or strategies used to enhance personal outcomes and organization outputs.
	With regard to personal outcomes, information technology, assistive technology, and individualized support strategies are used to reduce the discrepancy between a person's capability and the demands of his or her environment.
	With regard to organization outputs, information technology is used to collect, upload, analyze, download, and summarize personal outcome and organization output data.

dedication, honesty, innovativeness, teamwork, excellence, **accountability,** empowerment, quality, efficiency, and dignity. Although these values differ, they are also interconnected as reflected in

- The incorporation of current social-ecological models of **human functioning** and disability

- The emphasis on human potential, social inclusion, empowerment, equity, and self-determination

- The use of a system of supports to enhance personal outcomes

- The evaluation of the impact of interventions, services, and supports on personal outcomes and using that information for multiple purposes including reporting, monitoring, evaluation, and **continuous quality improvement**

Values also form the basis of **mental models:** the deeply ingrained assumptions, generalizations, and images for understanding the world. Mental models form the vision and culture of an organization. As discussed by Senge (2006), it is necessary to identify and understand these mental models, discuss their impact on individuals and organizations, and recognize that they frequently represent the limiting factor to organization change and thus, by inference, affect the successful redefinition of ID/DD organizations.

Organization change efforts frequently fail because, regardless of the intervention(s) tried, leaders and managers have failed to change the deeply ingrained assumptions, generalizations, and images that help organization personnel understand the world and experience (or visualize) the future. Mental models relate to what we think about both the clientele of ID/DD organizations and the organizations themselves. Some mental models facilitate change; others inhibit it. In general, the historically based mental models in Table 1.4 (p. 7) inhibit or prevent change, whereas those referred to in the table as "future oriented" facilitate change and support successful organization transformation and redefinition.

Table 1.4. Historically based and future-oriented mental models

Historically based	Future oriented
Disablement based on defectology	Social-ecological model of disability
Emphasis on segregation	Emphasis on social/community inclusion
Emphasis on control and power	Emphasis on self-empowerment
Organizations as mechanistic entities	Organizations as self-evaluating and improving systems
Vertically structured organizations	Horizontally structured organizations
Focus on process	Focus on outcomes
Change cannot happen	Change can happen
Leadership accountability	"Us" accountability
Success is leadership dependent	Success is dependent on everyone
Outcomes can't be measured	Outcomes can be measured

➤ Tool for Application

To better understand your organization's mental models, complete Organization Self-Assessment 1.3 (p. 16). The format is slightly different from the two previous assessments in that you need to rate your organization in reference to each of the mental models listed in Table 1.4 from *very characteristic* to *not characteristic at all*.

Your profile is very important for a number of reasons. First, it defines in part your organization's culture and how personnel within your organization approach a number of key issues related to the provision of services and supports to people with ID/DD. Second, it reflects greatly how your organization is organized and the respective roles that leaders and staff play in decision making within the organization. Third, it reflects your attitudes about processes versus outcomes and change versus no change. Hence, the profile is very informative regarding your organization's ideas about how best to implement the eight change strategies discussed in subsequent chapters. For example, if your profile has more checks toward the left than the right, you might want to focus first on Chapter 2 ("Expanding Thinking to Include Systems, Synthesis, and Alignment") and Chapter 9 ("Overcoming Resistance to Change"). The profile also reflects your organization's leadership—the second of our four catalysts. As we stress throughout the book, the first task of leadership is to change the mind-sets of organization personnel and stakeholders. As we discuss in the following section, the role performed by your organization's leadership is a major determinant of your organization's culture.

Leadership

Our approach to leadership distinguishes between management and leadership. As discussed by Kotter (1996), management is a set of processes that keep a complicated system of people and technology running smoothly. Management involves planning, budgeting, organizing, staffing, controlling, and problem solving. In distinction, leadership is about change. Leadership involves inspiring people and organizations to change, *to want to change*. Essential and sustained organization change and transformation is based on a collective effort. Thus, leadership should be participative and include personnel at all levels of the organization including the CEO, managers, and team members—including direct support staff. In addition, the first task of leadership is to change mind-sets on those mental models summarized in Table 1.4. Leadership also requires determination because a history of perseverance is frequently the best predictor of success.

Leadership Roles The management literature (see Print Resources, p. 13 and Guttman, 2008) discusses a few key roles that leaders play in any organization: mentoring and

Table 1.5.   Leadership roles and exemplary activities

Leadership role	Exemplary activities
Mentoring and directing	Presenting new ideas, information, and translation tools
Coaching and instructing	Introducing and explaining concepts, strategies, and specific skills
Inspiring and empowering	Providing a vision, clear communication, motivation, and delegation of tasks and authority
Collaborating and partnering	Instituting trust, respect, and a joint problem-solving mind-set

directing, coaching and instructing, inspiring and empowering, and collaborating and partnering. Exemplary activities involved in each of these roles are summarized in Table 1.5.

Leadership Functions   In addition to the four leadership roles summarized in Table 1.5, it has been our experience that good leaders perform critical **leadership functions** related to communicating a shared vision that answers the question, "What do we want to create?" Other critical leadership functions include encouraging and supporting the power of personal mastery so that people can grow and develop insight and skills, stressing a systems perspective that focuses on the major factors influencing a person's behavior, promoting a community life context for enhancing a person's life of quality of life and emphasizing the essential role of organizations as bridges to the community, monitoring personal outcomes and organization outputs and ensuring the transfer of knowledge throughout the entire organization to examine and understand ways that the organization can achieve enhanced personal outcomes and more efficient organization outputs, and promoting and monitoring the transformation/redefinition process.

➤ Tool for Application

Change and redefinition do not occur without effective leadership. Nor do they occur without an organization culture that supports inquiry, **innovation,** and risk taking. Because leadership is essential to all these endeavors, complete an organization self-assessment regarding your own leadership style. In the left column of Organization Self-Assessment 1.4 (p. 17), you will find the leadership roles and leadership functions listed above. The task is to evaluate your organization's leadership style.

A higher score indicates a more effective leadership style. As with the other organization self-assessments, information regarding your organization's leadership style can be used for multiple purposes. At the descriptive level, it provides a snapshot of where you are and, it is hoped, your goals for developing leadership roles and functions to bring about change and redefinition. In that regard, your organization's profile provides a teaching template. Effective leadership is based on being a good teacher who has a clear vision of where he or she wants to go, sets high goals, involves all stakeholders, maintains a clear focus, reinforces growth and development, and perseveres.

At the prescriptive level, your organization's leadership profile provides the second component of your organization's culture (the first being your organization's mental models profile—Organization Self-Assessment 1.3). One can define operationally—and thus describe—an organization's culture on the basis of mental models and leadership roles and functions. Although the management and ID/DD literature contain many definitions and descriptions of an organization's culture, our experiences suggest that a very simple operational definition of an organization's culture can be based on the mental models reflected in the organization's policies and practices and its leadership roles and functions.

Empowerment

All people—including service recipients and the staff of ID/DD organizations—want to feel important and be involved in planning and doing. Hence, empowering service recipients and organization personnel is a key change catalyst. Although the concepts of self-determination and empowerment are popular today in reference to an organization's clientele, they are equally important to organization personnel. According to self-determination theory, human systems function optimally when three basic psychological needs are met (Deci & Ryan, 2002):

- Sense of competence: The self-perception of being engaged in optimal challenges and experiencing the ability to effectively affect both physical and social worlds

- Sense of relatedness: The perception that one is both loving and caring for others while being loved by and cared for by others in the social system

- Sense of autonomy: The perception of having organized one's own experience and behavior; this self-organized activity maintains an integrated sense of self while serving to enhance the satisfaction of the other two needs

When these three psychological needs are met, people feel empowered. A sense of empowerment greatly influences the degree to which individuals want to be part of any activity. For example, personal outcomes associated with a sense of increasing empowerment are more predictive of longer–term well-being than outcomes associated with external motivations and threatened psychological need satisfaction. Similarly, causal relationships have been demonstrated between psychological need satisfaction and health care compliance, mental health, academic success, goal achievement, and prosocial activity (Deci & Ryan, 2002; Wasserman, 2010).

The relationship between empowerment and effective leadership should not be overlooked. At least 6 of the 10 leadership activities evaluated on Organization Self-Assessment 1.4 involve empowering all organization personnel to play significant roles in organization change and redefinition. This close relationship is also apparent in **high-performance teams** (see Chapter 4).

Technology

Technology is the fourth change catalyst that we incorporate into each chapter. Throughout the book, we approach the use of technology from two perspectives: to enhance personal outcomes and as a foundation for a **performance-based evaluation and management system.** From the personal enhancement perspective, we focus on using **assistive technology** in the provision of individualized supports (Chapter 5). Within that context, we view technology as making adaptations that allow people to do things by reducing the discrepancy between a person's capabilities and his or her environment's requirements. Thus, the reader is encouraged to view technology as a process and not just a device.

From a performance-based evaluation and management system perspective, we focus (especially in Chapters 3 and 7) on what information is required for reporting, monitoring, evaluating, and implementing continuous quality improvement. Thus, the reader is encouraged to view information technology in the broader context of assisting organization change and redefinition by facilitating evaluation and research efforts to collect, analyze, report, and use empirical data for multiple purposes including reporting, monitoring, evaluation, and continuous quality improvement.

CHARACTERISTICS OF REDEFINED INTELLECTUAL DISABILITY/DEVELOPMENTAL DISABILITY ORGANIZATIONS

For ID/DD organizations to be redefined, four things must occur. First, all organization person-nel must understand the challenges currently facing their organization. Second, these personnel and key stakeholders see that change is possible and that specific change strategies are avail-able to guide their efforts. Third, the catalysts for change (values, leadership, empowerment, and technology) are embedded in the change process. And, fourth, all stakeholders have a clear picture of what a redefined organization will look like. From our perspective and experiences, redefined ID/DD organizations are characterized as

- *Community based*—in reference to community living alternatives, integrated employment opportunities, inclusive education settings, and use of generic services and supports

- *Horizontally structured*—decision making shared among organization personnel, and the organization integrates high-performance teams

- *Support coordinators*—procuring or providing individualized supports based on the assessment of the profile and intensity of the person's needed supports and the implementation of a system of supports

- *Evidence-based practitioners*—using current best evidence obtained from credible sources to enhance clinical, managerial, and **policy decisions**

- *Knowledge producers*—creating value and knowledge through **systems thinking,** creativity, and a **learning culture** that synthesizes tacit and explicit information

- *Quality improvement oriented*—using performance-based information, **tacit knowledge,** and **explicit knowledge** to enhance an organization's effectiveness, efficiency, and sustainability

People do better and comprehend more when they "see the big picture." Figure 1.2 (p. 11) pro-vides such a view, showing how change strategies and change catalysts form the framework for a redefined ID/DD organization. The six characteristics of redefined ID/DD organizations just listed are embedded in material presented throughout the text and described more fully in Chapter 10.

▶ ACTION STEPS YOU CAN TAKE NOW

We anticipate that the primary readership of this book will be people who work at various levels of ID/DD organizations and regional or state systems, such as ID/DD state agencies including those referred to as policy makers, CEOs, division heads, managers, and members of high-performance teams (see Chapter 4). Our basic premise is that all of these people need to be involved in decision making and implementing the change strategies described in the following chapters. The book is intended to be a "leadership guide" that provides the rationale, methods, and real-life examples of how ID/DD organizations can use these strat-egies to redefine themselves. The term *redefining* reflects both the process and the outcomes of the strategies. As a process, the strategies require organizations to think differently about how they do business and the need to expand their thinking, focus on personal outcomes and organization outputs, develop high-performance teams, employ a system of person-

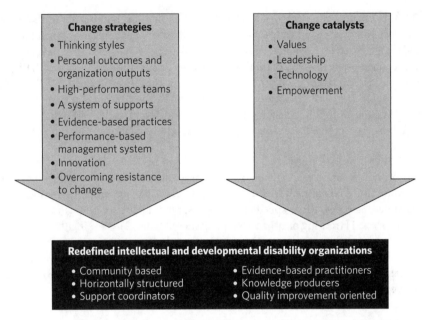

Figure 1.2. Change strategies, change catalysts, and characteristics of redefined organizations providing services and supports to people with intellectual and developmental disabilities. (*Key:* ID/DD, intellectual and developmental disability.)

centered supports, use evidence-based practices, implement a performance-based evaluation and management system, create value through innovation, and overcome resistance to change. By implementing these change strategies, organizations (and systems) will become more effective, efficient, and sustainable. To facilitate this process, at the end of each chapter we present a number of action steps that leadership can use for organization change and redefinition. Each proposed action step is based on information presented in the respective chapter as well as research-based knowledge and best practices. What follows is a description of four action steps you can take now to understand and meet the challenges facing your organization.

➤ *Action Step 1* Analyze and discuss the challenges your organization faces and how you scored on Organization Self-Assessment 1.1 regarding your familiarity with the 10 significant challenges that ID/DD organizations face today. Your familiarity with these 10 challenges will set the stage for how your organization adapts to them in the future. Thus, this first profile establishes your future agenda.

➤ *Action Step 2* Analyze and discuss your organization's familiarity with—and use of thus far—the eight proposed change strategies (Organization Self-Assessment 1.2). This information will help determine the progress you have already made toward organization change and redefinition. In addition, the information will assist strategic planning related to the desired direction of change/redefinition efforts, current and future benchmarks, and the resources your organization will need. In this process, do not forget that resources include more than money. As we discuss in Chapters 5, 7, and 9, resources include tacit and explicit knowledge, time, social and financial capital, and technology.

➤ *Action Step 3*   Begin to develop an action plan. In thinking about the "so what question," begin by reviewing your Organization Self-Assessments regarding mental models (1.3) and leadership style (1.4) and then begin to "think from right to left." This is a very productive—and change-oriented—way of thinking, which we discuss further in Chapter 3. **Right-to-left thinking** involves starting with the desired outcomes clearly articulated and then asking, "What needs to be in place for such outcomes to occur?" Thus, this action step requires that you ask, "What needs to be in place for the mental models and leadership styles to change?" Don't overlook the fact that these two profiles also describe your current organization culture.

➤ *Action Step 4*   Engage in strategic foresight. As discussed by Hines (2006), the strategic foresight process generally involves framing the key issues affecting your organization, scanning the environment to see what trends may play out, and envisioning possible and desirable outcomes. More specifically, futurists talk about six phases in the strategic foresight process: 1) framing or organizing the issues at hand, 2) scanning the environment and learning from others, 3) forecasting or creating alternative futures for your organization, 4) visioning or focusing on the "so what question" and establishing realistic future possibilities, 5) planning or building the bridge to those possibilities, and 6) acting and thereby crossing the bridge.

SUMMARY AND IMPORTANT POINTS

Throughout this chapter, we have emphasized the need for ID/DD organizations and systems to understand the challenges they face and to either begin or continue their efforts to become more effective in terms of personal outcomes and efficient in terms of organization outputs. In addition, we have stressed the importance of self-assessment as an essential tool in organization transformation and redefinition. As you have noticed, we have also shared our attitudes and beliefs that change is a positive value, that ID/DD organizations and systems need to change to remain viable, that one should learn from others, and that successful change and redefinition require the involvement of all key stakeholders.

Important Points We Have Made in This Chapter

➤ ID/DD organizations are currently facing during the early 21st century significant challenges related to dwindling resources, increasing need for services and supports, reorganization along horizontal lines of action, and demands for increased effectiveness and efficiency.

➤ Organizations and systems can evaluate the degree to which they currently are addressing these significant challenges and thus provide a baseline against which they can evaluate their change and redefinition efforts.

➤ Self-assessment information about the organization's familiarity and use of the eight change strategies can be used for multiple purposes that include gathering information for strategic planning and resource allocation.

➤ An organization's culture is best defined on the basis of the organization's mental models and leadership style.

RESOURCES

Print

Ashkenas, R., Ulrich, D., Jick, T., & Kerr, S. (2002). *The boundaryless organization: Breaking the chains of organizational structure.* San Francisco, CA: Jossey-Bass.

Blau, G.M., & Magrab, P.R. (Eds.). (2010). *The leadership equation: Strategies for individuals who are champions for children, youth, and families.* Baltimore, MD: Paul H. Brookes Publishing Co., Inc.

Giffords, E.D. (2009). An examination of organizational commitment and professional commitment and the relationship to work environment, demographic, and organizational factors. *Journal of Social Work, 9*(4), 386–404.

Hackman, J.R., & Wageman, R. (2007). Asking the right questions about leadership. *American Psychologist, 63*(2), 43–47.

Hamner, D., Hall, A.C., Timmons, J.C., Boeltzig, H., & Fesko, S. (2008). Agents of change in the disability field: Bridge-builders who make a difference. *Journal of Organizational Change Management, 21*(2), 161–173.

Kaiser, P.B., Hogan, R., & Craig, S.B. (2008). Leadership and the fate of organizations. *American Psychologist, 63*(2), 96–110.

Konzes, J.M., & Posner, V.Z. (2007). *The leadership challenge* (4th ed.). San Francisco, CA: Jossey-Bass.

Sternberg, R.J. (2007). A systems model of leadership. *American Psychologist, 63*(2), 34–42.

Electronic

Martinette, C.V., Jr. (2002). *Learning organizations and leadership style.* Retrieved from http://www.usfa.dhs.gov/pdf/efop/tr_02cm.pdf

MindTools. (2012) *Tools for organization change.* Retrieved from http://www.mindtools.com/AboutMindTools.htm

ORGANIZATION SELF-ASSESSMENT 1.1

Evaluating Your Organization's Status on Addressing Significant Challenges

Directions: Circle "1" if leaders, managers, and other personnel within your organization are aware of and have discussed the respective challenge, "2" if you have begun to address the challenge, "3" if some changes have been made to respond to the challenge, and "4" if your organization has successfully addressed (in your estimation) most of the challenges.

Challenge	Organization score (circle)			
1. Dwindling resources	1	2	3	4
2. Increased demand for services/supports	1	2	3	4
3. Movement from vertical to horizontal structure	1	2	3	4
4. Shift from general services to individualized supports	1	2	3	4
5. Emphasis on self-determination and self-direction	1	2	3	4
6. Focus on personal outcomes	1	2	3	4
7. Resource allocation based on assessed support needs	1	2	3	4
8. Use of natural supports	1	2	3	4
9. Emphasis on evidence-based practices	1	2	3	4
10. Calls for increased effectiveness and efficiency	1	2	3	4

Total score: _____

A Leadership Guide for Today's Disabilities Organizations: Overcoming Challenges and Making Change Happen
by Robert L. Schalock and Miguel Ángel Verdugo. Copyright © 2012 by Paul H. Brookes Publishing Co., Inc. All rights reserved.

14

Evaluating Your Familiarity and Use of the Eight Change Strategies

Directions: In the *Familiarity* column, circle "1" if you are not familiar with the strategy, "2" if you are somewhat familiar, and "3" if you are very familiar with the strategy. To evaluate the degree of use or implementation within your organization, in the *Use* column, circle "1" if the respective strategy is not currently being used in your organization, "2" if the strategy is used somewhat or partially being used, and "3" if the strategy is fully implemented.

Change strategy	Familiarity			Use		
Thinking styles	1	2	3	1	2	3
Focus on outcomes and outputs	1	2	3	1	2	3
High-performance teams	1	2	3	1	2	3
A system of supports	1	2	3	1	2	3
Evidence-based practices	1	2	3	1	2	3
Performance-based system	1	2	3	1	2	3
Creating value through innovation	1	2	3	1	2	3
Overcoming resistance to change	1	2	3	1	2	3

Total score: _____

Evaluating Your Organization's Mental Model

Directions: For each dyad (e.g., disability based on defectology versus social-ecological model of disability), place a checkmark next to the dimension that best reflects your organization's mental model.

Defectology _____ Social-ecology

Segregation _____ Inclusion

Control and power _____ Self-empowerment

Mechanistic organization _____ Self-organizing system

Vertical structure _____ Horizontal structure

Focus on process _____ Focus on outcomes

Change can't happen _____ Change can happen

Leadership accountability _____ "Us" accountability

Success dependent on leader _____ Success dependent on everyone

Outcomes can't be measured _____ Outcomes can be measured

Assessing Your Organization's Leadership Style

Directions: Use the following three-point rating key: 3 = very characteristic of leadership within the organization, 2 = somewhat characteristic, and 1 = not characteristic of leadership within the organization.

Leadership activity	Organization score (circle)		
Roles:			
Mentoring and directing	1	2	3
Coaching and instructing	1	2	3
Inspiring and empowering	1	2	3
Collaborating and partnering	1	2	3
Functions:			
Communicating a shared vision	1	2	3
Supporting personal mastery	1	2	3
Stressing a systems perspective	1	2	3
Promoting a community context	1	2	3
Monitoring personal outcomes and organization outputs	1	2	3
Promoting and monitoring the transformation process	1	2	3

Total score: _____

2

Expanding Thinking to Include Systems, Synthesis, and Alignment

What You Can Expect in This Chapter

➤ Examples of how systems thinking leads organizations to function as open systems, operate as bridges to the community, and use outcome predictor information

➤ Examples of how synthesis is used to make decisions regarding the format and content of individual supports plans and the allocation of resources based on the predictors of personal outcomes

➤ Examples of how alignment is used to position an organization's service components into a logical sequence for the purposes of reporting, monitoring, evaluation, and continuous quality improvement

➤ The use of program logic models for performance evaluation and management

➤ Five organization self-assessments regarding your organization's understanding and use of these three 21st century thinking styles

There is a wealth of published literature about **critical thinking skills.** You are probably familiar, for example, with the taxonomy of thinking skills proposed by Bloom (1956) and Passig (2003, 2007). This taxonomy involves thinking and learning skills related to knowledge, comprehension, application, analysis, **synthesis,** and evaluation. As critical as these thinking skills are, the challenges facing organizations that provide services and supports to people with ID/DD require expanding ones thinking to include 1) systems thinking, which focuses on the multiple factors that affect human functioning and organization performance; 2) synthesis, which involves the integration of information to improve the precision, accuracy, and **validity** of a decision; and 3) **alignment,** which positions the service delivery components of an ID/DD organization into a logical sequence for the purposes of reporting, monitoring, evaluation, and continuous quality improvement. Each of these three thinking styles, which we refer to as 21st century thinking styles, incorporates critical thinking skills. These associations are shown in Table 2.1 (p. 20).

Table 2.1.   Thinking styles and associated critical thinking skills

Thinking style	Associated critical thinking skills
Systems thinking	Distinctions, perspectives, and relationships
Synthesis	Analysis, evaluation, and interpretation
Alignment	Sequential relations, linear relations, and convergent thinking

The purposes of this chapter are to 1) describe these thinking styles and summarize their role in redefining ID/DD organizations, 2) explain how the associated critical thinking skills shown in Table 2.1 are used to **operationalize** each respective thinking style, 3) provide self-assessment exercises that allow the reader to evaluate his or her organization in reference to the use of the three thinking styles, and 4) discuss a number of **thinking errors** that diminish an organization's effectiveness and efficiency. As in Chapter 1, we conclude with a list of action steps that you can take now to expand your thinking by using 21st century thinking styles.

SYSTEMS THINKING

*Systems thinking focuses on the multiple factors that affect
human functioning and organization performance.*

Human functioning and organization performance are affected by both environmental and personal factors. Environmental factors stem from the *macrosystem* that includes the larger population, country, or sociopolitical influences and from the *mesosystem* that includes the neighborhood, community, or organization(s) providing services and supports. Personal factors are characteristics of a person such as age, gender, functional level, ethnicity, motivation level, lifestyle, education level, and past and current life events. These personal factors play out in the *microsystem* that includes the person, family, friends, colleagues, and close support staff. From a systems-thinking perspective, environmental factors interact with personal factors and thereby provide both the context within which ID/DD organizations operate and a framework for evaluating the factors that affect human functioning and organization performance. The advantages of systems thinking are that it leads to a more complete understanding of the systems within which ID/DD organizations function, allows one to recognize and address the complex relationships among the multiple parts of any system, and transforms and enhances the approach taken to evaluate personal outcomes and/or organization outputs.

Critical Thinking Skills

Systems thinking helps one to think holistically and incorporates the three critical thinking skills of seeing distinctions, recognizing perspectives, and understanding relationships (Cabrera, Colosi, & Lobdell, 2008).

Distinctions   Distinction making involves establishing an identity and a boundary that differentiates between who/what is inside and who/what is outside the set boundary—which in our case is an organization or system (e.g., a state ID/DD agency). Within our framework, we make a distinction between targeted individuals and the provider system. In addition, we distinguish among input variables, throughput or process variables, **short-term effects,** and **long-term impacts.**

Perspectives   Systems thinking allows organizations to recognize the different perspectives of key stakeholders and provides a framework for evaluating personal outcomes and organization outputs. The perspectives of key stakeholders vary. Clientele are most interested in having their needs met and experiencing enhanced personal outcomes. Organizations are typically most interested in effectiveness and efficiency and providing quality services and supports. Policy makers are most interested in short-term effects and increasingly in the long-term impacts of the services and supports that reflect a positive return on investment.

From an evaluation perspective, five points should be kept in mind regarding systems thinking. First, human service program outcomes depend on the relationships within and between systems that surround two groups of people: program providers and the individuals they support. Second, outcomes exist in the context of program participation and the specific services and supports provided to the clientele. Third, evaluation involves measuring or controlling for the functionality of these relationships and identifying significant variables that moderate or mediate personal outcomes and/or organization outputs. Personal outcomes or organization outputs are rarely related to—and explained by—only one factor. Fourth, systems thinking allows ID/DD organizations to begin to understand these functional relationships and, hence, be able to explain cause–effect relationships. This understanding puts ID/DD organizations in a better position to become knowledge producers and implement quality improvement strategies. Fifth, delineating and evaluating the systems relationships allows one to map potential measurements (referred to as *pulse points* because they indicate an organization's overall health). Examples include assessing the relationship of participant characteristics to personal outcomes and organization outputs, determining the influence of contextual variables on outcomes and outputs, and evaluating the quality of supports from an organization to its staff or program recipients (Cabrera et al., 2008).

Relationships   A system is a collection of related parts that interact to impact human functioning and organization performance. As presented throughout the book, these related parts are

- Input variables: targeted individuals, the provider system, and contextual variables

- Process variables: individual support strategies and **organization services**

- Short-term effects: personal outcomes and organization outputs

- Long-term impacts: socioeconomic position, health, and subjective well-being

Understanding and explaining the interaction of these related parts can be challenging. For the time being it is sufficient to understand two concepts: cause–effect relationships and mediator–moderator variables. At the beginning of the 21st century, social scientists are trying to understand the various input and process parts of a system that cause (i.e., affect) the results (i.e., effects). As reflected in the above-referenced short-term effects and long-term impacts, mediator and moderator variables are increasingly being identified that explain the relationship between what are referred to as independent variables (i.e., input and process variables) and dependent variables (i.e., short-term effects and long-term impacts). For our current purposes, mediator variables exhibit indirect causation, connection, or relation between an independent and dependent variable. Examples include attitudes, normative expectations, personality factors, the impact of the media, and one's belief system. A mediating effect is created when a third factor intervenes between the independent and dependent variable. In distinction, a moderator variable alters the relation or modifies the form or strength of the relation between an independent and dependent variable. Examples include gender, age, subgroupings such as **intellectual functioning** and **adaptive behavior,** and socioeconomic status (Schalock, Keith, Verdugo, & Gomez, 2010).

EXAMPLES OF SYSTEMS THINKING

We have selected two examples that show the importance and use of systems thinking in effective and efficient ID/DD organizations. The first relates to the impact of systems thinking on how an organization sees itself as an open system; the second involves the use of empirically based personal outcome predictors.

Organizations as Open Systems

Without the benefit of systems thinking, ID/DD organizations historically viewed themselves as singular entities that provided all things to all people. In this sense, they viewed themselves as closed systems in that they felt responsible for providing their own professional services, transportation (remember the yellow buses?), religious services, barbershops, bakeries, kitchens, laundry, and, yes, even a water tower. The error in this line of reasoning is the tendency to confound *special* (schools, education, employment, organizations) with a special place to be rather than as an approach to service/supports delivery in the natural environment. With the benefit of systems thinking, effective and efficient ID/DD organizations have begun to think of themselves as part of a larger system or resource network and to see their primary role as bridges to the community.

➤ Tool for Application

A community-based system provides resources for the organization, and it has been our experience that successful organizations plan for and use the resources of the community including social networks and natural supports to facilitate personal outcomes. Organization Self-Assessment 2.1 (p. 35) focuses on the degree to which community resources are used by your organization.

Analyzing your organization's profile can be very beneficial as you think about redefining your organization. In addition to reflecting the degree to which your organization is an **open system,** the analysis can also be used for two important redefinitional purposes: continuous quality improvement and discrepancy analysis. For example, even though the assessment might be skewed toward mainly 3s, what can be done to increase the access to and use of community resources? In that regard, ask organization personnel a series of questions: "Who is on the board? What are we doing to increase self-advocacy groups and connecting clients to community-based self-help groups? Have we really attempted to access social networks and natural supports?" Asking these types of questions and providing answers reflects an organization's serious commitment to redefining itself. The analysis can also focus on the discrepancy between what the community offers and the services/supports your organization provides. It is reasonable to assume that ID/DD organizations that are open systems should not provide the same services/supports found within the community. Reducing this discrepancy (i.e., reducing duplication) is a way for your organization to be more efficient. Remember: Having enhanced personal outcomes is a sign of an organization's effectiveness; reducing the amount of duplication is a sign of its efficiency.

Use of Personal Outcome Predictors

Many of the examples used in this book are based on the authors' (and their colleagues') work in the area of quality of life. During the first decade of the 21st century, quality-of-life researchers have begun to identify personal-, organization-, and systems-level factors that are statistically related to assessed quality of life–related personal outcomes. A listing of those significant predictors is presented in Table 2.2.

As summarized in Table 2.2, personal outcomes are affected by a number of personal, organization, and societal factors—in other words, the micro-, meso-, and macrosystems. By inference, these three systems also affect organization performance. The kind of information reported in Table 2.2 can be used for at least three important redefinitional purposes: reporting personal outcome information, using the outcome data for monitoring and evaluation, and using the data for continuous quality improvement. In reference to reporting, an ID/DD organization can report quality-of-life outcomes for their service recipients, and the system (e.g. a state ID/DD agency) can aggregate these data for further reporting and analysis. Examples of such reporting are found in Chapter 3. In reference to monitoring, the organization can use the identified predictor variables to determine whether those variables are being addressed in program policies and practices. Examples of this process are also found in Chapter 3. In reference to continuous quality improvement, the specific predictors (or predictor clusters) can be targeted for increased attention and resource deployment (time, money, expertise, and technology). Specific examples are found in Chapter 7.

➤ Tool for Application

Organization Self-Assessment 2.2 (p. 36) provides a baseline for how and to what degree your organization is using outcome predictors. If you are not currently measuring personal outcomes, you should still do the self-assessment and read Chapter 3 very carefully. In evaluating your current use, check all purposes that apply.

Keep the following points in mind when interpreting your self-assessment profile. First, the field of outcomes measurement is still in its infancy, and much remains unknown about all the factors that predict personal outcomes and the best way to operationalize and measure them. Thus, feel free to add additional predictors to those listed in Table 2.2 from your personal experience or reading of the literature. Second, assessing personal outcomes and using that information for strategic planning and program development is a time-consuming and potentially expensive process. Thus, if you are not currently assessing personal outcomes, your organization needs to be very clear about which outcomes to assess and how to assess them. We discuss the interrogatories of personal outcomes assessment in Chapter 3. Third, ask yourself, "How available is the information summarized in Table 2.2 and Organization

Table 2.2. Factors significantly affecting personal outcomes

Person-level factors	Health status
	Intellectual functioning and adaptive behavior level
	Amount of self-determination
Organization-level factors	Support staff strategies (facilitative assistance, including communication support and ensuring a sense of basic security)
	Support staff characteristics (teamwork, job satisfaction, staff turnover, job stress, and organization management practices)
	Employment programs (including opportunities for volunteerism)
Systems-level factors	Participation opportunities (contact with family members, friends, and people in one's social networks)
	Normalized community living arrangements
	Availability of public transportation

Sources: Schalock, Bonham, and Verdugo (2008); Schalock, Gardner, and Bradley (2007); and Walsh, Emerson, Lobb, Hatton, Bradley, Schalock, and Moseley (2010).

Self-Assessment 2.2 to organization personnel, and how widely is it being distributed and used in the organization?" A related question is, "Is the information understandable?" To be of value, information needs to be understood, distributed widely, and acted on. Fourth, regardless of your profile, use the information presented in Table 2.2 in your staff development activities to make a simple, yet profound, point: Personal outcomes result more from organization- and systems-level factors than from personal factors. This point underscores the need for ID/DD organizations to be open systems.

SYNTHESIS

*Synthesis involves the integration of information from multiple sources
to improve the precision, accuracy, and validity of a decision.*

ID/DD organization personnel need to get smarter in understanding and using the vast amount of available information to make good decisions. On a daily basis, organization personnel are making decisions about how to best integrate information about the **support needs** of their clientele into the development and implementation of individualized plans, how to integrate the vast amount of organization resources into efficient service delivery patterns, and how to demonstrate the relationship between input/process efforts and personal outcomes/organization outputs. These types of decisions require the use of synthesis.

To follow is an optimistic scenario as presented by Cascio (2009, p. 94). If the next several decades of the 21st century are as bad as some fear they could be, organization leaders can respond and survive the way our species has done time and again: by getting smarter and making good decisions. And how might leaders get smarter and make precise, accurate, and valid decisions while avoiding sensory clutter and cognitive fog? One approach would involve using the 21st century thinking style we refer to as synthesis. As used in this book, synthesis should not be confused with technologically based cognitive enhancement strategies inherent in assistive or information technology; nor should it be confused with interdisciplinary synthesis as reflected in systems engineering, industrial engineering, or operational research (Tow & Gilliam, 2009). As indicated previously, we define *synthesis* as a style of reasoning that integrates information from multiple sources to improve the precision, accuracy, and validity of a decision.

Critical Thinking Skills

The synthesis of information for the purpose of making good decisions involves the use of three critical thinking skills that allow one to gain insight into a phenomenon and thus make a better decision about it. These three critical thinking skills are analysis, evaluation, and interpretation. Collectively, they are increasingly being recognized as the cognitive engines driving the processes of knowledge development and leadership (Schalock & Luckasson, 2005).

- Analysis: Examine the case and its component parts and reduce the complexity of the case into simpler or more basic components or elements.

- Evaluation: Determine the precision, accuracy, and integrity of available information through careful appraisal and study. Seek additional information to reduce uncertainty, including the validity of premises and assumptions.

- Interpretation: Integrate the available information in light of the client's or organization's beliefs, judgments, or circumstances.

Decision Making

Decision making is an inferential process that requires the integration of all facts and is based on the analysis, evaluation, and interpretation of information. As reflected in the previously defined critical thinking skills, good decisions require more than intuition. Rather, good decisions require taking time to examine the case or issue at hand, determining the quality of the data and information that will be used to form a conclusion or recommendation, and basing the decision on one's interpretation of the relevance of the information to the organization or the organization's clientele.

The following examples demonstrate the importance of synthesis in two critical organization functions: 1) developing individual plans, which we will refer to in the book as **individual supports plans (ISPs)** although other terminology is commonly used, such as individual education plans, for other plans of this nature; and 2) deciding how to allocate resources in the provision of individualized supports based on knowledge regarding the significant predictors of personal outcomes. The first example focuses on the use of a template and computer-based drop-down boxes; the second emphasizes the key role that data-gathering strategies can have on decision making. Both examples reflect the three criteria for good decision making: systematic (i.e., organized, sequential, logical), formal (i.e., explicit, reasoned, and based on the three critical thinking skills described earlier), and transparent (i.e., apparent and communicated clearly).

EXAMPLES OF SYNTHESIS

As a basis for good decision making, synthesis involves identifying, connecting, and combining ideas or information from multiple sources. These sources can include personal experiences, professional standards, and published research. Good decision making and enhancing the organization's effectiveness and efficiency require that information be synthesized and acted on. This is especially true in reference to the two examples presented in this section: developing an ISP and using information about outcome predictors in resource allocation.

Developing an Individual Support Plan

Developing individual plans can consume countless hours of staff time and, unfortunately, can frequently result in very large documents that are filed rather than acted on or fully implemented. The research on the impact of individual plans on personal outcomes is just emerging; however, in the authors' experience, the impact has been limited in many organizations by two factors: lack of assessment data related to the support needs of specific individuals, and lack of access to—or knowledge of—individual support strategies. Our suggestion in the example that follows is to use a template and computer-based drop-

(1) Outcome categories	(2) Support needs assessment	(3) Support strategies	(4) Support objectives	(5) Outcome indicators
▼	▼	▼	▼	▼
Personal outcome categories (Table 3.1)	Support assessment areas (Table 5.2)	Individual support strategies (Table 5.3)	Exemplary support objectives (Table 5.7)	Personal outcome indicators (Table 3.2)

Figure 2.1.   A template for individual supports plan development.

down boxes (shown in Figure 2.1) to successfully address these two factors. Both strategies involve synthesis as a critical thinking skill and the use of information technology to assist staff in identifying, connecting, and combining information to make better decisions about the development and successful implementation of an ISP.

Figure 2.1 provides a template to understand and discuss the parameters of an ISP. This template is developed more fully in Chapter 5. For our purposes here, the columns within the template allow program staff to synthesize 1) information related to desired outcomes (Columns 1 and 5), 2) assessed support needs and individualized support strategies (Columns 2 and 3), and 3) **support objectives** that are used for reporting and monitoring (Column 4). The template also allows for the integration of assessment information (Columns 2 and 5) with specific supports provided (Column 3). This integration allows for evaluating the impact of support needs (Column 2) and supports provided (Column 3) on anticipated outcomes (Column 5).

The computer-based drop-down boxes shown along the bottom of Figure 2.1 provide staff with lists of current best practices related to the outcome categories (Column 1), support need areas (Column 2), individual support strategies (Column 3), staff-referenced support objectives (Column 4), and exemplary outcome indicators (Column 5). The content of these drop-down boxes will be shown and discussed more thoroughly in Chapters 3 and 5 (see table references beneath each drop-down box); here, it is important to see the big picture and how synthesis is essential in developing an ISP. Column 1 addresses the personal outcome categories around which the ISP is developed, implemented, and evaluated (Column 5). The specific outcome categories will depend on the organization and/or larger system's policies and targeted individuals. Potential outcome categories are discussed in Chapter 3 (Tables 3.1 and 3.2). Typical outcome categories relate to **quality-of-life domains** or public policy objectives such as increased independence, productivity, and community integration.

Columns 2 and 3 are critical in having staff efforts integrate assessed support needs with the individualized support strategies provided. Program staff involved in developing ISPs require such integration as well as access to specific individualized support strategies. Few organization personnel have information or knowledge regarding the plethora of available support strategies. Thus, there is a need for computer-based drop-down boxes that describe specific strategies such as task analysis, available assistive technologies, or the steps involved in implementing positive behavior supports. Integrating assessed support needs with specific support strategies increases the organization's effectiveness (by highlighting those strategies that have been demonstrated to enhance personal outcomes) and the organization's efficiency (by reducing time wasted on support strategies that are not related to the individual's assessed support needs).

➤ Tool for Application

Organization Self-Assessment 2.3 (p. 37) emphasizes the importance of templates and drop-down boxes in developing individualized plans. Answering the following questions regarding your ISP analysis will be very insightful. First, how are expected outcomes expressed, and where do they appear in the ISP? Do they drive the ISP (which is an example of right-to-left thinking), or are they stated only as behavioral objectives embedded somewhere in the document? Second, are specific, individualized support strategies listed, and do these strategies reflect best practices and a system of supports? Third, are specific support objectives associated with each support strategy? It is important to answer the third question. Historically, the focus within individualized plans has been on the client exhibiting certain behaviors that are expressed as behavioral objectives. Thus, the focus of monitoring and evaluating the success of the ISP was on the client and his or her reaching the behavior criterion. What is ineffective and inefficient about this line of reasoning? Two things: 1) The onus is on the service recipient and not the support staff who should be implementing specific support strategies, and 2) the effectiveness of an organization is evaluated on the basis of enhanced personal outcomes—not the individual meeting certain (and frequently very arbitrary) behavioral objectives. Finally, what is the relationship between the contents of a client's ISP as reflected in the columns in Figure 2.1 and the personal outcomes that the organization uses for reporting, monitoring, evaluation, and continuous quality improvement? These should be aligned, as discussed in the Alignment section later in this chapter.

Using Information About Outcome Predictors in Resource Allocation

ID/DD organizations have different levels of **evaluation capability,** or what the evaluation literature refers to as evaluation capacity. Some organizations are connected to a university or research center that can assist them in data gathering and data analysis. These organizations are in a good position to determine within their own organization (or system) the significant predictors of personal outcomes. For those organizations that do not have this capability, personnel can still benefit from research-based information regarding those factors—including individualized support strategies—that have a high probability of producing enhanced personal outcomes. The basic point of the following self-assessment is that research can help ID/DD organization personnel integrate what is known about outcome predictors into how they allocate the organization's resources.

➤ *Tool for Application*

Organization Self-Assessment 2.4 (p. 38) is based on information contained in Table 2.2, which summarizes the factors shown to significantly affect personal outcomes. Analyzing your organization's profile can be very informative and may result in creative thinking and problem solving about how to redefine the organization to be more effective and efficient. For example, it is not unusual to find that organizations allocate considerable resources to improving the health status of their clientele and self-determination but that they do not use assistive technology to enhance adaptive behavior and intellectual functioning. As discussed in Chapter 1, using assistive technology should be viewed as an effective and efficient way to reduce the mismatch between a person's capability and his or her environment's requirements. It is also not unusual for organizations to be concerned about staff turnover and job stress without devoting sufficient resources to fostering teamwork and changing management strategies that might lead to improved job satisfaction, reduced job stress, and, hence, reduced staff turnover.

In summary, synthesis is a critical 21st century thinking style. As exemplified in the organization self-assessments, it involves making good decisions related to ISP development and resource allocation after identifying, connecting, and combining information from multiple sources. But two broader issues also need to be addressed. One is the need to help staff understand how they can use information not just for decision making but also for managing their time more effectively and efficiently. The second issue is that the prefix *multi-* will become increasingly important in redefined ID/DD organizations. Thus, as we embrace a multidisciplinary, multivariate, and multisystems approach to problem solving and service delivery, synthesis as a 21st century thinking style will be even more important for integrating information to improve the precision, accuracy, and validity of a leader's decision. It will also lead to increased scientific understanding and positive social effects. The same can be said of the third 21st century thinking style: alignment.

ALIGNMENT

Alignment positions the service delivery components of an ID/DD organization into a logical sequence for the purposes of reporting, monitoring, evaluation, and continuous quality improvement.

When first introduced to the term *alignment,* many readers might think of the front ends of cars and tires. As suggested in our definition, alignment also involves coming into precise adjustment or correct relation and proper positioning or state of the adjustment of parts. Although alignment's primary purpose as a thinking style is to position the service delivery components of an ID/DD organization into a logical sequence for the purposes of reporting, monitoring, evaluation, and continuous quality improvement, its importance can be more generally viewed from the perspective of the individual and the organization.

For individuals, alignment is accomplished when individual supports provisions are in line with the person's assessed support needs and the evaluation of personal outcomes. Diagrammatically, this alignment requires

Assessment of Support Needs >> ISP>> Outcome Evaluation

An organization is aligned when the team is committed to a common direction, the organization focuses on business and deliverables that evolve from that direction, the organization's teams are clear about their roles and responsibilities, business relationships are open, the organization avoids siloism, and decision-making practices are in place. Alignment as a thinking style is critical in redefining ID/DD organizations. As stated by Guttman, "Alignment is not only about reconstituting the performance context (e.g., strategy, goals, accountability, and protocols), but it is also about reshaping business relationships." (2008, p. 192).

Critical Thinking Skills

Three critical thinking skills are involved in alignment: sequential or serial thinking, wherein service delivery components are arranged in a sequence that involves an input, throughput/processes, and output; linear thinking, which allows one to relate outcomes and outputs to inputs and throughputs/process; and convergent reasoning, which allows one to reduce the complexity of organizations and systems to a workable conceptual and measurement framework. The most commonly used measurement framework to operationalize these three critical thinking skills is a **program logic model.**

PROGRAM LOGIC MODELS AND ALIGNMENT

Traditionally, program logic model components have included inputs (i.e., resources), processes, and program outcomes/outputs. As shown in the prototypic program logic model presented in Figure 2.2, these traditional components have been modified slightly to align better with current systems-related thinking and terminology. Specific details follow.

- Input variables are divided into targeted individuals, the provider system, and contextual variables.

- Process variables are viewed from the perspective of individual support strategies, organization services, and management strategies. This reconceptualization has resulted from the pervasive impact on ID/DD organizations of the supports **paradigm,** the key role that community living alternatives play in personal outcomes, the important distinction between short-term effects and long-term impacts, and the organization's formal linkages.

- Short-term effects are evaluated in terms of personal outcomes and organization outputs.

- Long-term impacts reflect more permanent changes in the person's socioeconomic position (e.g., education status, employment status, income), health indicators (e.g., longevity, wellness, access to health care), and subjective well-being (e.g., life satisfaction, positive affect such as happiness and contentment, absence of negative affect such as sadness, worry, or helplessness).

- Input and process variables are considered as affect (i.e., antecedent or causal), and short-term effects and long-term impacts are considered as effect (i.e., consequence or resultant).

Key Concepts and Terms

Understanding the key concepts and terminology used in program logic models is essential to their successful application by an ID/DD organization to align its input, process, and outcome/output processes. In Table 2.3 (p. 30), we define the key terms used in our prototypic model presented in Figure 2.2.

Value of Program Logic Models

Chapter 7 discusses in considerable detail how the information obtained from a program logic model framework can be used for the purposes of reporting, monitoring, evaluation, and quality improvement. For our current purposes, it is sufficient to understand the value of a program logic model in aligning an organization's input, process, and outcome/output components. In that regard, a fully operationalized program logic model 1) articulates the operative relationships among program services; 2) provides an important tool for program evaluation and quality improvement; 3) enables organizations to understand what must be done to achieve the desired short-term effects while continuing to focus on the long-term impacts of their services and supports; 4) identifies critical factors that can influence short-term effects and long-term impacts and recognizes critical players whose cooperation/partnering is key to success; 5) identifies core processes that reengineering, quality improvement, and enhanced perfor-

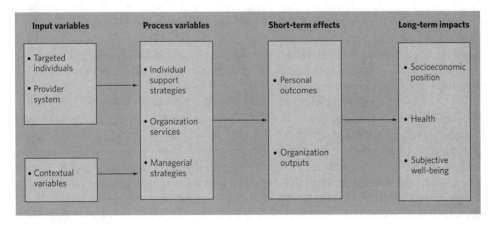

Figure 2.2. Prototypic program logic model.

Table 2.3. Program logic model key terms and concepts

Input variables	*Targeted individuals:* client characteristics including diagnosis, age, gender, and assessed support needs
	Provider system: organization characteristics including philosophy and goals, resources, and evaluation capability
	Contextual variables: organization culture, community factors, political environment, economic situation, family variables, location, formal linkages
Process variables	*Individual support strategies:* incentives, cognitive tools, environmental accommodation, skill development, learning aids, engagement opportunities
	Organization services: community living alternatives, employment/education options, community-based activities, transportation, professional services
	Managerial strategies: leadership style, 21st century thinking styles, performance-based evaluation and management system, high-performance teams, evidence-based practices
Short-term effects	*Personal outcomes:* the benefits to program recipients that are the result, direct or indirect, of a system of supports and program services
	Organization outputs: the products that result from the resources a program uses to achieve its goals and objectives and the processes implemented by an organization to produce these products
Long-term impacts	Social indicators such as socioeconomic position, health, and subjective well-being

mance can improve; 6) provides a framework for analyzing alternative strategies for achieving desired personal outcomes and organization outputs; and 7) clarifies for stakeholders the sequence of organization-based events and processes to allow for a fuller understanding of organization performance (Donaldson, 2007; Dyehouse, Bennett, Harbor, Childress, & Dark, 2009; Helitzer, Hollis, Hernandez, Sanders, Roybal, & van Deusen, 2010; Millar, Simeone, & Carnevale, 2001; Schalock & Bonham, 2003).

➤ *Tool for Application*

Effective and efficient ID/DD organizations have well-defined program logic models that enhance performance evaluation and management. Other organizations have all of the pieces but have not integrated them; still others have models that are not logical. Thus, your organization's status regarding Organization Self-Assessment 2.5 (p. 39) can provide beneficial information for redefining how you position or align your service delivery components into a logical sequence for reporting, monitoring, evaluation, and continuous quality improvement. A typical profile or pattern of responses emerges when we use this organization self-assessment with ID/DD organizations that are in our estimation effective and efficient compared with those that are less so. Effective and efficient organizations are more likely to answer mainly *yes* on the clear delineation questions, and generally *yes* on the operational data sets. Frequently, however, even effective and efficient organizations have paid less attention to contextual variables, the distinction between personal outcomes and organization outputs, and the importance of being sensitive to long-term impacts.

We suggest the following four guidelines regarding how your organization might use the results of Organization Self-Assessment 2.5. First, look at the results regarding the clear delineation of your critical pathways (i.e., components). If they are not clear to organization personnel, the first thing to do is develop a system that has clearly articulated input, process, and outcome/output components. Second, if you have about an equal number of *yes* and *no* responses on the delineation section, focus on identifying and implementing those missing components. Third, focus on the development of specific data sets within each component to include in a performance-based evaluation and management system (see Chapter 7). Fourth, once your system is in place, ask a very important question: Do organization personnel think about how input variables affect process variables, which in turn influence short-term effects and long-term impacts? If the answer is no, review two of the important leadership functions discussed in Chapter 1: communicating a shared vision and stressing a systems perspective.

► ACTION STEPS YOU CAN TAKE NOW

Our intent in this chapter has not been to denigrate anyone's way of thinking. Rather, our primary purpose has been to suggest that 21st century organizations require using three critical thinking styles that are essential to redefining ID/DD organizations. Regardless of how your organization scored on the five organization self-assessments presented in this chapter, there are at least four action steps you can take now to further the positive impact on your organization of expanding your thinking to include systems, synthesis, and alignment.

➤ *Action Step 1*   Evaluate the possibility of thinking errors within your organization. Ethical practice is a part of personal decency, professional honor, and responsibility to others. Leaders have especially important obligations to act ethically and to engage in the kind of thinking that enhances accuracy. An important way to enhance accuracy is to avoid thinking errors. The level of self-awareness, reflection, personal development, knowledge, and skills required to be a good leader demands clear and error-free thinking.

What are common types of thinking errors, and how do they undermine a leader's good thinking? Ten of the most common are summarized in Exhibit 2.1, along with an example of how the respective thinking error might appear in an organization.

The purpose of avoiding thinking errors is not merely to avoid mistakes but also to increase ethical practices and enhance the quality and robustness of one's decisions. Within ID/DD organizations, with so much at stake for clients, families, communities, and employees, clear thinking is a must. The insight to identify one's own thinking errors or the thinking errors of others can strengthen the organization, maximize scarce resources, build trust among those associated with the organization, and enhance the ability of the organization to accomplish its mission.

➤ *Action Step 2*   Review your use of generic community resources as evaluated in Organization Self Assessment 2.1. Develop specific action plans to access these generic resources. As discussed earlier, effective and efficient ID/DD organizations will be open systems whose primary function is to provide a bridge to the community.

➤ *Action Step 3*   Begin to identify significant predictors of personal outcomes. In this action step, use both tacit and explicit knowledge that is available to you. Tacit knowledge includes know-how gained by the practice, study, **wisdom,** and judgment derived from the accumulated daily experiences of all levels of personnel within the organization. In distinction, explicit knowledge is based on facts and data contained in publications, manuals, web sites, databases, and annual reports.

In addition, begin the process of mentoring, directing, coaching, and instructing organization personnel to realize that the most important predictors of personal outcomes are related to organizational policies/practices and societal factors. This is also a good opportunity for coaching and instructing regarding the potential that assistive technology has to enhance adaptive behavior and augment deficits in intellectual functioning.

EXHIBIT 2.1

Common Thinking Errors

Type of thinking error	What is it?	How might this appear in an organization?
Affective error	Your feelings, such as incorrect stereotypes, misplaced empathy, or what you wish were true	An employee you like shows signs of addiction. You miss the signs and do not take action because you like her.
Anchoring error	The first bit of information anchors your mind on an incorrect conclusion	The reimbursement rate of 10 years ago covered relevant expenses, but today it does not cover expenses. Your budget thinking, however, is anchored in the past and you do not reevaluate the line.
Availability error	What happened recently or most dramatically	The last 25 families each had a mother who was the primary caregiver and who managed the individualized plan. In the 26th family, the father is the primary caregiver, but you miss that important fact.
Blind obedience	What the authority figure said	The governor has stated that certain families at the poverty line are cut from child care. You blindly comply instead of pursuing alternative funding.
Commission bias	What removes a problem quickest	Ralph spat at a young staff member. Ralph's individualized habilitation plan (IHP) was inadequately developed and implemented. You angrily dial the police to handle the problem immediately.
Confirmation bias	What you expect to find	You heard through the grapevine that 30-year-old Suza has relationship "problems." Without a current assessment, you include relationship problems in her IHP.
Diagnosis momentum	Piling on after an initial diagnosis of a condition	Carey was diagnosed with bipolar disorder by another agency in the past. On intake, you skip the thorough evaluation and social history and just do a screen for bipolar disorder.

(continued)

EXHIBIT 2.1   *(continued)*

Framing effects	Mistakenly influenced by the context	When asked for references, the well-dressed and well-spoken applicant states that her current supervisor is on vacation. She urges that you talk instead with a former colleague. You decide that because she looks like a great candidate you will skip your usual reference call to a current supervisor.
Premature closure	Deciding too soon	On Friday afternoon, before the final investigation report arrives, you tell Maxine she has nothing to worry about and send her home.
Representativeness error	What is typically true	Family members always love the services you provide. To speed things up, you put Myron into a work setting without parental consent.

For more information, contact Ruth Luckasson (ruthl@unm.edu).

➤ *Action Step 4*   Diagram your organization's program logic model. If you need help beyond that provided in Figure 2.2 and Table 2.3 (and later in Figure 7.1), step-by-step directions are found in Gugiu and Rodriguez-Campos (2007).

SUMMARY AND IMPORTANT POINTS

Our message in this chapter has been very simple: 21st century ID/DD organizations need to use 21st century thinking styles. Systems thinking allows organizations to focus on the multiple factors that affect human functioning and organization performance; synthesis allows organization personnel to integrate vast quantities of information to improve the precision, accuracy, and validity of a decision; and alignment allows ID/DD organizations to position their service delivery components into a logical sequence for the purposes of reporting, monitoring, evaluation, and continuous quality improvement.

Important Points We Have Made in This Chapter

➤ The three 21st century thinking styles of systems thinking, synthesis, and alignment are essential in redefining ID/DD organizations because they allow organization personnel to understand and communicate better about the multiple factors that affect organization performance, more effectively solve problems and thus become knowledge producers, and align their services and supports for multiple purposes.

➤ Effective and efficient ID/DD organizations need to view themselves as open systems whose major purpose is to bridge to generic services and supports in the community.

➤ The synthesis of information to make good decisions involves three critical thinking skills: analysis, evaluation, and interpretation.

➤ Individual supports planning will show the influence of the synthesis of information, the implementation of assistive technology, and the use of right-to-left thinking. This will occur through structuring the ISP around desired outcomes, aligning the assessment of support needs with the provision of individualized supports, and providing real-time best practices to support staff.

RESOURCES

Print

Ellermann, C.R., Katooka-Yahiro, M.R., & Wong, L.C. (2006). Logic models used to enhance critical thinking. *Journal of Nursing Education, 45*(6), 220–227.

Leischow, W.J., Best, A., Trochim, W.M., Clark, P.I., Gallagher, R.S., Marcus, S.E., & Matthews, E. (2008). Systems thinking to improve the public's health. *American Journal of Preventive Medicine, 35*(2, Supplement 1), 196–203.

Mingers, J., & White, L. (2009). A review of the recent contribution of systems thinking to operational research and management science. *European Journal of Operational Research, 207*(3), 1147–1161.

Electronic

Flex Monitoring Team, University of Minnesota. *Creating program logic models: A toolkit for state flex programs.* (2012) Retrieved from http://www.flexmonitoring. org/documents/PLMToolkit.pdf

Learning from logic models: An example of a family/school partnership program. (2012) Retrieved from http://www.hfrp.org/publications-resources/browse-our-publica-tions/learning-from-logic-models-an-example-of-a-family-school-partnership-program

Community Anti-Drug Coalitions of America. (2012) *Planning primer: Developing a theory of change, logic models, and strategic and action plans.* Retrieved from http:// www.actmissouri.org/PDF%20Files/Planning.pdf

Theory of change and logic models. (2012) Retrieved from http://learningforsustain-ability.net/evaluation/theoryofchange.php

Using logic models for program development. (2012) Retrieved from http://edis.ifas. ufl.edu/wc041

Using the logic model for program planning. (2012) Retrieved from http://www.lri.lsc. gov/pdf/other/TIG_Conf._Materials/EMcKay_Logic_Model_Intro_LSCpdf

Use of Generic Community Resources

Directions: In the assessment, circle 3 if your organization or center uses the respective community resource is used extensively in your organization, 2 if used somewhat, and 1 if used very little or not at all. As you will see, your profile and score reflect the degree to which your organization is an open system.

Community resource	Degree of use (circle)		
Health/nutrition	1	2	3
Housing	1	2	3
Employment (job or volunteer)	1	2	3
Education	1	2	3
Transportation	1	2	3
Mental/behavioral health	1	2	3
Leisure	1	2	3
Social capital (e.g., self-help groups, advocacy groups)	1	2	3
Natural supports	1	2	3
Religious organization(s)	1	2	3
Other public/private agencies	1	2	3
Others (please list)	1	2	3

Total score: _____

Use of Personal Outcome Predictor Information

Directions: Place a checkmark beneath the current use (i.e., reporting, monitoring, evaluation, and/or continuous quality improvement) of each of the predictor variables listed in the left column.

Predictor cluster	Current use (check all purposes used)			
	Reporting	Monitoring	Evaluation	CQI
Personal level				
Health status				
Adaptive behavior level				
Intellectual functioning level				
Self-determination level				
Organization level*				
Support staff strategies				
Support staff characteristics				
Employment options				
Societal level*				
Participation opportunities				
Living arrangement				
Transportation				

*See Table 2.2 (p. 23) for specific examples.

Analysis of Your Individual Supports Plan (ISP)

Directions: Randomly select one of your client's ISPs (or whatever you call the plan). Place the selected ISP adjacent to Figure 2.1 (the format or template used by your organization may differ, but this is unimportant). Analyze the degree to which the listed ISP components have been integrated into the sample ISP. Circle 3 if there is good evidence of integration or synthesis, 2 if there is some evidence of synthesis, and 1 if there is no evidence of integration or synthesis.

ISP component	Evidence of synthesis or integration		
Outcome categories specified	3	2	1
Assessment of support needs	3	2	1
Specification of individualized support strategies	3	2	1
Listing of support objectives	3	2	1
Listing of outcome indicators	3	2	1

Allocation of Resources Based on Predictors of Personal Outcomes

Directions: Evaluate the degree to which your organization's resources are directed at each outcome predictor. Circle 3 if your organization allocates significant resources (defined as time, money, expertise/experience, and technology) to the respective predictor, 2 if it allocates some resources, and 1 if it allocates few if any resources.

Predictor cluster	Degree of resource allocation		
Person-level predictors			
Improving health status	3	2	1
Enhancing adaptive behavior level	3	2	1
Augmenting intellectual functioning level	3	2	1
Enhancing self-determination	3	2	1
Organization-level predictors			
Fostering teamwork	3	2	1
Improving job satisfaction	3	2	1
Reducing staff turnover	3	2	1
Changing management styles	3	2	1
Developing employment programs	3	2	1
Reducing job stress	3	2	1
Societal-level predictors			
Increasing participation opportunities	3	2	1
Developing normalized community living arrangements	3	2	1
Increasing available transportation	3	2	1

Score: _____

Use of a Program Logic Model
Conceptual and Measurement Framework

Directions: This organization self-assessment has two parts. The first part asks whether the specific components shown in Figure 2.2 are clearly delineated. The second part asks you to evaluate whether specific data sets (e.g., those listed in Table 2.3) are associated with the respective components. For this self-assessment, the rating system used is very straightforward: Circle *yes* or *no*.

Component	Clear delineation		Operationalized data sets	
Input variables				
Targeted individuals	Yes	No	Yes	No
Provider system	Yes	No	Yes	No
Contextual variables	Yes	No	Yes	No
Process variables				
Individual support system	Yes	No	Yes	No
Organization services	Yes	No	Yes	No
Managerial strategies	Yes	No	Yes	No
Short-term effects				
Personal outcomes	Yes	No	Yes	No
Organization outcomes	Yes	No	Yes	No
Long-term impacts				
Socioeconomic position	Yes	No	Yes	No
Health	Yes	No	Yes	No
Subjective well-being	Yes	No	Yes	No

3

Measuring and Using Personal Outcomes and Organization Outputs

What You Can Expect in This Chapter

➤ A conceptual and measurement framework for personal outcomes and organization outputs

➤ Assessment instruments for measuring personal outcomes and organization outputs

➤ A discussion of the multiple uses of personal outcomes and organization outputs including their use in quality assurance, monitoring systems change, reporting, evaluation, and continuous quality improvement

➤ Exhibits showing how personal outcomes and organization outputs can be measured and used for reporting, monitoring, and continuous quality improvement

The challenges discussed in Chapter 1 highlight the need for organizations that provide services and supports to people with ID/DD to be more accountable in terms of results and efficient in terms of resource use. Operationally, this means that organization personnel need to focus on the measurement and use of personal outcomes and organization outputs. Personal outcomes and organizational outputs are designed as follows:

- *Personal outcomes* are the benefits derived by program recipients that are the result, direct or indirect, of program activities, services, and supports.

- *Organization outputs* are organization-referenced products that result from the resources a program uses to achieve its goals and the actions implemented by an organization to produce these outputs.

From our perspective, personal outcomes and organization outputs are critically important to readers of this book for two reasons. First, they can be used for multiple purposes related to reporting, monitoring, evaluation, and continuous quality improvement, and thus provide information that is necessary for an ID/DD organization to redefine itself. Second, they play an essential role in operationalizing **quality assurance** and **systems change**.

In reference to quality assurance, all ID/DD organizations and state systems are interested in quality services and quality outcomes. The following three examples represent significant efforts by three different entities to define quality services and supports. What is common to the three is a similar conceptual and measurement framework that addresses quality assurance on the basis of clearly operationalized and measured personal outcomes and organization outputs. First, many ID/DD organizations use the Council on Quality and Leadership's Personal Outcome Measures for quality assurance and quality improvement. There are 25 outcome measures that include the following seven domains (each with associated measurable indicators): identity, autonomy, affiliation, attainment, safeguards, rights, and health and wellness (Council on Quality and Leadership, 2010; Gardner & Caran, 2005).

As a second example, many state systems use the National Core Indicators developed by the National Association of State Directors of Developmental Disabilities Services and the Human Services Research Institute (Bradley & Moseley, 2007). The domains (each with associated measurable indicators) are consumer outcomes; systems performance; health, welfare, and rights; staff stability and competence; family indicators; and case management. Consumer core domains (with associated indicators) are work, community inclusion, choices and decisions, self-determination, relationships, and satisfaction.

The third example is the Quality Framework proposed by the U.S. Centers for Medicare and Medicaid Services (U.S. Department of Health and Human Services, 2010). This framework has two dimensions. The first includes the quality assurance components of participant access, participant-centered service planning and delivery, provider capacity and capability, participant safeguards, participant rights and responsibilities, participant outcomes and satisfaction, and systems performance. The second dimension includes four management functions that should be aligned with each component: design, discovery (data collection), remediation (use of data to respond to immediate problems), and improvement (use of data to improve services and supports at the systems level).

Each of these three examples of using personal outcomes and organization outputs for quality assurance involves delineating clear outcome and output categories and their associated measurement indices and aligning key quality assurance functions with the respective measures of personal outcomes and organization outputs. Furthermore, each of the entities referenced above uses either personal outcome data and/or organization output information for multiple purposes analogous to those described later in this chapter. From a quality assurance perspective, these measures provide useful organization and/or systems-referenced information regarding provider capabilities, service/supports planning and implementation, participant safeguards, and organization- or systems-level monitoring and performance. An additional critical commonality is the use of personal outcome and organization output information to define quality.

In reference to systems change, one can best characterize the ID/DD service delivery system in the early part of the 21st century as a highly complex support system that is found in smaller and smaller programs and facilities. This change in where and how ID/DD services and supports are delivered is reflected in the expansion and dispersal of services and supports, the growth of the home and community-based waiver, the growth of performance indicators in other fields, the movement toward consumer-directed funding, and the increasing consensus about what constitutes quality. This change has also brought with it a significant need for ID/DD organizations to report personal outcomes and organization outputs so that their multiple constituencies can better understand organization- and systems-level performance and thereby monitor and evaluate systems change.

Regardless of the specific personal outcome and organization output measures used to monitor systems change, the specific measures selected should meet the following four criteria:

- They have utility and can be used for multiple purposes including reporting, monitoring, evaluation, and continuous quality improvement.

- They are robust in that they are based on a supportable conceptual and measurement framework, and the assessment of the indicators is done reliably and validly.

- They are understandable. The service delivery system is complex enough. The indicators must be clear enough for all stakeholders to understand their meaning, measurement, relevance, and potential use.

- They are relevant to their intended use.

The purpose of this chapter is to present a conceptual and measurement framework for organizations to use as they incorporate personal outcomes and organization outputs into their thinking and acting. The chapter is organized around three questions ID/DD organization personnel frequently ask: "What are personal outcomes and organization outputs?" "How are personal outcomes and organization outputs measured?" and "How can my organization use personal outcome and organization output-related information?" The exhibits and self-assessments presented in the chapter are based primarily on our research conducted from 1990–2010 in the field of quality of life–related personal outcomes and our extensive experience with ID/DD service providers over the last decade as they have formulated and tested organization output measures. We also include literature-based references where appropriate and conclude the chapter with a list of electronic resources.

PERSONAL OUTCOMES: THEIR CONCEPTUALIZATION AND MEASUREMENT

Personal outcomes are the benefits derived by program recipients that are the result, direct or indirect, of program activities, services, and supports. As shown in Table 3.1, there are a number of ways to conceptualize personal outcomes.

Table 3.1.   Personal quality of life–related outcome categories

Outcome category	Domains and exemplary indicators
Person-referenced quality-of-life domains	See Table 3.2.
Family-related quality-of-life domains[a]	Family interaction (time together, talks)
	Parenting (helps individual, teaches)
	Emotional well-being (friends, outside help)
	Personal development (education and employment opportunities)
	Physical well-being (health, nutrition, recreation/leisure)
	Financial well-being (transportation, income)
	Community involvement (activities, membership)
	Disability-related supports (school/workplace, home, friends)
Social indicators[b]	Socioeconomic position (education, occupation, income)
	Health (longevity, wellness)
	Subjective well-being (life satisfaction, positive affect [happiness, contentment], absence of negative affect [sadness, worry, helplessness])

[a]*Sources:* Isaacs, Clark, Correia, and Fannery (2009) and, Summers, Poston, Turnbull, Marquis, Hoffman, Mannan, and Wang (2005).

[b]*Sources:* Emerson, Graham, and Hatton (2006) and, Mackenbach, Stirbu, Roskam, Schapp, Menvielle, and Kunst (2008).

Table 3.2.   Quality-of-life related personal outcome domains and exemplary indicators

Domain	Exemplary indicators
Independence factor	
Personal development	Education (achievements, education status)
	Personal competence (cognitive, social, practical)
	Performance (success, achievement, productivity)
Self-determination	Autonomy/personal control
	Goals and personal values (desires, expectations)
	Choices (opportunities, options, preferences)
Social participation factor	
Interpersonal relations	Interactions (social networks, social contacts)
	Relationships (family, friends, peers)
	Supports (emotional, physical, financial)
	Recreation
Social inclusion	Community integration and participation
	Community roles (contributor, volunteer)
	Social supports (support networks, services)
Rights	Human (respect, dignity, equality)
	Legal (citizenship, access, due process)
Well-being factor	
Emotional well-being	Contentment (satisfaction, moods, enjoyment)
	Self-concept (identity, self-worth, self-esteem)
	Lack of stress (predictability and control)
Physical well-being	Health (functioning, symptoms, fitness, nutrition)
	Activities of daily living (self-care, mobility)
	Physical activities including recreation
Material well-being	Financial status (income, benefits)
	Employment (work status, work environment)
	Housing (type of residence, ownership)

Our approach to operationalizing personal outcomes is based on an empirically validated conceptual and measurement quality-of-life framework that lists the major quality-of-life domains and exemplary indicators. The eight domains listed in the table above have been validated through extensive cross-cultural research (Jenaro, Verdugo, Caballo, Balboni, Lachapelle, & Otrebski, 2005; Schalock, Verdugo, Jenaro, Wang, Wehmeyer, Xu, & Lachapelle, 2005; Wang, Schalock, Verdugo, & Jenaro, 2010). The eight domains are also closely aligned with both the rights addressed in the United Nations Convention on the Rights of Persons with Disabilities (United Nations, 2006) and those associated with desired public policy outcomes for people with ID/DD (Schalock et al., 2010a; Shogren & Turnbull, 2010). As shown in Table 3.2, the eight domains can be grouped into three higher order quality-of-life factors: independence, social participation, and well-being (Wang et al., 2010).

Measuring Personal Outcomes

There is an extensive literature regarding quality-of-life measurement (Brown, Schalock, & Brown, 2009; Schalock, Gardner, & Bradley, 2007; Verdugo, Schalock, Keith, & Stancliffe, 2005). The measurement interrogatories summarized in Table 3.3 have emerged from that literature.

Table 3.3. The interrogatories of quality-of-life measurement

Interrogatory	Key factor
What to measure	Quality-of-life domains and indicators
	Quality outcomes-valued personal experiences and circumstances that is, 1) follow as a result or consequence of some activity, intervention, or service, and 2) are measured on the basis of quality indicators
How to measure	Subjective appraisal (e.g., satisfaction or importance)
	Objective assessment (e.g., objective indicators of personal experiences and circumstances)
Who should be involved	Individuals with intellectual and/or developmental disabilities
	People who know the individuals well
Where to assess	Natural environment
When to assess	Depends on questions asked
Research method	Multivariate designs and observational studies that focus on individual and environmental predictors of personal outcomes
	Methods that take into account the effects of individual choice

The authors have been involved in the development, validation, and use of a number of quality of life–related personal outcome scales. One that is widely used internationally and across diagnostic groups is the quality of life measurement GENCAT scale (Verdugo, Arias, Gomez, & Schalock, 2010), which is described in Exhibit 3.1 (p. 46). Other examples can be found in Bonham et al. (2004); Edmonton (2011); and van Loon, van Hove, Schalock, and Claes (2010).

➤ Tool for Application

In studying the outcome categories, domains, and exemplary indicators listed in Tables 3.1 and 3.2 and shown in Exhibit 3.1, the reader might ask, "What personal outcomes does my organization champion, and what is their current status?" Completing Organization Self-Assessment 3.1 (p. 57) will answer these questions.

The analysis of the self-assessment profile will be very informative regarding your conceptualization and measurement of personal outcomes. If your organization has clearly articulated personal outcomes and has measured them, then you should ask, "What are we using the personal outcome information for?" If you have not measured them, the question is "Why not?" If you need to develop personal outcome measures, then 1) specific guidelines can be found in Brown, Schalock, and Brown (2009), Claes, van Hove, van Loon, Vandevelde, and Schalock (2010), and Verdugo et al. (2005); and 2) numerous references to developed personal outcome scales are found in Exhibits 4.4, 6.3, and 7.5, and summarized in Schalock et al. (2007).

ORGANIZATION OUTPUTS: THEIR CONCEPTUALIZATION AND MEASUREMENT

Organization outputs are the organization-referenced products that result from the resources a program uses to achieve its goals and the actions implemented by an organization to produce these outputs. Our approach to the conceptualization and measurement of organization outputs is based on two factors. The first is the concept of performance management as reflected in policy initiatives such as the Centers for Medicare and Medicaid Services (U.S. Department of Health and Human Services, 2010), Government Performance and Results Act (U.S. General Accounting Office, 1999), the U.S. Department of

EXHIBIT 3.1

Example of a Quality-of-Life Measurement Scale (GENCAT)

The GENCAT scale is an instrument for the objective evaluation of quality of life–related personal outcomes of adult users of social services; it is designed according to the eight quality-of-life domains summarized in Table 3.2. The GENCAT assesses 69 objective indicators related to the eight domains that encompass a person's quality of life and that may be the focus of customized support programs provided by different types of social services. The scale is completed by professional staff who know the person well and who have had recent opportunities to observe that person over prolonged periods of time and in different facets of the person's life.

The GENCAT is a self-administered questionnaire in which professionals answer objective, observable questions based on the specific domain-referenced indicator. The scoring key for each item involves four frequency options: *never or hardly ever, sometimes, often,* and *always or almost always.* As shown below, the composite scores recorded in each dimension and for the overall scale are converted into standard scores ($M = 10$; $SD = 3$), into percentiles, and into a quality-of-life index ($M = 100$; $SD = 15$). The resulting profile summarizes the individual's personal outcomes across the eight quality-of-life domains and can be used for reporting, developing individualized support plans (see Chapter 5), and providing a reliable measure for monitoring the program's progress and results.

					Section 1b. Quality of Life (QOL) Profile					
Percentile	EW	IR	MW	PD	PW	SD	SI	RI	QOL Index	Percentile
99	16-20	16-20	16-20	16-20	16-20	16-20	16-20	16-20	>130	99
95	15	15	15	15	15	15	15	15	122-130	95
90	14	14	14	14	14	14	14	14	118-121	90
85	13	13	13	13	13	13	13	13	114-117	85
80									112-113	80
75	12	12	12	12	12	12	12	12	110-111	75
70									108-109	70
65	11			11	11	11	11	11	106-107	65
60									104-105	60
55									102-103	55
50	10	10	10	10	10	10	10	10	100-101	50
45									98-99	45
40									96-97	40
35	9		9	9		9	9		94-95	35
30									92-93	30
25	8	8	8	8	8	8		8	89-91	25
20									86-88	20
15	7	7	7	7	7	7	7	7	84-85	15
10		6	6	6	6	6	6	6	79-83	10
5	5	5	5		5	5	5	5	69–78	5
1	1-4	1-4	1-4	1-4	1-4		1-4	1-4	<68	1

Key: EW = Emotional well-being, IR = Interpersonal relations, MW = Material well-being, PD = Personal development, PW = Physical well-being, SD = Self-determination, SI = Social inclusion, RI = Rights

For more information, contact Miguel Ángel Verdugo (verdugo@usal.es).

Education (Individuals with Disabilities Education Improvement Act of 2004; 2006), and the Urban Institute (Hatry, 2000). The second factor is our experience with numerous redefined ID/DD organizations that have synthesized findings from management and research-based literature; tacit knowledge; and organization-referenced, evidence-based practices to formulate and evaluate the six organization output categories and their associated exemplary indicators listed in Table 3.4.

Measuring Organization Outputs

The measurement of organization outputs is based on the assessment of a comprehensive set of indicators such as those listed in Table 3.4. The Organization Outputs Scale shown in Exhibit 3.2 (p. 48) has been developed and validated by the authors as part of an international program planning and evaluation consortium. The scale's development and validation have been based on meeting the following scale-development criteria: 1) feasibility in that the indicators assessed are typically part of the organization's management information system; 2) utility in that the performance areas and indicators can be used for multiple purposes; 3) robustness in that the indicators are clearly defined and, thus, can be measured reliably; 4) understandable in that the indicators are clearly defined and can be aggregated into easy-to-understand output categories; and 5) relevant with regard to their use in redefining ID/DD organizations.

The Organization Outputs Scale enables organizations to assess organization outputs and to use that information for reporting, monitoring, evaluation, and continuous quality improvement. The scale is administered by a trained, organization-based interviewer who interviews two well-informed staff members to determine whether evidence exists regarding each indicator.

Table 3.4. Organization output categories and associated exemplary indicators

Output category	Exemplary indicators
Personal outcomes	Quality-of-life domain scores
	Quality-of-life factor scores
Effort	Units of service/support provided
	Number of clients placed into more independent, productive, and community-integrated environments
Efficiency	Cost per unit
	Administrative overhead
	Overhead cost rate
	Percentage of budget allocated to client-referenced supports
	Use of information science
	Number of networks/partners
Staff-related indicators	Staff development activities
	Employment duration/tenure
	Job satisfaction
Program options	Employment alternatives
	Community living alternatives
	Educational alternatives
Network indicators	Partners/interagency agreements
	Consortia membership
	Data-sharing agreements
	Shared eligibility/case management

EXHIBIT 3.2

Organization Outputs Scale

Directions: Evidence exists within the organization that data are collected (or information is available) regarding the respective output indicator. Circle 2 of there is considerable evidence, 1 if there is some evidence, and 0 if there is no evidence for each organization output indicator.

Output category	Output indicator			
Personal outcomes	Quality-of-life domain scores	2	1	0
	Quality-of-life factor scores	2	1	0
Effort	Units of service/support	2	1	0
	Number of clients placed into more independent, productive, and community-integrated environments	2	1	0
Efficiency	Cost per unit	2	1	0
	Administrative overhead rate	2	1	0
	Overhead cost rate	2	1	0
	Percentage of budget allocated to client-referenced supports	2	1	0
	Use of information systems	2	1	0
	Number of networks/partners	2	1	0
Staff-related measures	Staff development activities	2	1	0
	Employment duration/tenure	2	1	0
	Job satisfaction	2	1	0
Program options	Employment alternatives	2	1	0
	Community living alternatives	2	1	0
	Education alternatives	2	1	0
Network indicators	Partners/interagency agreements	2	1	0
	Consortia membership	2	1	0
	Data-sharing agreements	2	1	0
	Shared eligibility/case management	2	1	0

Total score _____

Percentage score

(score/40) _____

➤ *Tool for Application*

Evaluating your organization's current status on the Organization Outputs Scale will provide valuable information regarding how your organization has addressed organization outputs and their measurement. In analyzing the profile obtained in Exhibit 3.2, you might want to focus not just on your total and percentage scores but also on those specific output categories where you are strong (and can build on) and on those where you are weak (and need further development). In addition, evaluate whether the exemplary indicators are part of your management information system or are either not available or available only in a file cabinet—a sure sign that your organization is data rich but information poor.

USING PERSONAL OUTCOMES AND ORGANIZATION OUTPUTS FOR REPORTING, MONITORING, EVALUATION, AND CONTINUOUS QUALITY IMPROVEMENT

When we are asked questions about how organizations can use personal outcomes and organization outputs, our first response is always that it depends on four factors. First, what questions are you asking, and what is your intended use of the information? Second, what information/data do you have readily available, and are the data psychometrically sound (i.e., with regard to **reliability** and validity)? Third, what format is the data in, and is this format understandable to your staff? In reference to this third question, and because most organization personnel are not statisticians, we often suggest that the organization provide data tutorials to help personnel understand relevant statistical concepts and how best to interpret data regarding personal outcomes and organization outputs. Fourth, have you considered ways to translate the information into practice? Once the four questions are answered satisfactorily, we explain and provide examples of the following common uses of personal outcomes and organization outputs information: reporting, monitoring, evaluation, and continuous quality improvement.

Reporting

Reporting involves the description of key variables associated with the organization's service delivery system and gives an account of measurable personal outcomes and organization outputs. Its major purpose is to communicate to multiple stakeholders by using descriptive information.

Report writing is not new to ID/DD organization personnel. The relevant question is "What is in the report?" Consistent with the need for ID/DD organizations to address the challenges discussed in Chapter 1, we suggest that ID/DD organizations employ what are commonly referred to as *provider profiles* to meet needs related to accountability requirements, quality assurance standards, and systems change monitoring.

Initiated in Nebraska and Maryland (see the Resources section for web addresses), these provider profiles report multiple data sets that are published annually both in hard copy and electronically for all ID/DD agencies receiving state funds. A summary of the key components of a provider profile is presented in Exhibit 3.3.

Different data sets included in an agency's profile are used for different purposes. The section on agency information is straightforward and describes the services and supports provided. The next three sections (II–IV) are important organization outputs that indicate the organization's commitment to staff training, continuous quality improvement, and quality assurance. The fifth section summarizes assessed quality-of-life scores on those domains referenced in

Table 3.2 and Exhibit 3.1. This information can also be used for multiple purposes including the establishment of empirical benchmarks. The average quality-of-life scores for all organization clientele are presented sequentially so that the organization has an empirical benchmark regarding client changes in each quality-of-life domain. A second empirical benchmark is obtained when comparing the organization averages with those of the larger system. The third empirical benchmark is obtained by comparing the organization's and/or system's assessed quality-of-life scores with those of community members who do not have disabilities.

From a reporting perspective, provider profiles yield useful information for all key stakeholders. Clients receive information regarding the effectiveness of their organization in enhancing their personal well-being and the organization's commitment to continuous quality improvement and quality assurance. As public information, the profiles can also be used by clients in selecting specific service/support organizations. For organizations, the profiles provide documentation of their quality assurance and quality improvement activities and a standardized way to report personal outcomes. For policy makers and funders, the profiles provide information that they can use to judge the social returns on investment. To date, the authors are aware of few organizations that report all of the organization outputs summarized in Table 3.4 and assessed on the Organization Outputs Scale (Exhibit 3.2). The primary reason for this lack of consistent reporting is the variability in organization purposes and structure, licensing certification requirements, and/or lack of easily retrievable information regarding output indicators.

Monitoring

Monitoring is an interactive oversight process whose primary purpose regarding personal outcomes and organization outputs is to ensure the precision, accuracy, and integrity of the information that is used for reporting, evaluation, and continuous quality improvement. One way to accomplish this purpose is to determine how information regarding personal outcomes and organization outputs is collected. Information obtained from a reliable and valid assessment instrument is more precise and accurate than information obtained anecdotally or from a nonstandardized assessment or survey instrument.

EXHIBIT 3.3

Key Components of a Provider Profile

   I.   Agency information (location, number of people served per service/support component, listing of service/supports offered, number of employees)

  II. Training activities for direct support staff (e.g., health, safety, individual supports plan development and implementation)

 III. Quality improvement activities (e.g., team development, data tutorials, quality circles, environmental scans)

 IV. Quality assurance activities (e.g., first aid certification, CPR certification)

  V. Quality-of-life scores

     a. Agency averages per quality of life domain (see Table 3.2) shown for each calendar year

     b. Agency averages per domain compared with statewide averages

     c. Agency averages per domain compared with community members without disabilities

➤ *Tool for Application*

Organization Self-Assessment 3.2 (p. 58) provides a template for determining your organization's sources of information regarding personal outcomes and organization outputs. In completing the survey, use the operational definitions found in Tables 3.2 and 3.4. Analyzing your profile will provide important information regarding 1) whether you are actually measuring personal outcomes and/or organization outputs (and, if so, which ones); 2) the strategies you are using for the outcomes and outputs you are measuring; and 3) the need to potentially use survey instruments such as those presented in Exhibits 3.1 and 3.2.

Evaluation

Contrary to the popular conception of evaluation as an assessment for qualitative or quantitative judgments, within the context of organization change, evaluation is defined as the process of carefully and systematically appraising the status of performance indicators and studying the impact of independent variables (e.g., client characteristics, support strategies, and/or organization characteristics) on dependent variables (e.g., personal outcomes or organization outputs). Within this context, the three primary purposes of evaluation are to provide important information for data-based decision making and managing results, provide data for continuous quality improvement, and determine the significant predictors of personal outcomes and/or organization outputs.

Most ID/DD organizations do not view themselves as evaluators; rather, their role historically has been to be evaluated. One essential component in redefining ID/DD organizations involves developing the organization's evaluation capability so that the organization can both evaluate personal outcomes and organizational outputs for reporting and monitoring and, equally important, use that information for continuous quality improvement. Thus, evaluating personal outcomes and organization outputs becomes one of the major catalysts in redefining ID/DD organizations.

This section of the chapter moves beyond the assessment of personal outcomes and organization outputs and toward viewing them as dependent variables. As dependent variables, these measures can be used for multiple evaluation purposes that include: 1) determining the significant predictors of these outcomes and outputs, 2) providing an outcomes/outputs framework for transdisciplinary research, 3) providing a common language to communicate to stakeholders, and 4) implementing a vehicle to monitor the transitional process.

Clearly defined and measured dependent variables such as personal outcomes and organization outputs are critical in evaluation studies that determine the significant predictors of the targeted outcomes/outputs. This type of evaluation is also an integral part of continuous quality improvement. For example, return for a moment to Table 2.2 (p. 23), which summarizes the literature-based factors that significantly affect quality-of-life related personal outcomes. The evaluation studies on which this table is based used well-defined, well-measured personal outcomes (frequently aggregated into a total score) as the dependent variable against which the various potential predictors (e.g., personal characteristics, organization-level variables, societal-level variables) were evaluated for their significant contribution to the outcomes. As discussed in the following section, continuous quality improvement is based in part on explicit knowledge that stems from the determination of significant outcome/output predictor variables. An organization can use this evidence to reallocate resources (time, money, expertise, and technology) that focus on specific quality improvement strategies related to these significant predictors so as to increase the probability of improved outcomes/outputs. Furthermore, and as discussed in Chapter 6, evidence-based practices require well-defined outcome/output measures that are used as dependent variables in the determination of the effectiveness of a particular practice. The role of these measures in performance evaluation and management will be discussed in Chapter 7.

Continuous Quality Improvement

From our perspective, continuous quality improvement incorporates three critical factors. The first involves using tacit knowledge that comes from experience and explicit knowledge that is research based to enhance an organization's effectiveness and efficiency. The second is the use of empirically derived benchmarks, such as the total score or percentage obtained on the Organization Outputs Scale (Exhibit 3.2), as standards against which to evaluate current organization performance. Although benchmarks are frequently based on comparisons with other organizations (Schalock, 2001), we feel that the more meaningful use of benchmarks in redefining ID/DD organizations involves 1) focusing on self-comparison and identifying what works best generally within the organization, 2) using the empirically derived benchmark(s) as a goal that directs quality improvement activities, and 3) using benchmarks to monitor the change process (Schalock, Verdugo, Bonham, Fantova, & van Loon, 2008).

The third factor incorporated into continuous quality improvement is right-to-left thinking. Although it may be clear that results follow particular activities, people typically do not start from anticipated results and work backward. By and large, people are linear thinkers who have been taught to read, write, and think sequentially. Although linear thinking is a critical skill in alignment and program logic models (see Figure 2.2, p. 29), there are significant advantages from a performance management perspective to engage in right-to-left thinking. As we use the term, right-to-left thinking is a two-phase process. First, it involves clearly identifying desired personal outcomes and organization outputs. Second, it requires organization personnel to ask and answer a performance-guiding question: "What needs to be in place in terms of organization and systems-level processes for these desired outcomes and outputs to occur?" In essence, right-to-left thinking allows your organization to begin with the end in mind.

There are at least five advantages to using right-to-left thinking as an essential component of continuous quality improvement. First, it establishes the mind-set among personnel within an organization that change is possible by beginning with the question, "What needs to be in place?" This question implies two things: that change is possible and that the primary purpose of quality improvement is to bring about change. The net result is that personnel come to realize that thinking how to make changes is the first step after defining what you want. Second, an organization positions itself to learn from others when personnel ask a related question: "What have similar organizations done to enhance personal outcomes and organization outputs, and what does the literature say?" Answering this question involves creating a culture of learning and what we refer to in Chapter 4 as a *learning organization*. Third, right-to-left thinking focuses personnel's efforts on support strategies that have a demonstrated relationship to enhanced personal outcomes and management strategies that enhance organization outputs. As such, right-to-left thinking leads to increased organization effectiveness by streamlining the service/supports delivery process, reducing duplication, and using best practices. Fourth, the organization gains time by having a clear focus on using effective support strategies. Steven Jay Gould (as quoted in Mauboussin, 2010, p. 27) says it well: "I had asked the right question and found the answers. I had obtained, in all probability, the most precious of all possible gifts in the circumstances—substantial time." And, fifth, establishing clear goals regarding personal outcomes and organization outputs provides an initial benchmark against which the organization can monitor and evaluate the transformation process.

The goal of continuous quality improvement is to enhance an organization's effectiveness and efficiency by focusing on changing organization policies, practices, and training within the context of values guiding innovation: dignity, equality, self-determination, nondiscrimination, and inclusion. Quality improvement is incremental and requires not only clearly operationalized and measured personal outcomes and organization outputs (such as those described in Tables 3.1–3.4 and shown in Exhibits 3.1–3.3) but also the implementation of a system of supports (Chapter 5), the use of evidence-based practices (Chapter 6), the availability of a performance-based evaluation and management system (Chapter 7), and high-performance teams (Chapter 4) to develop, implement, and evaluate a **quality improvement plan.** For this reason, and given that we have yet to discuss these areas, a more detailed discussion of continuous quality improvement and quality improvement plans is deferred to Chapter 7 (see Exhibit 7.3, p. 131). However, it is not too early to think about what a quality improvement plan would look like based on the contents of Chapters 1–3.

EXHIBIT 3.4

Quality Improvement Plan Template

Component	Brief description/text reference
1. Targeted area	Personal outcomes (Tables 3.1 and 3.2) Organization outputs (Table 3.4)
2. Goal	To enhance personal outcomes and organization outputs measured against specific benchmarks
3. Strategy	Some examples: values training to change mental models, data tutorials to increase understanding and knowledge, assistive technology devices to reduce the mismatch between a person's capability and environmental demands and/or provide opportunities for inclusion, self-determination, and empowerment
4. Rationale	Why the specific quality improvement strategy would logically enhance the targeted area and thus facilitate goal attainment
5. Responsibility center	Identification of specific high-performance support team (see Chapter 4) or person to implement the strategy
6. Role of leadership	What role(s) will leadership play in implementing and evaluating the impact of the quality improvement strategy (see Table 1.5)
7. Empirical base	Specification of the objective evidence and/or measure(s) used to evaluate the impact of the quality improvement strategy
8. Values governing the process	Dignity, equality, self-determination, nondiscrimination, inclusion

Exhibit 3.4 summarizes the eight components of a quality improvement plan. The plan begins with a clear statement of the targeted area followed by a measurable goal whose attainment will be evaluated by objective evidence (empirical base—Component 7). The specific strategy is specified (Component 3), followed by a brief rationale section that explains why the **quality improvement strategy** should logically and positively affect the targeted area. The three remaining components relate to the assignment of the responsibility center (Component 5), the role of leadership in the process (Component 6), and the values that will guide the development and implementation of the plan (Component 8).

➤ Tool for Application

Quality improvement plans need to address specific realities within the organization's operating environment. Specifically, each ID/DD organization or system has its own culture and requirements for reporting and accountability. In addition, some organizations/systems already have data and performance management systems in place that include clearly operationalized outcome and output measures. We are not proposing that all organizations/systems rush to use the proposed template shown in Exhibit 3.4. However, the framework outlined there should have heuristic value to all readers as personnel within ID/DD organizations continue to think about redefining their organizations and the role that quality improvement plays in that process. This is the purpose of Organization Self-Assessment 3.3.

Analyzing your profile will help frame any changes you need to make regarding your quality improvement efforts. First, if you have a preponderance of *no* responses, you may need to focus more on the purposes and components of your current approach to quality improvement. Second, you may need to think, "What is it that we are trying to improve?" Personal outcomes and organization outputs will provide that important framework. Third, you may discover that your current approach to quality improvement is based on deductive reasoning (i.e., armchair discussions, committee meetings, and intuition) and not on empirical information obtained from the assessment of personal outcomes and organization outputs. Thus, you should carefully review the rationale and empirical base components in Exhibit 3.4. Our experience has been that viewing continuous quality improvement from the perspective of these eight components also results in productive discussions centered around the role of leadership and the values guiding the quality improvement effort. We have also observed that the most effective quality improvement plans are short: usually only 3–5 pages, with copies distributed to all relevant personnel.

➤ ACTION STEPS YOU CAN TAKE NOW

Most ID/DD organizations and systems are data rich but information poor. Thus, one of the essential tasks in measuring and using personal outcomes and organization outputs for the multiple purposes described in this chapter is to think clearly and logically about the organization/system's desired outcomes and outputs and about how objective indicators of those can be assessed and used for reporting results relative to each, monitoring the key aspects of the organization/system to ensure compliance with best practices, evaluating the potential causes of those outcomes and outputs, and using those empirically based outcomes and outputs as a basis for continuous quality improvement. Although the task is potentially daunting, it is doable—and, whether the task is daunting or not, measuring and using personal outcomes and organization outputs is an essential component in redefining ID/DD organizations.

Throughout this chapter, we have presented text material, organization self-assessments, and exhibits that collectively provide the basis for the following four action steps that you can take now to measure and use personal outcomes and organization outputs.

➤ *Action Step 1*   Identify the personal outcomes and organization outputs that you are currently using. Although your data sets may not be exactly the same as those we propose in Tables 3.1, 3.2, and 3.4, they should meet the following definitional criteria: 1) Personal outcomes are the benefits derived by program recipients that are the result, direct or indirect, of program activities, services, and supports; and 2) organization outputs are the organization-referenced products that result from the resources a program uses to achieve its goals and the actions implemented by an organization to produce these outputs. If the outcomes and outputs you are using do not meet these criteria, rethink your currently assessed and reported outcomes and outputs, using those summarized in Tables 3.1 and 3.4 as a guide. As you discuss this issue, return to Exhibits 3.1 and 3.2.

➤ *Action Step 2*   Specify how you are currently using your assessed personal outcomes and organization outputs. Are they being used for reporting, monitoring, evaluation, and continuous quality improvement? If so, how? If not, how can they be used for multiple purposes? Use Exhibits 3.3 and 3.4 as guides.

➤ *Action Step 3*   Analyze what is missing in your data system and determine whether your current—or additional—data sets can be used for multiple purposes. If so, how? Remember that using the same data sets for multiple purposes reduces duplication and the expense of collecting and analyzing redundant information—thus increasing your organization's efficiency.

➤ *Action Step 4*   Discuss with organization personnel how your organization can approach quality improvement from the perspective outlined in Exhibit 3.4. This framework will help not just with the selection of personal outcomes and organization output classes but also with the alignment of data sets to the strategies used in the quality improvement plan. Furthermore, it will allow you to specify the importance of the plan's rationale, responsibility center, leadership, empirical base, and the values guiding the quality improvement process. If needed, you might want to refer to Exhibit 7.3 (p. 131), which presents a more complete exemplary quality improvement plan.

SUMMARY AND KEY POINTS

Redefining ID/DD organizations begins with a clear vision of desired results and a mind-set that growth, change, and transformation are both possible and necessary. Personal outcomes and organization outputs provide that clear vision and mind-set. This chapter has focused on personal outcomes and organization outputs and how they can be conceptualized, measured, and used.

Important Points We Have Made in This Chapter

➤ ID/DD organizations and systems need to be more accountable in terms of personal outcomes and organization outputs and efficient in terms of resources used.

➤ Information about personal outcomes and organization outputs is important for reporting, monitoring, evaluation, quality assurance, continuous quality improvement, and monitoring systems change.

➤   Information about outcomes and outputs must be readily available and
    easily understood for it to be acted on. Involving clientele and support staff
    enhances the meaningfulness and use of the information.

RESOURCES

Electronic

Bonham Research. *AskMe! Maryland survey.* Retrieved from http://www.bonhamre-
    search.com/Level%201/AskMe.htm

Council on Quality: Quality measures. *Better services, better outcomes, stronger com-
    munities.* Retrieved from http://www.cql.org

Human Services Research Institute. *National Core Indicators.* Retrieved from http://
    www.nationalcoreindicators.org

Maryland provider profile. Retrieved from http://dhmh.maryland.gov/dda_mdre-
    portable/nl/askorgreport

Nebraska Department of Health and Human Services. *2008 Nebraska developmental
    disabilities provider profiles.* Retrieved from http://www.hhs.state.ne.us/dip/ded/
    ProviderProfile.pdf

Current Status on Personal Outcomes and Their Measurement

Directions: Place a check in the column that best describes whether the specific personal outcome is measured, not measured, or needs to be developed.

Outcome category	Current status		
	Measured	Not measured	Need to develop
Person-referenced domains			
Personal development			
Self-determination			
Interpersonal relations			
Social inclusion			
Rights			
Emotional well-being			
Physical well-being			
Material well-being			
Family-referenced domains			
(see Table 3.1 if your organization provides family services/supports)			
Societal indicators			
Socioeconomic position			
Health			
Subjective well-being			

Monitoring Template for Personal Outcomes and Organization Outputs

Directions: Circle the current status level that best describes the measurement strategy used for each of the outcomes/output categories listed below.

Outcome/output area	Outcome/output category	Current level			
Personal outcomes	Quality-of-life domain scores	3	2	1	0
	Quality-of-life factor scores	3	2	1	0
Organization outputs	Personal outcomes	3	2	1	0
	Effort indicators	3	2	1	0
	Efficiency indicators	3	2	1	0
	Staff-related measures	3	2	1	0
	Program options	3	2	1	0
	Network indicators	3	2	1	0

3 = Currently measured via a reliable and valid instrument

2 = Currently measured by a survey or instrument without demonstrated reliability and validity

1 = Currently measured by anecdotal information

0 = Not measured

Organization's Approach to Continuous Quality Improvement

Directions: This self-assessment requires that you use a current quality improvement plan developed by your organization as the basis for the assessment. The assessment is based on the quality improvement template presented in Exhibit 3.4. Evaluate your status on the eight quality improvement questions listed below by checking *Yes* or *No*.

Component	Question and response
Targeted area	Is there a clearly identified and defined targeted area? Yes__ No__
Goal	Is there a clearly defined goal that is measurable? Yes__ No__
Strategy	Is there a description of the specific quality improvement strategy? Yes__ No__
Rationale	Is there a clearly articulated rationale as to why the specific quality improvement strategy would logically enhance the targeted area and, thus, facilitate goal attainment? Yes__ No__
Responsibility center	Is a responsibility center clearly identified? Yes__ No__
Role of leadership	Is there a clearly stated role that leadership will play in the implementation and evaluation of the plan? Yes__ No__
Empirical base	Are objective measures or other evidence indicators clearly specified? Yes__ No__
Values	Are the values guiding the quality improvement process clearly articulated? Yes__ No__

4

Developing High-Performance Teams

What You Can Expect in This Chapter

➤ Discussion of five contextual factors that indicate the need for organizations to develop high-performance teams

➤ Description of what high-performance teams do within organizations that provide services and supports to people with intellectual and developmental disabilities

➤ Explanation of the five essential characteristics of high-performance teams

➤ Suggestions as to how to develop high-performance teams

➤ Discussion of operating principles and accountability requirements of high-performance teams

The time is right for organizations that provide services and supports to people with ID/DD to develop what we refer to in this chapter to as *high-performance teams.* Although organizations use teams for multiple purposes such as individual supports planning, supports provision, quality improvement, quality assurance, and staff development, the question many organizations are asking is "Are these teams currently functioning in ways that enhance the organization's effectiveness and efficiency?" In some organizations, the answer is *yes;* in others, *maybe;* and in still others, a definite *no.*

Teams, whether they are interdisciplinary, intradisciplinary, or cross-disciplinary, consume a significant amount of an organization's resources and attention. They also potentially garner the significant expertise to successfully implement the organization's services and supports. In our estimation, the real challenge to today's ID/DD organizations is to develop high-performance teams that ensure quality services and enhance an organization's effectiveness and efficiency. As discussed in this chapter, such teams 1) typically perform key functions related to supports assessment, individual plan development, information processing, evaluation of person-referenced outcomes and organization outputs, continuous quality improvement, and crisis management; and 2) are characterized by their being involved, informed, organized, accountable, and empowered.

To appreciate the importance of developing high-performance teams, it is necessary to understand the context within which ID/DD organizations operate. That context can be described in terms of five influencing **contextual factors.** First, there has been a transformation in the culture of professional services to people with ID/DD. Traditionally, professional expertise (e.g., medical, psychological, nursing, educational, social work) represented a central authority in organizations. For many decades, this expertise provided the knowledge, standards, protocols, and practices to direct the caregiving and rehabilitation processes with a reasonable degree of autonomy and professional independence. Beginning in the last decade of the 20th century, this situation has changed in that professionals are now perceived more as organization/agency employees and are expected to act in the interest of the organization's goals and targets, including viewing clients as consumers (Noordegraaf, 2007; Reinders, 2008).

The second contextual factor has been the emergence of new public management that views the market as the prime regulatory instrument in the public domain. Public goods, such as the well-being of people with ID/DD, are seen as products that are open to market mechanisms of demand, supply, and price. Features of the new public management are market mechanisms, decentralization, quality control, measures of performance, and an emphasis on results, efficiency, and cost-effectiveness. As a result, agency/organization personnel need to spend considerable time in detailed administration and documentation (DiRita, Parmenter, & Stancliffe, 2008).

Third, education and rehabilitation services and supports are more client and family driven. This contextual factor is playing out in the purchase of services/support agreements between clients and/or families and service and support providers. Self-directed funding also reflects this contextual factor.

Fourth, there has emerged a mind-set that the provision of services and supports should not be a function of satisfying consumer support wants but, rather, of meeting client support needs. As discussed in Chapter 5, the formulation of the individual's support is the result of a common endeavor that involves both client input and professional assessment. The same is true for the delivery of supports. Therefore, within ID/DD organizations, conditions should be created that foster a productive and satisfying dialogue as reflected in a sustainable partnership characteristic of high-performance teams.

The fifth contextual factor relates to the continuing need for tenure-related stability of organization personnel. ID/DD organizations are facing significant staff turnover, and there is no sign that staffing continuity is improving (Lakin & Stancliffe, 2005). However, there is evidence that a significant part of support staff discontinuity as experienced by clients and families is not related to external (labor market) factors but, rather, to the service organizations' design and management practices (Buntinx, 2008). The stability of an organization's personnel is crucial for providing quality services and supports related to effective practices. One good way to increase personnel stability is to pay special attention to recruiting new members, teaching and involving them in client-related activities, promoting continuous training, and involving them as members of high-performance teams.

These five contextual factors indicate that the time is right for ID/DD organizations to develop high-performance teams. The purpose of this chapter is to summarize what high-performance teams do within ID/DD organizations, describe the characteristics of such teams, and explain how they can be developed. At the outset, it is important to stress the key role that mental models play in the development of high-performance teams. Six of the future-oriented mental models summarized in Table 1.4 are basic to the successful development and implementation of high-performance teams: an emphasis on self/personal empowerment, organizations as self-organizing systems, horizontally structured organizations, a focus on outcomes, "us" accountability, and a shared understanding that success is dependent on everyone.

WHAT HIGH-PERFORMANCE TEAMS DO

High-performance teams reflect the structural changes that are occurring in both public and private organizations. These changes stem from top-down hierarchies that are built along vertical lines of authority to organizations built along horizontal lines of action. High-performance teams have emerged in the human services field within the context of the transformation of professional services, the emergence of new public management, the focus on consumer-driven and consumer-centered supports, and the need to increase the involvement and tenure-related stability of organization personnel. These teams represent an effective and efficient way to integrate client, professional, and managerial interests. By integrating support processes, cost-effectiveness, and quality improvement practices into the same, high-performance teams are in a better position to maintain quality, continuity, and flexibility. But, what do they do?

What high-performance teams do within any specific ID/DD organization is determined by two factors and one piece of reality. The first factor is the need to implement the respective organization's mission and goals. Some organizations provide multiple services and supports including diagnostic services, education/rehabilitation supports, case management, and follow-along contacts. Others may be engaged only in residential or employment programs. Thus, the composition and focus of the team will vary depending on the organization's mission and goals. The second factor is that specific team functions may be governed by statutory requirements. This relates to clinical functions such as who can diagnose, who can prescribe medication or develop behavior intervention programs, and who can engage in specific education or rehabilitation practices. The piece of reality is that in most ID/DD organizations, 90% or more of a client's waking hours are spent with support staff, who are increasingly regarded as professional because of their tacit knowledge and essential role in implementing a system of supports.

For the majority of ID/DD organizations with which we are familiar, high-performance teams are organized around the following six primary functions summarized in Table 4.1.

CHARACTERISTICS OF HIGH-PERFORMANCE TEAMS

The management literature focuses extensively on how organizations can foster the successful development of high-performance teams. On the basis of our reading of the management literature as well as our personal experiences observing high-performance teams in

Table 4.1. Primary functions of high-performance teams

1. Assessment teams who conduct the assessment of the client's support needs and are involved in the functional analysis of behavior related to the application of positive behavior supports. Specific members may be involved in diagnosis and/or eligibility determination.

2. Individual supports teams who are involved in the development and implementation of a system of supports. This team develops the plan based on the assessment of support needs and the alignment of support strategies to the client's personal goals and interests. The three key players in the plan's implementation are the client, the support staff, and case management personnel. Clients, family members, and essential support staff and teachers are members of this team.

3. Information systems teams who are responsible for data gathering, processing, analysis, and reporting. The information generated by this team is used for reporting, monitoring, evaluation, and continuous quality improvement. Information technology personnel are essential to this team.

4. Outcomes evaluation teams who partner with research consultants or universities to evaluate the impact of the organization's services and supports on personal outcomes and organization outputs. Individuals with knowledge of research design, statistics, and data-analysis strategies are essential to this team.

5. Quality improvement teams who are integrally involved in developing the goals, strategies, and rationale for quality improvement strategies. They also typically have primary responsibility for implementation of these strategies. All relevant stakeholders such as the client, members of the client's family, direct support staff, and a supports coordinator or case manager should be members of a quality improvement team.

6. Crisis management teams who provide 24-hour support to line and program staff to minimize crisis situations and provide professional assistance in handling challenging behaviors. Professionals with expertise in chemical intervention, applied behavior analysis, and behavioral intervention are essential to this team.

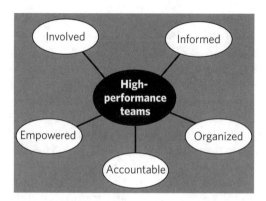

Figure 4.1. Characteristics of high-performance teams.

action, we suggest that high-performance teams can be defined according to the five characteristics shown in Figure 4.1. This section of the chapter describes these characteristics and explains how each contributes to an organization's effectiveness and efficiency.

Involved

Psychologists use the concept of locus of control to explain why it is critical for people to be involved in decisions about their lives and to control their destiny as much as possible. The term *internal locus of control* is used when we are involved and feel we have control. If we feel that others control us and do not include us in decisions and life activities, the term used is *external locus of control.* People who experience internal locus of control are more motivated, have a more positive self-concept, and exhibit a sense of ownership in both processes and outcomes/outputs.

The microunit concept provides a good vehicle to increase the involvement of organization personnel and enable more of an internal locus of control (Buntinx, 2008; Nelson, Batalden, & Godfrey, 2007). Microunits refer to teams that provide specific functions within an organization. They include the relevant stakeholders such as service recipients, direct support staff, and professionals but also include key elements of the human resources and financial control systems of the organization. There is no formula for the size of the microunit, but it should encompass all relevant functions within an organization (see Table 4.1).

The basic idea in a high-performance team whose members are highly involved is that the services and supports provided by the organization can be no better than the quality of the services and supports generated by the frontline microunit. Through their involvement, the team members share the same coordinating process, information system, and orientation toward valued personal outcomes. Because they operate at the client-service interface of the organization, they should also maintain relations with relevant settings of their clients such as family, school, work, and leisure. The primary orientation of team members is to maintain productive client relationships that enhance personal growth and valued outcomes. In addition, the increased involvement of all organization personnel provides an efficient way for an organization to address human resource management and financial control challenges. Specifically, a high-performance team with members who are highly involved provides a model for structuring interdisciplinary support teams that: 1) combine the expertise of frontline staff and relevant experts; 2) meet on a regular basis to discuss and evaluate client needs, support strategies, and outcomes; 3) share the same information about the client's assessed needs and available resources; 4) participate autonomously in internal resource allocation and efficiency monitoring; and 5) self-manage and monitor their efforts and results regarding continuous quality improvement.

Informed

People who are informed make better decisions. Organizations that are informed about best practices and their implementation are definitely more effective and generally more efficient. High-performance teams can function only in an organization where both tacit and explicit knowledge are recognized and appreciated. Tacit knowledge is the wisdom that comes from personal experiences among staff; explicit knowledge is based on research.

The distinction between tacit and explicit knowledge and the role they play in high-performance teams is important. Reinders (2010) has stressed that overemphasizing explicit, empirically based information might render the personal dimension of professional knowledge invisible, thereby excluding it from attention and support. Although we return to this issue in Chapter 6 in our discussion of evidence-based practices, all organization personnel—and especially direct support staff who spend the greatest amount of time with the client—bring to the team insight regarding how to interpret behavior and nonverbal communication, empathy, and insight into the client according to their experiences with the person.

Both tacit and explicit knowledge provide the basis for what Senge (2006) refers to as a learning organization, which is essential to the successful operation of high-performance teams. A learning organization fosters mentoring within the group, uses resources/information based on research literature and experience-based knowledge and insight, creates potential solutions, implements actions to improve performance, evaluates results, and rewards the team's efforts. Learning organizations also take risks, partner with others to increase their knowledge base and learning potential, scan the environment to find new ways to do things, encourage learning by involving all organization personnel, and reinforce curiosity and openness to new approaches.

In efforts to inform team members, it is important to realize that people process information differently. That is, they have different cognitive learning styles. For example, people can gather information by attending to details (receptive) or looking for general points or relationships (perceptive). Analogously, people can process information by being systematic or intuitive. Some team members will be systematic-receptive (and need more time and information before making a decision), and some will be perceptive-intuitive (and need less time and information to make a decision). This important distinction between cognitive learning styles underlies the key concept in the highly successful book, *Blink: The Power of Thinking without Thinking* (Gladwell, 2005). On the basis of material presented in that book, we suggest that high-performance team members are most informed when they: 1) look for cues, general points, patterns, and relationships; 2) are willing to use trial and exploration; 3) avoid preconceptions; 4) rely on a delicate balance between deliberation and intuition; and 5) reduce things to the simplest possible elements in their decision making.

Organized

Sustainable organizations need to function on a "loose–tight" basis. However, if high-performance teams are to increase an organization's effectiveness and efficiency, there needs to be "tightness" in their operations. That is, specific protocols need to be developed around the following six key issues: communicating effectively, organizing team meetings, achieving synergy, being persuasive, preventing cognitive traps, and overcoming **conflict.** Team efforts can be jeopardized if appropriate protocols are not developed to address these issues. We define *protocol* as a clear understanding of an issue and a shared response to address the issue.

As discussed by Guttman (2008, p. 148–149), there are many ways to establish protocols and thereby manage key issues within high-performance teams. According to Guttman, key issues are best managed through defining each issue, clarifying the issue, determining the priority of action based on the impact of the issue to the organization's effectiveness and efficiency, and developing a plan of action. This process typically involves selecting a subteam whose goal is to reach closure; identifying a process- and outcome-oriented team member who is focused, is able to depersonalize, has sufficient time, and is adept at involving others; determining major steps needed to gain closure; agreeing on key deliverables; establishing time lines and milestones; and communicating the results to the team and organization. To various degrees, these general approaches can be used to establish protocols regarding each of the six key issues discussed below. As discussed later in the chapter, strong leadership is typically required initially to establish these protocols.

Communicating   High-performance teams do not have time for pseudo-communication: They need effective communication. Essential aspects of such communication are clarity, authenticity, accuracy, efficiency (i.e., being direct and to the point), completeness, timeliness (i.e., being relevant to the issue at hand), focus on decisions and deliverables, and openness. This last aspect occurs in organizations with supportive cultures that reward candor.

Team Meetings   Team meetings can be an organization's greatest time robber. High-performance teams use time productively and sparingly. In a survey (reported in *USA Today*, June 9, 2010, p. A1) of the biggest workplace peeves, poor time management was ranked as the most common pet peeve among 43% of the 1,037 workers surveyed. The next two highest ranked peeves involved gossip (36%) and messiness (25%). Most readers likely have spent countless hours in team meetings (and can appreciate the term *meetingitis*) and wished more than once that there were better, agreed-on protocols. The management literature (and personal experience) suggests the following parameters for effective and efficient team meetings: 1) The meeting starts on time; 2) all members are present or send a representative; 3) cell phones and laptops are barred except for relevant data retrieval; 4) there are preestablished time allotments per agenda item, and the chair sticks to them; 5) there are no side conversations; 6) everyone participates; and 7) the meeting ends on schedule with closure and deliverables.

Synergy   Steven Covey (2004) introduced the concept of synergy as a principle of creative cooperation that is built on trust and cooperation. The process can save significant time and lead to increased effectiveness and efficiency. Creative cooperation (i.e., synergy) is facilitated in high-performance teams through three processes: build on one another's strengths and contributions (there is no reason to keep reinventing wheels); be proactive and involve others in creative endeavors and overcoming challenges; and think "win–win" so that, through collaboration, everyone wins.

Persuasiveness   High-performance team members need to understand the process of persuasion and its impact on attitude change. The process of persuasion essentially boils down to who (the source) communicates what (the message) by what means (the channel) to whom (the receiver). Key factors influencing each of these processes include the following: (Petty & Wegener, 1998)

- Source factors: credibility, expertise, trustworthiness, likeability, attractiveness, and similarity. These factors relate not only to the person attempting to persuade others but also to how others feel about themselves regarding credibility (e.g., good judgment), expertise (e.g., do you have the facts?), and trustworthiness (e.g., do you accept your own judgment?).

- Message factors: fear versus logic (logic is better), one-sided versus two-sided argument (two-sided is better), and repetition. The popular book *Made to Stick: Why Some Ideas Survive and Others Die* (Heath & Heath, 2009) expands on these source and message factors. In this book, the authors explain how to get people to pay attention to what you say and suggest specifically that you create traction by presenting your idea as a story that is simple, unexpected, concrete, credible, and emotional.

- Channel factors: in person (by far the best), phone/texting (effectiveness depends on many factors), or computer (quite effective, but if the message is important, most people will want a hard copy and/or follow up with a call)

- Receiver factors: expectations (it is good to forewarn) and prior knowledge of the issues

Cognitive Traps   Six cognitive traps can be very detrimental to high-performance teams. First, in "all-or-nothing thinking," the team sees things in black-and-white categories, and if a situation is anything less than perfect, it is viewed as a total failure. The reality is that most of life is a shade of gray. Second, in "overgeneralization," the team sees a single event as a never-ending pattern of defeat by using words such as always or never. Third, team members sometimes use a "mental filter" in which they pick out a single negative detail and dwell on it exclusively. Each team meeting should begin by celebrating successes! Fourth, when teams fall into the cognitive trap of emotional reasoning, they act quickly on the basis of how they feel at the moment rather than analyzing the true facts or the available information. Fifth, when teams use "should statements," watch out: They feel that things should be the way they hoped or expected them to be rather than the way they actually are. Teams should be optimistic and set high goals, but they should not fall into the cognitive trap of equating "should" with feelings of guilt. The sixth cognitive trap relates to "personalization and blame," in which the team members hold themselves personally responsible for events that are not entirely under their control.

Conflict   Differences in attitudes, opinions, and approaches are the basis of conflict. From a proactive and positive perspective, the key thing in addressing conflict is to recognize it and resolve it. We know this is easier said than done, but conflict resolution is one of the hallmarks of a high-performance team. The Thomas–Kilmann approach to understanding and resolving conflict is very applicable to high-performance teams. Thomas and Kilmann's two-dimensional model (as presented in Thomas, 1976) involves assertiveness (which varies from unassertive to assertive) and cooperativeness (which varies from uncooperative to cooperative). Visualizing these two dimensions as a 2 × 2 matrix, one can envision five ways to address conflict: competing, accommodating, avoiding, compromising, and collaborating. Competing implies being assertive and uncooperative; accommodating entails being unassertive and cooperative; avoiding is being unassertive and uncooperative; compromising involves being less assertive but cooperative; and collaborating involves being both assertive and cooperative. Collaboration is the preferred and most productive conflict resolution strategy in high-performance teams.

Conflict resolution also involves crucial conversations. These conversations involve 1) staying focused to get better results, 2) continuing to have a dialogue that minimizes defensiveness among those involved, 3) stepping out of the "conflict content" and resolving

EXHIBIT 4.1

**Key Components of Being
Organized and Following Established Protocols**

Communication: clarity, authenticity, accuracy, efficiency, completeness, timeliness,
   focus, openness

Team meetings: start on time, all members present, no distractions or side
   conversations, time specified for agenda items, full participation, closure,
   deliverable(s)

Synergy: build on one another's strengths, be proactive, think "win–win"

Persuasion: understand source, message, channel, receiver factors

Cognitive traps: avoid by recognizing the fallacies of all-or-nothing thinking,
   overgeneralization, mental filters, emotional reasoning, should statements,
   personalization and blame

Conflict: approach and resolve by focusing on collaborating, by being both assertive
   and cooperative, and by engaging in crucial conversations

the conflict through a shared purpose, 4) exhibiting positive emotions that make people
want to return to the dialogue, and 5) applying problem-solving skills.

Exhibit 4.1 summarizes the essential points about the six protocols associated with being
organized. When used by high-performance teams and incorporated into high-performance
team meetings and team-related processes, these six protocols can make ID/DD organizations more effective and efficient.

Accountable

What are high-performance teams accountable for? Certainly not the legal and financial stability of the organization (that is the board of directors' responsibility); not the day-to-day
management of the organization (that is the CEO's responsibility); nor are they responsible
for the culture of the organization (that is everyone's responsibility). High-performance
teams cannot be held accountable if they are not involved, informed, and empowered. Our
proposal is that high-performance team members should work within the team at their
highest level of licensure, certification, and competency and are accountable for the eight
outcome categories summarized in Table 4.2.

➤ *Tool for Application*

The accountability requirements summarized in Table 4.2 should both serve as an impetus for
high-performance team development and implementation and summarize the key ingredients in redefining ID/DD organizations. Organization Self-Assessment 4.1 (p. 78) begins that
process.

Analyzing this profile will be informative and provide a catalyst for either developing
or further enhancing high-performance teams. If you scored mainly 3s, then you already
have developed and implemented high-performance teams but, perhaps, did not use that
term or understand all their characteristics. Even if you marked mainly 3s, do not overlook
another characteristic of high-performance teams: they are constantly raising the perfor-

Table 4.2.   Accountability requirements of high-performance teams

1. Being fully aware of the organization's desired personal outcomes and expected organization outputs
2. Being involved in the synthesis of assessed client support needs and aligning those needs to the provision of a system of support
3. Being knowledgeable about best practices and evidence-based practices and how those strategies can be used in supports planning
4. Being involved in the development and measurement of personal outcomes and organization outputs
5. Being organized in reference to understanding and following the six protocols summarized in Exhibit 4.1
6. Involving service recipients in team meetings and subsequent actions
7. Constantly monitoring personal outcomes and asking, "What can the team do to enhance these?"
8. Setting a high-performance bar regarding time use, team and protocol development, networking, and personal and team mastery

mance bar and focusing continuously on quality improvement. If your profile is mixed (3s, 2s, and 1s), target those accountability areas that are partially in place or not in place and carefully read the section on developing high-performance teams later in this chapter. If you scored primarily 1s, then it is probably time to address key sustainability issues related to vertical versus horizontal structure of the organization, control mechanisms used within the organization, perceived accountability and responsibility centers, the role of the line staff in the organization's service delivery process, and the clarity of the organization's desired outcomes and outputs. Regardless of one's status on the self-assessment, the profile should be used as a benchmark for judging subsequent organization change and transformation.

Empowered

Within the context of high-performance teams, empowerment means that all organization personnel (including those clients who are so inclined) are involved in activities related to reporting, monitoring, evaluation, and continuous quality improvement. This does not mean that everybody does everything—which might equate to nobody does anything. From our perspective, empowerment means the following:

- Team members have adequate information to act wisely and contribute. Two exhibits (5.2 and 5.3, p. 89 and 92) presented in Chapter 5 reflects this. Exhibit 5.2 shows how a client's complex support needs data can be simplified and put into a supports action plan that line staff can implement. Exhibit 5.3 shows how the same information can be used to develop a client's "My Support Plan"; the plan is provided to the client, who then can monitor the receipt of needed and appropriate supports. It is only reasonable to assume that an organization will be more effective when all members of the high-performance team are on the same, clearly communicated track.

- People who arrange the funding for individual supports plans (e.g., case managers) should be in face-to-face contact with those who develop and implement the individual plan, rather than placing these two key processes into a "silo" within which decisions need to be approved by someone else. This siloism is common in many systems. If the funding parameters are clear, and if the pattern and intensity of the individual's support needs are available, then the high-performance team should be empowered to put the two together and get on with developing and implementing the individual supports plan.

- Crisis management is done at the staff level nearest the client.

- Support staff are expected, encouraged, and rewarded for advocating on behalf of their clientele and interfacing to the maximum degree possible with both generic agencies and each client's natural support network.

Reasonable people operate according to reasonable guidelines. The same is true for high-performance teams. We suggest that empowerment should not lead to justifying poor-quality services and supports, that it should not be a vehicle for stereotypes and prejudices or a substitute for insufficiently explored questions and answers, and that it should not be an excuse for incomplete information or a way to solve conflicts or in-house political problems. Rather, the following two criteria should guide how organizations approach empowering high-performance teams. First, empowerment needs to be systematic in that it is organized, sequential, and logical; second, the empowering process is transparent in that it is apparent and communicated clearly.

There is another side to empowerment. At the personal level, empowerment and the heightened performance that accompanies it involve having maximum control over how one's time is used. To that end, we present in Exhibit 4.2 some helpful aphorisms based on published time management and stress management literature (Schalock & Verdugo, 2010). Our premise is that people who use time well are more productive, creative, and efficient and experience less negative stress. The same can be said of high-performance teams.

In summary, one expected result of high-performance teams who manifest the five characteristics shown in Figure 4.1 is an improvement in the quality of services and supports provided to the organization's clientele. Exhibit 4.3 describes how two high-performance teams within the FEAPS quality model have increased the participating organizations' effectiveness and efficiency. FEAPS is the main Spanish nonprofit, family-based movement for people with ID/DD. It is an umbrella organization composed of 891 nonprofit associations throughout Spain. FEAPS supports 235,000 families and 106,700 people with ID/DD. FEAPS's vision is to be a united group of qualified social organizations with a common ethical code for all member organizations. Since 1996, FEAPS has deployed a complex process of organizational develop-

---

EXHIBIT 4.2

Time and Stress Management Aphorisms

- Schedule time for personal rewards and regular exercise.
- Be proactive; anticipate upcoming issues and problems...and plan ahead.
- Use technology to simplify routine tasks and enhance personal efficiency and effectiveness.
- Use prime production time for just that—productivity.
- Do things right the first time so they do not have to be redone.
- Look for "two-fers," "three-fers," and so forth, to get multiple benefits addressed from one's investment effort.
- Always look for the smallest task that will produce the largest effect.
- Invest your time in making the time of others more productive.
- Balance opportunities with how well they match personal values, life goals, and the development of others.
- Give yourself personal time.

Sources: Schalock & Verdugo, 2010

EXHIBIT 4.3

FEAPS Quality Network and
FEAPS Consultancy Network: Two High-Performance Teams

- **The FEAPS Consultancy Network** is based on the organizational development model. This type of consulting is not an expertise model (in which the consultant is the expert and offers solutions to the client organization) but, rather, a process model, in which the organization, through the consultant, is engaged in finding best solutions and becomes a learning organization. The mission of this network is to provide organization support to develop strategies to enhance individual and family quality of life and to promote individuals' inclusion as full citizens in a fair and supportive society. Currently, the members of this team are 38 professionals with master's degrees in organizational development from different FEAPS entities. FEAPS has an agreement enabling the organizations to develop this consulting work (maximum: 30 days per year). The Consultancy Network management is certified under the ISO 9001:2008. Services of the FEAPS Consultancy Network are low cost for FEAPS organizations.

- **The FEAPS Quality Network** helps orient organizations toward a quality model that involves the quality-of-life model (as outcomes), total quality management (as process), and the FEAPS Code of Ethics (as strategy and values). The mission of the Quality Network is to promote the continued development of FEAPS quality in all FEAPS organizations. Currently, the members of this team are 24 experts in FEAPS quality from different FEAPS entities (one from each Spanish region). All support given to FEAPS entities through this network is free of charge.

These two networks/high-performance teams have the following five characteristics in common: 1) high operational independence (horizontal functioning) and elevated ethical commitment; 2) all members share the same mental models (quality of life, ethics, intellectual disability conceptualization) as a result of ethical commitment and scientific knowledge; 3) all members have an elevated trust in the effectiveness and intentions of their network colleagues; 4) high cohesion among members of each network, based on commitment and affection; and 5) a high degree of mutual support and readiness among the members of each network. Since their inception, these two networks/high-performance teams have increased the organizations' effectiveness and efficiency in the following four ways: 1) promoting awareness and need of cultural change, change thinking, and change actions in organizations through self-evaluation, feedback systems, and deliberation processes to change mental models; 2) pursuing alignment of every organization with FEAPS's mission, vision, values, and strategies to enhance quality-of-life outcomes; 3) developing shared systems of support and good practices, and disseminating best common knowledge to member organizations; and 4) instilling within organizations a high degree of enthusiasm, energy, and loyalty to FEAPS projects.

For more information, contact Javier Tamarit (calidad@feaps.org).

ment that continues today. One consequence of this process was the creation of networks to support the development of associations and promotion of FEAPS quality. In 2001, the FEAPS Quality Network and FEAPS Consultancy Network were created. Both are high-performance teams that facilitate increased organization effectiveness and efficiency.

DEVELOPING HIGH-PERFORMANCE TEAMS

High-performance teams do not just happen. Rather, they occur within high-performance organizations that have particular characteristics such as a clear vision, clearly stated goals and objectives, a learning culture, and a constant emphasis on building organization momentum. Although high-performance teams may emerge at different speeds and take on the unique flavor of their respective organizations, their development involves the four change catalysts discussed in Chapter 1: values, leadership, technology, and empowerment.

Values

Values, which constitute the basis for ethical action regarding personal conduct, also form the vision and culture of an organization and its staff use patterns. Values also serve as high-performance teams' operating principles in that they provide the framework for best practices and the criteria against which decisions are made and action plans are implemented. Table 4.3 lists five high-performance team operating principles based on the values held by future-oriented ID/DD organizations and those expressed throughout this book.

Leadership

High-performance teams do not happen without strong leadership based on an organization culture that fosters and reinforces innovation. Leadership is essential in supporting and directing high-performance team members as they become effective partners through a shared commitment to goals and objectives, a focus on quality innovation, and a sense of interprofessional trust and respect (West & Markiewicz, 2004). Leadership is also required as the team moves through four predictable developmental stages (Guttman, 2008): testing; infighting; getting organized; and, finally, functioning as a high-performance team. Through the testing and infighting stages, leadership needs to perform the four leadership roles described in Chapter 1: mentoring and directing, coaching and instructing, inspiring and empowering, and collaborating and partnering.

As the team begins to organize itself and become a high-performance team, the leadership (at all levels of the organization) needs to demonstrate the six leadership functions described in Chapter 1. More specifically, initially they need to mentor, direct, coach, instruct,

Table 4.3.   High-performance team operating principles

1. A social-ecological model of human functioning and disability should guide the interpretation and use of assessment information and provide the framework for education and habilitation strategies.
2. Intervention and habilitation efforts should emphasize human potential, social inclusion, empowerment, equity, self-determination, and community inclusion.
3. An individual system of supports that encompasses multiple strategies should be based on the standardized assessment of the person's profile and intensity of needed supports.
4. The impact of interventions, services, and supports should be evaluated on both personal outcomes and organization outputs.
5. Outcome and output information should be used in activities related to reporting, monitoring, evaluation, and continuous quality improvement.

and collaborate with potential team members to develop protocols that provide the parameters for communicating more effectively; organizing their team meetings to be more effective and efficient; building on one another's strengths and contributions (and, thereby, implementing the synergy equation: $1 + 1 = 3$); becoming more persuasive in communicating; implementing the high-performance team principles summarized in Table 4.3; avoiding cognitive traps that result in defeatist attitudes and low expectations; and overcoming conflict within the team through collaboration. Through these organizing and implementing processes, leaders also need to communicate a shared vision, ensure the transfer of knowledge throughout the organization, and encourage and support the power of personal mastery.

Technology

High-performance teams use technology for two major purposes. The first is to use electronic and assistive technology (AT) to provide a system of supports. This use of technology enables people to do things by reducing the discrepancy between a person's capability and the requirements of his or her environment. AT devices range from sensory-motor prosthetics to computer- and video-based instructional systems. As learning organizations, high-performance teams need to constantly scan the environment for new and effective strategies and devices related to skill training, AT, and prosthetics.

The second use of technology by high-performance teams involves using information technology to collect, upload, analyze, and summarize real-time information that provides relevant data for reporting, monitoring, evaluation, and continuous quality improvement. Figure 2.1, for example, shows how computer-based drop-down boxes can be used by supports planning teams to obtain best practices information related to personal outcome categories, support assessment areas, individual support strategies, exemplary support objectives, and personal outcome indicators. Data for the provider profiles discussed in Chapter 3 (see Exhibit 3.3, p. 50) were obtained via the use of laptop computers for data acquisition and reporting (the analysis was done via a systems-level real-time management information system). Although laptops should be turned off during team meetings, they should be used extensively for the major functions undertaken by high-performance teams. They are essential for staff training, updating, knowledge, and learning new strategies.

Empowerment

High-performance teams can't function effectively if they are overly controlled and severely limited in how they function. Granted, some teams may not reach their expectations, but to function well they need to have a sense of competence, relatedness, and autonomy. More specifically, as evaluated in Organization Self-Assessment 4.1, they need to be involved in the synthesis of support needs and support provision, involved in the measurement of personal outcomes and organization outputs, and be part of the monitoring of both personal outcomes and organization outputs.

There is one additional aspect of high-performance teams that we have not yet discussed. They are not limited to only activities within an organization or to personnel from only that organization; they can be composed of members from different stakeholder and transdisciplinary groups, including research and training centers. This is shown clearly in Exhibit 4.4 (p. 74), which explains how the regional Persons with Developmental Disabilities (PDD) board in Edmonton, Canada, developed a high-performance team whose deliverable was a quality of life–referenced personal outcomes scale (*My Life: The Personal Outcomes Index*).

EXHIBIT 4.4

The Use of High-Performance Teams in the Development of a Personal Outcomes Scale

The Persons with Developmental Disabilities Edmonton Region Community Board (PDD Edmonton) is a government agency responsible for funding services to adults with intellectual disabilities in the province of Alberta, Canada. PDD Edmonton had been receiving increasing pressure from elected and senior government officials to better account for both expenditures and program outcomes. The organization created a project to improve its evaluation and information systems and decided to start by evaluating personal outcomes.

A small core leadership team consisting of five people internal to PDD Edmonton was created. The project was supported by the CEO and the board of directors and managed by the assistant CEO. A clear vision was articulated, and a project management–based work plan was developed. Leadership for the core elements of the plan was shared among the team. External partnerships were developed as required at various stages of the project plan. To create support for the project and promote contributions from key stakeholders, a marketing and communication plan was developed and implemented throughout the life of the project.

The project was driven by a core set of values that focused on supporting individual empowerment, independence, and community inclusion for adults with intellectual disabilities.

The *My Life: Personal Outcomes Index* was developed as a key customer-outcomes measurement survey. The survey tool was rigorously piloted and refined. To live up to the values of the project, information was collected directly from the people who receive services, and the survey was designed in such a way that some of the recipients of services could be hired as surveyors. In the course of developing the survey instrument, partnerships were formed with the people who receive services and their families, staff from service provider organizations, and experts in the area of survey methodology, all of whom contributed to its development.

From the PDD Edmonton experience, the top 12 organizational musts to promote high-performance teams follow:

➤ Clear, common vision aligned to program mission

➤ Commitment of leadership

➤ Commitment of cross-organizational human resources

➤ Commitment of financial resources

➤ Common core values

➤ Common understanding of the importance of the continual development of external relationships

➤ Commitment to a continuous improvement cycle

➤ Diversity of experience, skill set, and knowledge of team members

➤ Shared roles and responsibilities of team membership

➤ Effective communication strategies

➤ Accountability of team for results

➤ Clearly identified actions for execution

(continued)

> EXHIBIT 4.4   *(continued)*
>
> Although far-reaching in its scope and broad in its engagement, the project was tightly managed by the internal leadership team. Team members were recruited from different parts of the organization and had different core roles and responsibilities; leadership and accountability were shared, and each member of the team was empowered to carry out his or her work.
>
> For more information, contact Sean McDermott (sean.mcdermott@gov.ab.ca).

▶ *ACTION STEPS YOU CAN TAKE NOW*

One premise of this chapter has been that although all ID/DD organizations have a plethora of teams, many of them do not function as high-performance teams. For those organizations and systems that appreciate the contribution that such teams can make to an organization's effectiveness and efficiency, there are at least four action steps that will facilitate their development and successful implementation.

➤ *Action Step 1*   Evaluate how your current teams are structured and how they function. To what degree do they reflect the five characteristics of high-performance teams: involved, informed, organized, accountable, and empowered? If they do not reflect these five characteristics then focus initially on Action Step 2, progressing thereafter to Action Step 3.

➤ *Action Step 2*   Determine how high-performance teams can best be developed within your organization's leadership style as assessed in Organization Self-Assessment 4.1. In addition, identify potential team leaders who are currently performing those four leadership roles that are essential to developing high-performance teams: mentoring and directing, coaching and instructing, inspiring and empowering, and collaborating and partnering. Your selection of organization personnel may surprise you. Some of these roles can be performed by existing leaders and managers; however, remember the critical importance of encouraging and supporting the power of personal mastery among all personnel, including service recipients. A sage word of advice: People with a disability know more about disabilities than those without a disability.

➤ *Action Step 3*   Begin establishing protocols that are functional, relevant, and outcome oriented. In this process, do not use rules and regulations as your model—they send the wrong message. The protocols should be simple; distribute them throughout your organization and within the evolving high-performance team(s) as ways to deal with key issues. Before beginning this process, review the key components of being organized and following protocols (Exhibit 4.1), your organization's status on accountability areas (Organization Self-Assessment 4.1), and the operating principles of high-performance teams (Table 4.3).

➤ *Action Step 4*   Learn from others. Contact those contributors who provide real-life examples of high-performance teams (Exhibits 4.3 and 4.4). They have been there, done that, and are willing to share their experiences and suggestions.

SUMMARY AND IMPORTANT POINTS

In conclusion, the concept of high-performance teams and their development and implementation embody a broader challenge in redefining ID/DD organizations. This broader challenge relates to the question of how to create a culture that fosters creativity and innovation, captures change thinking, fosters learning, focuses on outcomes and outputs, orients itself horizontally, is consumer directed, views profit as enhanced personal outcomes and maximized organization outputs, and views loss with regard to lost opportunities, suboptimal functioning, and lack of incentive. High-performance teams can successfully address those broad challenges, as does each of the following five chapters.

As discussed in this chapter, ID/DD organizations operate within an environment that is not only very dynamic but also very different from the environment experienced historically. Today's environment and challenges are not just political and financial: They also require changes in mind-sets and expectations. The five contextual factors discussed at the beginning of this chapter have forced organizations to rethink how they can benefit from the expertise that resides within all levels of the organization: the transformation in the culture of professional services, the new public management, the movement toward self-directed services and funding, the focus on meeting client support needs, and the emergence of the microunit concept. Each factor leads logically to the further development and use of high-performance teams.

Important Points We Have Made in This Chapter

➤ High-performance teams are characterized by involving all organization personnel, being informed and fostering a learning organization, being organized and operating on the basis of established protocols, being accountable, and being empowered to make decisions and act on them.

➤ High-performance teams typically are responsible for assessment, individual supports plan development, information gathering and analysis, outcomes evaluation, continuous quality improvement, and crisis management.

➤ Established protocols are essential for high-performance teams to function effectively and efficiently and to manage key issues. The six protocols discussed in this chapter deal with communication, team meetings, synergy, persuasiveness, cognitive traps, and conflict.

➤ Developing high-performance teams involves four change strategies: values, leadership, technology, and empowerment.

RESOURCES

Print

Caldwell, J. (2010). Leadership development of individuals with developmental disabilities in the self-advocacy movement. *Journal of Intellectual Disability Research, 54*(11), 1004–1014.

Gray-Stanley, J.A., Muramatsu, N., Heller, T., Hughes, S., Johnson, T.P., & Ramirez-Valles, J. (2010). Work stress and depression among direct support professionals:

The role of work support and locus of control. *Journal of Intellectual Disability Research, 54*(8), 749–761.

Heath, C., & Heath, D. (2005). *Made to stick: Why some ideas survive and others die.* New York, NY: Random House.

Jelphs, K., & Dickinson, H. (2008). *Working on teams.* Bristol, UK: Policy Press.

Schwartz, T. (2010). *The way we're working isn't working: The four forgotten needs that energize great performance.* New York, NY: Free Press.

Electronic

Aston Business School. Aston organisation development. (2012) Retrieved from http://www.astonod.com

Consortium for Research on Emotional Intelligence in Organizations. (2012) Retrieved from http://www.eiconsortium.org/

Society for Industrial and Organizational Psychology, Inc. (Division 14 of the American Psychological Association). (2012) Retrieved from http://www.siop.org

High-Performance Team Status on Accountability Areas

Directions: For each accountability area, circle 3, 2, or 1 to indicate whether the area is fully in place (3), partially in place (2), or not in place (1). Use your current team(s) composition and functioning as the basis for the self-assessment.

	Fully in place	Partially in place	Not in place
Aware of outcomes/outputs	3	2	1
Involved in synthesis of support needs	3	2	1
Knowledgeable about best practices and evidence-based practices	3	2	1
Involved in developing and measuring outcomes and outputs	3	2	1
Uses established protocols	3	2	1
Involves clients in organization practices	3	2	1
Monitors personal outcomes	3	2	1
Sets a high performance bar	3	2	1

5

Employing a System of Supports

What You Can Expect in This Chapter

➤ Definitions of supports, support needs, and a system of supports

➤ Ways to assess the support needs of people with intellectual and developmental disabilities

➤ Elements of a system of supports

➤ Components of a personal planning process

➤ Principles that underlie the development of an individual supports plan

Since the mid-1980s, the supports paradigm has brought together the related practices of person-centered planning, personal development and growth opportunities, community inclusion, self-determination, and empowerment. During that time, we have seen significant progress in our conceptualization and measurement of the support needs of people with ID/DD; the way we think about what a system of supports entails; the process we use to develop, monitor, and evaluate an individual's supports plan; and a clearer focus on what the desired outcomes should be in an individual planning process. Simultaneously, as we discussed in the previous chapter, we have seen the development of high-performance teams that can effectively be involved in the development, implementation, monitoring, and evaluation of an individual's supports plan. The purposes of this chapter are to 1) discuss the prerequisites for an organization to employ a system of supports, 2) outline the components of the individual supports planning process, and 3) provide examples of how organizations have successfully overcome challenges related to the provision of individualized supports. Throughout the chapter, the following definitions will be used (Thompson et al., 2009):

- *Supports:* Resources and strategies that aim to promote the development, education, interests, and personal well-being of a person and enhance individual functioning. Services are one type of support offered by professionals and agencies.

- *Support needs:* A psychological **construct** referring to the pattern and intensity of supports necessary for a person to participate in activities linked with normative human functioning

- *System of supports:* The planned and integrated use of individualized support strategies and resources that encompass the multiple aspects of human performance in multiple settings. A system of supports model provides a structure for an organization to provide individualized supports that enhance human performance and personal outcomes.

- *ISP:* A logical, sequential, and transparent process for developing, implementing, monitoring, and evaluating the use of best support strategies to enhance personal outcomes

PREREQUISITES TO EMPLOYING A SYSTEM OF SUPPORTS

There are four prerequisites to employing a system of supports to enhance human functioning and personal outcomes. The first is a way to measure an individual's support needs. The second is a system of supports that addresses the assessed support needs. The third is a personal outcomes conceptual and measurement model that is used to assess personal outcomes affected by the system of supports provided. The fourth is the availability of a high-performance team that uses 21st century thinking styles.

Measuring Support Needs

An individual's support needs can be measured with varying degrees of accuracy by self-report, direct observation, or a standardized instrument such as the Supports Intensity Scale (SIS); (Thompson et al., 2004). This instrument is used as an example in this chapter because it is a well-standardized and researched instrument and has been used in multiple jurisdictions (Kuppens, Bossaert, Buntinx, Molleman, & Van-Abbeele, 2010; Schalock et al., 2010; Thompson, Tasse, & McLaughlin, 2008; Verdugo, Arias, Ibanez, & Schalock, 2010).

Before briefly describing the SIS, it is important to distinguish between scales that measure adaptive behavior versus those that measure support needs. As shown in Table 5.1, these two types of scales are very different in terms of their intended uses, item stems, and item responses. The two primary differences relate to use (diagnosis versus determining the individual's support needs) and item responses (proficiency in relation to adaptive skills versus pattern and intensity of support needs).

As a prerequisite to employing a system of supports, it is critical to use a support needs scale that provides information for determining and reporting the profile and intensity of a person's support needs and for providing information relevant to the development of an ISP. The SIS fulfills these two purposes by assessing the pattern and intensity of support needs in areas related to life activities, protection and advocacy, and exceptional medical and behavioral support needs. A brief overview of these areas is presented in Table 5.2 (Thompson et al., 2004). Later in this chapter, we describe how the extensive amount of information obtained from the SIS can be summarized and consolidated into a support action plan administered by support staff.

System of Supports

A system of supports needs to be implemented since it provides three essential functions in a redefined ID/DD organization. First, it compiles potential support strategies into an

Table 5.1.   Comparison of scales measuring adaptive behavior versus support needs

Feature	Adaptive behavior scale	Support needs scale
Uses	As part of determining a diagnosis of intellectual disability	To determine a person's support needs
Item stems	Skills needed to successfully function in society	Life activities in which a person engages when participating in society
Item responses	Level of mastery	Intensity and pattern of support needs

Sources: Thompson et al. (2004), Schalock et al. (2010a).

Table 5.2. Support need areas assessed in the Supports Intensity Scale (SIS)

Area	Components
Life activities	Home living, community living, lifelong learning, employment, health and safety, social
Protection and advocacy	Advocacy, money management, protection from exploitation, decision making
Exceptional medical needs	Respiratory care, feeding assistance, skin care, other
Exceptional behavioral needs	Externally directed destructiveness, self-directed destructiveness, sexual, other

Sources: Thompson et al. (2004)

organized system through which individualized supports can be planned and implemented based on the individual's assessed support needs. The elements and exemplary components summarized in Table 5.3 present a system of supports encompassing the multiple aspects of human performance in multiple settings. The support strategies summarized in Table 5.3 are based on work in **human performance technology** and systems design (Thompson et al., 2009). As discussed later in the chapter, when used in an ISP, a particular component becomes a supports objective.

Second, a system of supports provides a framework for coordinating the procurement and application of specific supports across sources of support that include natural supports, technology, environmental accommodation, staff-directed activities, professional services, and organization- and societal-level policies and practices. The left column of Table 5.4 depicts how this coordination can occur across the sources and system components. This framework also shows the importance of ID/DD organizations becoming support coordinators.

Table 5.3. Elements and exemplary components of a system of supports

Element	Exemplary component
Cognitive	Assistive and information technology (e.g., communication devices, calculators, computers, global positioning system, learning/memory devices, medication dispensing devices, medical alert monitors, speech recognition devices)
Prosthetics	Sensory aids and mobility devices
Skills and knowledge	Task analysis, applied behavior analysis, education and training strategies such as universal design for learning
Environmental accommodation	Ramps, braille, push buttons, modified counters and workspaces, modified transportation, sense of basic security, adapted texts and signs, environments that are conducive to learning
Incentives	Roles, status, involvement, recognition, appreciation, money, personal goal setting, empowerment, self-directed individual supports plan, community participation
Personal characteristics	Choice making, decision making, interests, motivation, skills and knowledge, positive attitudes and expectations
Natural supports	Support networks, advocacy, befriending, community involvement, social engagement and interactions
Professional services	Physical therapy, occupational therapy, speech therapy, medical, psychological, psychiatric, nursing
Positive behavior supports	Functional assessment of challenging behavior and focusing on altering the environment before a problem behavior occurs, teaching appropriate behaviors
Policies and practices (organizational)	Aligning staff and professionals' work, increasing staff involvement, reducing turnover and continual change of direct care workers, establishing "a reference person" for each client, partnering with universities and other research and training centers
Policies and practices (societal)	Resource allocation patterns, transportation, interagency networks, public relations campaigns, tax incentives, information services

The third essential function provided by a system of supports is to provide a framework for evaluating the impact of specific supports on the individual's functioning and quality of life and on the organization's effectiveness, efficiency, and sustainability. The right column of Table 5.4 lists these potential impacts. From an evaluation perspective, these potential impacts become dependent variables in evidence-based practices research (Schalock, Verdugo, & Gomez, 2011).

Personal Outcomes Conceptual and Measurement Model

The third prerequisite to employing a system of supports is to assess personal outcomes so that the impact of the specific supports can be evaluated. As discussed in Chapter 3, personal outcomes can be assessed from the perspective of the individual, family, or society (see Table 3.1, page 43). In this chapter, we use the quality-of-life conceptual and measurement framework

Table 5.4. Framework for coordinating and evaluating specific supports

Source/component	Impact on
Natural sources	
Family and friends	Social inclusion
Colleagues	Interpersonal relations
Generic agencies and businesses	Emotional well-being
Technology based	
Assistive technology	Cognitive functioning
Information technology	Independent living
Smart technology	Self-determination
Prosthetics	Living and employment status
	Sensory-motor functioning
Environment based	
Environmental accommodation	Personal development
	Social inclusion
Staff directed	
Incentives	Behavior skills
Skills/knowledge	Increased motivation
Positive behavior supports	Personal development
	Emotional well-being
Professional services	
	Personal development
	Interpersonal relations
	Physical well-being
	Emotional well-being
	Communication
	Adaptive behavior
Policies and practices (organization)	
Aligning staff and professional work	Organization effectiveness and efficiency
Increasing motivation and tenure	
Partnering and networking	
Transportation	
Policies and practices (societal)	
Resource allocation patterns	Opportunities to enhance organization sustainability
Interagency networks	
Public relations campaigns	
Tax incentives	
Public information	

summarized in Table 3.2. This framework includes eight quality-of-life core domains (personal development; self-determination; interpersonal relations; social inclusion; rights; and emotional, physical, and material well-being) with associated indicators. The assessment of culturally sensitive indicators associated with each domain results in measures of personal outcomes. The quality-of-life conceptual and measurement framework summarized in Table 3.2 has been validated through extensive cross-cultural research (Wang, Schalock, Verdugo, & Jenaro, 2010) and is closely aligned with both the articles contained in the U.N. Convention on the Rights of Persons with Disabilities (United Nations, 2006) and the desired personal outcomes associated with public policy (Shogren & Turnbull, 2010).

High-Performance Teams

The fourth and final prerequisite is determining who will actually implement the system of supports. The previous chapter discussed the role that high-performance teams play in the planning and delivery of individualized supports. Functioning as microunits within and across organizations and functions, high-performance teams provide an effective and efficient model for structuring interdisciplinary support teams that combine the expertise of frontline staff and relevant experts; meet on a regular basis to discuss client support needs, support strategies, and personal outcomes; share the same information about the client's assessed support needs and available resources; participate autonomously in internal resource allocation and efficiency monitoring; and self-manage and monitor their efforts regarding evaluation and quality improvement. The additional value that high-performance teams bring to employing a system of supports is their use of the three 21st century thinking styles discussed in Chapter 2: systems, synthesis, and alignment. By way of review, systems thinking focuses on the multiple factors that affect human functioning and organization performance; synthesis involves the integration of information to improve the precision, accuracy, and validity of a decision; and alignment positions the service delivery components of an ID/DD organization into a logical sequence for the purposes of reporting, monitoring, evaluation, and continuous quality improvement. Alignment involves clearly relating assessed support needs to the provision of a system of supports and to the evaluation of personal outcomes.

In summary, providing individualized supports through a system of supports requires a clear understanding of what such a system entails as well as the three other prerequisites for its successful deployment: the measurement of the individual's support needs, a personal outcomes conceptual and measurement framework, and high-performance teams who understand and apply 21st century thinking styles.

➤ Tool for Application

Organization Self-Assessment 5.1 (p. 99) allows personnel within your organization to evaluate the current status of the four prerequisites to employing a system of supports. Your profile should be interpreted in reference to your current individual supports planning process and the perceived effectiveness of that process. If your profile has a lot of *not in place* responses and your planning process is effective, could adding the specific components referenced in Tables 5.2–5.4 improve its effectiveness? If there are a lot of *not in place* responses and you perceive that your **individual supports plan process** needs improving, the quality improvement action steps are clear. If you have lots of *planned* responses, ask yourself, "For how long have they been planned?" Time passes quickly, and the challenges mount.

In addition to the prerequisites evaluated on Organization Self-Assessment 5.1, every organization needs a logical, sequential, and transparent process for developing, implementing, monitoring, and evaluating the use of best support practices and strategies to enhance personal outcomes. The vehicle for doing so is referred to as an ISP. The six components involved in that process are described next. However, before reading the following section, you might want to review how you scored on a previous organization self-assessment (Organization Self-Assessment 2.3: Analysis of Your ISP).

COMPONENTS OF THE
INDIVIDUAL SUPPORTS PLANNING PROCESS

Individualized planning terms and documents differ widely as reflected in "individual… supports, service, education program, transition, written rehabilitation, habilitation, family support…plan." The term used between *individual* and *plan* generally denotes the age group, focus area, or funding source. Some planning documents include legally mandated components, others are structured by the core philosophical values of the organization, and still others are artifacts of past practices and traditions.

At the outset, it is important to distinguish between a supports plan and an achievement plan. A supports plan is developed around personalized goals and assessed support needs, support strategies, support objectives, and personal outcomes. The intent of a supports plan is to procure and/or provide those supports required for the person to be successful in major life activity areas, maintain or improve his or her medical condition, and/or prevent or minimize challenging behaviors that impede human functioning. Collectively, the intent of individualized supports is to enhance personal outcomes. In distinction, achievement plans, as prominent parts of individualized education programs (IEPs) and individualized written rehabilitation plans, focus on learning and/or achieving observable and measurable skills. Achievement plans target skills and levels of mastery. Unlike achievement plans, supports plans are not characterized by long-term goals and short-term behavioral objectives that specify achievement milestones for the individual. Rather, because the function of a supports plan is to identify and employ the resources and strategies that will bridge the gap between the challenges that a person with ID/DD encounters in life activity areas and the personal outcomes that the individual values, staff-referenced support objectives are developed and monitored rather than client-referenced behavioral objectives. These differences will become increasingly apparent as we next discuss the six components of the supports planning process. These components, which are shown in Figure 5.1, are analogous to other planning models found in the management literature. Such models typically include four phases or components: planning, doing, checking, and reassessing (Grol, Baker, & Moss, 2008).

Component 1: Assessment of Support Needs

Two approaches are typically used to assess individual support needs. One is to use a standardized instrument such as the SIS (see Table 5.2). A second is to use a consensus approach to assess the pattern and intensity of support needs according to a particular conceptual model. This approach is shown in Table 5.5 (p. 85) in reference to eight core quality-of-life domains. We recognize that such a consensus approach is potentially less reliable than a standardized instrument. However, when the assessment is based on clearly conceptualized and operationalized indicators that are used by individual members of high-performance teams who are trained in valid assessment procedures, the consensus approach can be used to reliably assess the support needs of individuals.

Table 5.5. A consensus approach to determining level of support needs per quality of life domain

Domain	Indicator	Level of support need		
		High	Medium	Low
Personal development	Activities of daily living*			
	Cognitive skills			
	Social skills			
	Practical skills			
Self-determination	Decision making			
	Personal goals			
	Choice making			
Interpersonal relations	Social interactions			
	Social relations			
Social inclusion	Community participation			
	Accessing natural supports			
	Community integration			
Rights	Human			
	Legal			
Emotional well-being	Enjoyment			
	Self-esteem			
	Safety and security			
Physical well-being	Fitness			
	Nutrition			
	Wellness			
	Leisure/recreation			
Material well-being	Employment			
	Ownership			

*Self-care skills and mobility.

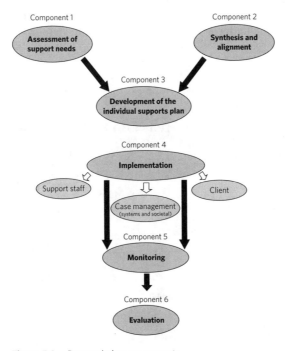

Figure 5.1. Personal plan components.

Component 2: Synthesis and Alignment

Once the individual's support needs are determined, three team actions need to occur. First, the assessment information needs to be integrated (i.e., synthesized) into a personal outcomes framework that will facilitate the development, monitoring, and evaluation of the ISP. That framework would logically be the life activity areas summarized in Table 5.2 or the quality-of-life domains summarized in Tables 3.2 and 5.5. In some jurisdictions with which the authors are familiar, the life activities assessed on the SIS are integrated into the quality-of-life domains, as shown in Exhibit 5.1.

The second team action involves aligning the support needs to specific support strategies. This action requires that team members be very familiar with the components of a system of supports (Tables 5.3 and 5.4) and use logical reasoning to connect needed supports to support strategies. For example, if the person's support needs relate to mobility and access, then the logical support strategies are a mobility device (e.g., wheelchair) and environmental accommodation. Analogously, if the person's support needs relate to lifelong learning, then individualized support strategies will involve assistive and information technology and teaching–learning strategies. For a person whose support needs center on challenging behaviors, positive behavior supports are required along with psychiatric services. The principle involved in this second team action is simple: understand the individual's specific support needs and align those needs to a system of supports.

The third team action step involves identifying the sources of support. This step is critical because it focuses team efforts to identify support resources (including the client). Once identified, obtaining these supports becomes the basis for establishing support objectives and coordinating the provision of supports. Consistent with systems thinking, the source of support can be the individual, the organization, or society. As shown in Table 5.6, such an approach will maximize the employment and coordination of supports, enrich team members' thinking and creativity, and thereby enhance personal outcomes.

As discussed earlier, support objectives are used in an ISP rather than behavioral objectives because the purpose of a supports plan is to obtain and provide those supports for a person to be successful in life activities and, thereby, experience enhanced personal outcomes. Table 5.7 provides examples of support objectives associated with the three sources of supports shown in Table 5.6.

EXHIBIT 5.1

Integration of Life Activity Areas into Quality-of-Life Domains

Quality-of-life domain	Support Intensity Scale (SIS) area
Personal development	Lifelong learning, home living activities
Self-determination	Protection and advocacy (Items 1, 5, 7)
Interpersonal relations	Social activities
Social inclusion	Community living activities
Rights	Protection and advocacy (Items 2–4, 6, 8)
Emotional well-being	Exceptional behavior support needs
Physical well-being	Health and safety, exceptional medical needs
Material well-being	Employment activities

Source: Thompson et al. (2004)

Table 5.6. A systems approach to support resources

Source	Exemplary support
Individual	Skills, knowledge, inherent ability, interests, motivation
Organization	Assistive and information technology, environmental accommodation, incentives, prosthetics, professional services, easy-to-read texts, policies and practices that focus on the organization being a bridge to the community, partnerships
Society	Natural supports, policies and practices, environmental accommodation, technology

Component 3: Development of the Individual Support Plan

The development of an ISP can be approached from three perspectives. The first is the plan's format. Collectively, we have probably seen a hundred different formats that have been developed on the basis of system requirements, organization policies and practices, and pure creativity. From our perspective, the particular format is not particularly important as long as it facilitates good planning; clear communication; and effective implementation, monitoring, and evaluation. Thus, it would be presumptuous to suggest a standardized ISP format.

Second, the principles that guide the development of an ISP are important because they reflect the individualization and person-centered philosophy underlying current policies and practices. The five development principles summarized in Table 5.8 reflect both the intended purpose of an ISP and best practices regarding its development.

The third perspective regarding the development of a personal plan relates to the content of the plan. Specific information regarding data sets used in the development of the plan can be found in the following tables:

- Support assessment areas: Tables 5.2 and 5.5

- Support strategies: Tables 5.3 and 5.4

- Support objectives: Table 5.7

- Outcome categories and indicators: Tables 3.1 and 3.2

Table 5.7. Examples of support objectives

Source	Exemplary support objectives
Individual	Use personal goal setting to promote social inclusion.
	Provide a behavior supports plan to increase incentives.
	Implement computer- and video-based instruction on food preparation and safety skills.
	Implement a positive behavior support program to reduce self-injurious behavior.
	Use local self-advocacy groups and smart phones to increase community involvement.
	Use Facebook or other social networks.
Organization	Use video-based instruction to increase functional skills.
	Use a medical alert device and mobile support team to allow semi-independent living.
	Use a computer-based augmentative communication system to increase expressive language.
Societal	Advocate for community-based environmental accommodation to increase mobility access.
	Develop online communities to increase social interaction and community participation.
	Network with community-based self-help groups to increase social inclusion.
	Use Facebook or other social networks to recruit allies within the community.
	Gain access to community and neighborhood support groups to facilitate successful community living.

Table 5.8.   Individual supports plan development principles

1. The client is actively involved in the plan's development and implementation.
2. Priority is given to those outcome areas that both reflect the person's goals and address health and safety issues.
3. A holistic approach is used that reflects the multidimensionality of human behavior.
4. Support objectives are referenced to specific support strategies composing a system of supports and not to person-specific attitudes or behaviors.
5. Personal outcomes are assessed in terms of the benefits derived by program recipients that are the result, direct or indirect, of individualized, person-centered support strategies.

Component 4: Implementation

For many organizations, the implementation component is less than optimal. A typical scenario is that a sophisticated plan is developed and is then either filed away to be reviewed in 3, 6, or 12 months or else implemented by support staff who have had no input into its development or who do not understand the complexity (or relevance) of the plan. The net result is a waste of considerable time and effort due to a lack of organization and coordination, an inability to relate the supports plan to any outcome, and a lack of confidence among clients and family members that the organization is making a significant difference in the person's life.

Overcoming these deficits is not easy. However, attending to the three implementation agents referenced beneath *Implementation* in Figure 5.1 holds promise. These three agents are likely to be most involved in effectively implementing the personal plan: case manager, support staff, and the individual. Within most organizations, case management plays a critical role in systems-level issues and in fulfilling those societal-level exemplary support objectives listed in Table 5.7.

Direct support staff spend the most time with clients and know them the best. The challenge is to make the ISP clear and doable by these personnel, including the supports they are to provide to the person and the support objectives they need to implement and monitor. Exhibit 5.2 shows how a large supports provider, Arduin in the Netherlands, has met these challenges by developing and implementing a support action plan. This plan is based on information obtained from the individual or advocate during a pre-ISP development interview, and the type of support per activity of daily living is obtained from the most recent administration of the SIS. Within the person's ISP, this information is shown for each quality-of-life domain summarized in Table 3.2. In Exhibit 5.2, this information is shown only for the domain of self-determination.

The real buy-in required for the successful implementation of an ISP is that of the client, who should have been involved in its development and on whose behalf it is written. As discussed previously, research in the area of inclusion and empowerment shows clearly that personal involvement leads to better compliance and more positive outcomes. Thus, clients should be actively involved in the implementation of their supports plans. A vehicle for doing so is presented in Exhibit 5.3 (p. 92), which shows how the Arduin program in the Netherlands provides a one-page laminated copy (*My Support Plan*) to each service recipient. Such a simple step not only provides specific goals related to the concept of involvement and empowerment but also reflects an important aspect of how an organization monitors its ISP process.

The *My Support Plan* example shown in Exhibit 5.3 summarizes the person's expressed support needs related to each quality-of-life domain. The format is based on the client's preference—a laminated version, an online version, or both. It is not limited to written information; there is also the option of adding figures, photos, pictograms or even spoken words. The information in the *My Support Plan* document is exactly the same as in the ISP and urges personal assistants to write down information in easy-to-read sentences. The starting point of transparency is the person understanding his or her own supports plan. This can be further achieved by giving the individual unlimited access to his or her *My Support Plan* document, electronically or on paper.

To monitor staff as to whether the plan's objectives are actually implemented and the specified supports are actually provided, the client will, on an ongoing basis but at least every 3 months, evaluate the information on each of the topics in a conversation with the support worker (assisted by his or her personal assistant). For more information, contact Mr. Remco Mostert (rmostert@arduin.nl).

EXHIBIT 5.2

Support Staff Action Plan

Section I. A general summary of the individual's support needs

Activities of Daily Living	
Verbal/gestural prompting	
Medical	
Infectious diseases	some support needed
Seizure management	some support needed
Therapy services	some support needed
Other(s)	some support needed
Behavioral	
Assault or injuries to others prevention	extensive support needed
Property destruction prevention	extensive support needed
Self injury prevention	some support needed
Emotional outbursts prevention	some support needed
Maintenance of treatments	extensive support needed

Section II. Individual's goals and wishes regarding life expectations

Domain: **Self-determination**
ADL: Partial/physical assistence
         2 instructions, 1 learning objective

Additions **Protection and Advocacy Activities**	
Advocating for self	**Full physical assistance (4 / 4)**
LEARNING OBJECTIVE: John has more motivation on house activities when staff is not present. Help John to stay motivated when staff is present. Learning goal: Let John go to the toilet on his own with the help of the color clock.	
Exercising legal responsibilities	**Full physical assistance (4 / 4)**
Let John use his own front door key when he comes home.	
Making choices and decisions	**Partial physical assistance (3 / 4)**
John is able to choose between two things if you show them. Other choices are hard to express for him, but you can make them up by his behavior. You can see if he likes it or not.	

(continued)

EXHIBIT 5.2   *(continued)*

Section III. Support needs per quality-of-life domain (only self-determination shown)

Home Living Activities
October 22, 2008 – John needs more support while executing home activity tasks.
He needs to learn how to move freely in his home while staff is present.

Community Living Activities
October 22, 2008 – Maintain current situation.

Lifelong Learning Activities
October 22, 2008 – Stay open for possibilities in this area. Because of his level of
Intellectual Disabilities, courses are quite difficult. John has trouble over viewing
consequences.

Employment Activities
October 22, 2008 – Because John cannot overview consequences, support will always
be needed, now and in the future.

Health and Safety Activities
October 22, 2008 – Because John cannot overview consequences, support will always
be needed, now and in the future.

Component 5: Monitoring

The monitoring of an ISP should focus on the successful implementation of support objectives and strategies rather than behavioral objectives. As discussed in Chapter 3, monitoring should lead to empirical benchmarks. From this perspective, monitoring provides a standard against which to evaluate organization performance and a goal that directs future continuous quality improvement efforts. Monitoring is a key part of the transformation/redefinition process and requires that high-performance teams establish empirically based benchmarks, implement support strategies and support objectives, and use the empirical benchmarks to monitor the change process.

This suggested approach to monitoring is much different than that done typically with achievement plans. Specifically, rather than monitor the status of the person's behavioral objectives, the high-performance team monitors the status of the support strategies listed in the ISP. To emphasize this point, note the verbs used in the exemplary support objectives presented in Table 5.7. They are action verbs related to the team's efforts and responsibilities. The format and process for monitoring the ISP and the support objectives are organization- and system specific. The essential notion is that support objectives are monitored and that information from the monitoring process becomes a benchmark to monitor the change process and develop quality improvement strategies to improve the level of implementation and the effectiveness of the ISP.

Component 6: Evaluation

Evaluating the results of a system of supports should involve the periodic (e.g., yearly) evaluation of personal outcomes that are aligned during the ISP development process with the outcome categories. We are realistic about the amount of change that occurs in personal outcomes over time. The personal outcomes profiles are typically variable and do not always show a linear improvement from one evaluation period to the next. The data contained in the provider pro-

Table 5.9. Factors affecting the effectiveness of an individual supports plan (ISP)

1. Assessment of the individual's support needs
2. Synthesis and alignment are used to integrate the information into a personal outcomes framework that facilitates the development and monitoring of the ISP.
3. Support needs are aligned with support strategies and the source(s) of support identified.
4. The ISP uses a framework that encompasses outcome categories, support assessment areas, support strategies, support objectives, and outcome indicators.
5. The ISP is fully implemented and monitored by high-performance teams, with action plans developed for direct support staff and relevant aspects of the plan incorporated into the individual's My Support Plan document.

files from Nebraska and Maryland discussed in Chapter 3 reflect this variability; nevertheless, they provide useful information and generally show enhanced personal outcomes over time (see Exhibits 6.2 and 6.3).

Evaluating an ISP's effectiveness should also involve determining whether critical parts of the ISP process have been implemented. Table 5.9 lists implementation factors that should be incorporated into the evaluation. If key factors are not implemented, then doing so should become a major focus of subsequent quality improvement efforts.

In summary, the effectiveness and efficiency of an individual plan depend on how well its components are clearly understood by all stakeholders. To facilitate this understanding, we summarize in Table 5.10 the major activities associated with each of the six personal plan components shown in Figure 5.1.

OVERCOMING CHALLENGES RELATED INDIVIDUAL SUPPORT PLANS

An organization's ISP represents both a contract with its clientele and the heart of its service/supports delivery system. Developing and implementing individual plans can consume a large percentage of an organization's budget and staff time. Organizations are challenged to develop plans that are realistic, effective, efficient, and flexible and that provide continuity across staff and service/support providers. Although there are potentially numerous ISP-related challenges, this section of the chapter discusses (with examples of how best practices can be used to address them) five that we have observed frequently. The five challenges are related to: 1) how to implement an ISP to enhance its impact, 2) what to monitor and evaluate, 3) how to incorporate futures planning for students transitioning into adult services, 4) how to maximize assistive and information technology into the ISP process, and 5) how to develop and implement a personal plan within a large facility and across diagnostic groups.

Table 5.10. Major activities associated with each personal plan component

Component	Major activities
Assessment of support needs	Assessing support needs to determine the profile and intensity of needed supports
Synthesis and alignment	Integrating support needs information into an individual supports plan personal outcomes framework
	Aligning support needs to support objectives and sources of support
Development	Incorporating five principles into individual supports plan
Implementation	Implementing support objectives via case management, direct support staff, and the client
Monitoring	Determining the specific support strategies used and their implementation status
Evaluation	Periodically assessing personal outcomes and determining the impact of support strategies on personal outcomes

EXHIBIT 5.3

My Support Plan

I am Ard and this is My Support Plan. In this is written down how I am doing, what my wishes and goals are, what important is for me in my life and what supports I need. Every month we will take a look at how all this is doing. We means the support worker and I, together with my personal assistant. If you have a question, ask me or my personal assistant. The name of my personal assistant is:

Date: January 2nd 2011

**These are my
Personal Outcomes**

These are my Wishes and Goals

1. I wish to have more friends.
2. I want to be a member of the local football club.
3. I wish to be taken seriously. Therefore I want to be more able to express myself.
4. I wish to live on my own.
5. I wish to have a paid job.

Is this improving?

YES - NO

Date 1: _____

YES - NO

Date 2: _____

This is important for my life:

PD   Personal Development—Learning new things

Continuously doing courses like writing, accounting, cooking and drawing is important for me. I also like to experience all daily activities. Music making, especially drums, is what I like most!

SD   Self-Determination—Making my own choices

I want to be the one who makes decisions about my own life. Support me in doing that and be patient.

IR   Interpersonal Relations—Family and friends

I love my family and want to be part of my family in every occasion. I have less friends and find it difficult to create new friendships. Support me in creating friendships. I like the people I meet at the music group.

SI   Social Inclusion—Being part of the community

For me it is important to know my neighbors and that they know me. I also want to do my shopping as much as possible in my own neighborhood. I like to be a volunteer (I am pretty good in music).

R   Rights—What I am allowed to do

I want to know more about my rights. I want to spend my own money.

EWB   Emotional Well-Being—How I feel

I can worry quickly and can feel unsure about myself.

PWB   Physical Well-Being—Being healthy

I like food but do not always know what is best for me. My favorite sport is Football. I do not like exercising on my own.

MWB   Material Well-Being—Having money and goods

I am proud to work 5 days a week as a shop assistant but wish it to be a paid job. Going to the beach during the summer holiday is important for me. I like buying presents for my family.

These are the supports that I need:

PD   Personal Development—Learning new things

- Give me an overview of available courses about writing, accounting, drawing, cooking. Let me choose what course I like to do.
- Ask me to assist you in housekeeping, cooking, gardening, and so on...
- While assisting, explain me what you do and tell me how I am doing. Be an example for me!

SD   Self-Determination—Making my own choices

- When a choice is needed, ask me. First let me try on my own. If it is to difficult for me, then explain me what possible options there are to choose. Be patient and only decide for me when I ask you to do so.

IR   Interpersonal Relations—Family and friends

- Create a birthday calendar for me.
- Support me in sending cards for special moments.
- Support me to invite people at home.

SI   Social Inclusion—Being part of the community

- Support me in becoming a member of the local football club. Introduce me there. Especially in the beginning it is important for me that you also come to the training and the first matches.
- Take me out. Teach me what shops there are in my village and how I get there.

R   Rights—What I am allowed to do

- Support me in getting an overview of my money. Tell me, explain to me, what my rights are.

EWB   Emotional Well-Being—How I feel

- Talk with me about my day in the morning and evening. Tell me what I am good at!

PWB   Physical Well-Being—Being healthy

- Support me in preparing healthy meals. Let us eat together.
- Support me in exercising (e.g. cycling, walking to the shops).

MWB   Material Well-Being—Have money and goods

- Support me in getting a paid job. (Especially getting paid for the job I have now).

Is support given?

PD	YES - NO
SD	YES - NO
IR	YES - NO
SI	YES - NO
R	YES - NO
EWB	YES - NO
PWB	YES - NO
MWB	YES - NO

Date 1: _____

Is support given?

PD	YES - NO
SD	YES - NO
IR	YES - NO
SI	YES - NO
R	YES - NO
EWB	YES - NO
PWB	YES - NO
MWB	YES - NO

Date 2: _____

Implementing to Enhance Impact

Exhibits 5.2 and 5.3 addressed this challenge through the use of a support staff action plan (Exhibit 5.2) and *My Support Plan* (Exhibit 5.3). These two strategies have enhanced personal outcomes because everyone is involved in working together from assessing support needs to planning, developing, monitoring, and evaluating the impact of the plan. And because the high-performance team is focused on one product, there is a cycle of continuous quality improvement that also results in enhancing the organization's effectiveness and efficiency.

Monitoring and Evaluation

Overcoming this challenge is best done by having a clear understanding of what should be monitored and evaluated and developing a data-based system for doing so. That system should have the following parameters:

- What to monitor: support objectives that emphasize actions by case managers and direct support staff. This approach to monitoring better fulfills the intent of an ISP, which is to provide supports required for the person to be successful in major life activity areas, maintain or improve his or her medical condition, and/or prevent or minimize challenging behaviors.

- What to evaluate: personal outcomes that are consistent with the organization's mission and goals and that provide information for reporting, evaluation, and continuous quality improvement

Futures Planning

This challenge involves how to successfully transition students from special education programs to adult service agencies without losing the significant information and productive work reflected in the student's IEP and transition plans. In some jurisdictions, the information cannot be shared; in others, the eligibility and intake process begins anew when the former student applies for adult services and supports; and, in still other jurisdictions, the student drops by the wayside. These practices are not effective, efficient, or rationale. Systems are complex, and we understand that. However, if the individual education and transition plans contain transition support objectives, and if there is **networking** and interagency involvement (which is a significant predictor of postsecondary school personal outcomes for special education students), then the transition process should be more successful. Exhibit 5.4 summarizes best practices regarding the individualized transition plan process.

Maximizing Assistive Technology

Assistive technology (AT) is a critical component of a system of supports and frequently employs smart technology. As discussed by Storey (2010), smart technology involves a variety of systems such as computers, cell phones (i.e., smart phones), personal digital assistants, voice activation systems, or touchpad controllers. Control can be through physical manifestation, radio frequency, infrared extension units, sip-n-puffs, eye commands, or the use of smart phone applications. As a support, smart technology can be used across environments to facilitate independence or semi-independent living, integrated employment, and community inclusion (Gentry, 2009; Helal, Mokhtari, & Abdulrazak, 2008).

EXHIBIT 5.4

The Transition Individualized Education Program (IEP) Process

When a student turns 16, his or her IEP expands to include measurable goals relevant to the student's postsecondary life and a listing of needed services that will contribute to later education, employment, and independent living. Writing a transition IEP requires that new members be added to the educational team beyond the general and special educators, the related service representatives, and the student and his or her parents. Often, these individuals come from outside adult service agencies or employment agencies, but they also may include people particularly important in the student's life who can contribute to transition planning. Expanding the team allows the student and family members to make connections with services and supports that will replace public school services after the student finishes school. Somewhat similar to IEP planning, transition planning involves several steps: 1) conducting transition assessment, including person-centered planning, so as to identify a student's strengths, needs, and preferences as well as the student's current level of performance; 2) writing goals pertaining to postschool life and IEP goals that mirror the results of the transition assessment; and 3) finding the transition services that will enable the student to reach his or her postschool goals (Test & Mazzotti, 2011). In most states, students become adults and attain the age of majority at age 18; if they are considered to be legally competent, they then can exercise their legal rights without parental supervision. Being competent means that an individual is able to make personal decisions and to communicate them to others. Prior to turning age 18, a student's IEP team must help the student (and the parents) understand his or her legal rights and how to exercise them (Individuals with Disabilities Education Improvement Act of 2004, **PL** 108–466).

For more information, contact Martha E. Snell (snell@virginia.edu).

AT is a process and not just a device. AT involves making either technical or environmental adaptations that allow people to do things. Organizations should view adaptations as allowing staff to reduce the discrepancies between their clients' capabilities and environmental requirements. Guidelines for doing so are found in Exhibit 5.5.

Implementation in Large Facilities and Across Diagnostic Groups

Large organizations sometimes face significant challenges related to their size, multiple settings, multiple diagnostic groups, and history. Our observation is that siloism is more common among large organizations—especially if they are structured vertically. The example shown in Exhibit 5.6 explains how one large program in Spain (Lantegi Batuak) has addressed significant challenges in implementing ISPs. By way of background, Lantegi Batuak is a nonprofit organization with more than 25 years of experience. Its mission is to generate job opportunities for people with ID/DD, mental health disorders, or traumatic brain injuries. It operates 19 centers and as of 2011 serves 2,200 clients, 70% of whom have ID/DD.

EXHIBIT 5.5

Guidelines for Using Assistive Technology (AT)

1. Determine the setting-specific demands that require discrete and interrelated abilities. Once setting-specific demands have been understood, the focus shifts from the task to the individual.

2. Evaluate the person's functional strengths and limitations. By identifying factors that facilitate or inhibit performance, one paves the way for making adaptations that allow people to participate more fully in their surroundings. Some adaptations involve nontechnical strategies (e.g., reading to the person), whereas others involve devices. AT devices can help compensate for the missing requisite skills.

3. Selection of the assistive technology device should be guided by the setting-specific demands, the capabilities a person must possess to use the device, and the individual's functional limitations for which compensation will occur by using the device. During the process of matching the adaptation to the person's needs, certain evaluation criteria should be considered. Chief among these are ease of use; amount of training required; cost to purchase and maintain; technological features such as needed software programs, performance of the device, and use across environments; and promotion of the person's independence.

4. When possible, family members should be actively involved in both the decision-making and implementation processes and also should be aware of the expected outcomes. Furthermore, the viewpoint and motivation level of the consumer and the family are also critical.

5. Once an AT device has been obtained, the consumer and others must be trained on the device, its capabilities and intent, and the vocabulary related to the device.

6. Someone needs to be identified to work with the consumer and monitor the overall use and impact of the device. Three important monitoring criteria are suggested: 1) the ease with which the technology adaptation is being implemented and whether the consumer is using the device as instructed, 2) the reliability and durability of the device, and 3) whether the adaptation is working and producing the desired results.

For more information, contact Brian R. Bryant (brianrbryant@aol.com).

► ACTION STEPS YOU CAN TAKE NOW

Our assumption in writing this chapter is that you already understand the concept of an individual plan and the role it plays in your organization's service delivery system. Furthermore, we assume that your current individual planning process is at least reasonably effective and that your organization is not about to introduce a whole new approach to supports planning and implementation. Thus, the five action steps you can take now focus on how to improve on what you have.

EXHIBIT 5.6

**Example of Implementing Individual Supports Plans
in Multiple Facilities and Across Different Diagnostic Groups**

Objective: Implement individual supports plans that incorporate the concepts of person-centered planning, self-determination, individualized supports, and quality of life–related personal outcomes

Conceptual basis: Supports paradigm, International Classification of Functioning, Disability, and Health **ecological model** of disability, quality-of-life concept

Process:

1. Initiated a pilot study in 2005 to demonstrate that the objectives and conceptual basis were relevant and obtainable. Results indicated that they were.

2. Strong leadership was provided that encouraged and reinforced implementing the new approach to support planning and provision. Leadership also addressed the concerns of professionals, families, and the clients.

3. Based on the success of the 2005 pilot study, the new approach was introduced. We no longer decide what the person needs; rather, we ask him or her, and this involves an effort to improve the global operation of the centers as reflected in flexible times, encouraging rotations, support in the transition to employment, and readdressing unattended areas.

4. Staff positions have been redefined to include job coaches, section assistants, workshop and service managers, and technicians.

Results:

1. After 5 years of progressive implementation, 100% of people with intellectual disabilities and mental illness have their own individual supports plans.

2. This change marks an advance in the individualization of Lantegi Batuak's programs by integrating all of the support that the organization offers to each individual with the objective of improving his or her quality of life.

For more information, contact Txema Franco (tf@lantegi.com).

➤ *Action Step 1*   Review your profile from Organization Self-Assessment 5.1 and think about the four prerequisites to employing a system of supports. What is not in place, and what is planned but needs to be implemented?

➤ *Action Step 2*   Analyze how you are currently assessing the support needs of your clientele. Does your current approach use a standardized assessment instrument or a consensual approach, and does it produce information that can be used in the development of an individual's ISP? Do support staff understand the content and the relevance of the information, and does the ISP include support objectives?

➤ *Action Step 3*   Share the elements and exemplary components shown in Tables 5.3 and 5.4 with members of the high-performance teams who are developing or implementing individual plans. Encourage them to add more exemplars. In any case, the information provided in Tables 5.3 and 5.4 should be readily available to supports planning teams to better organize, coordinate, and evaluate the plan.

➤ *Action Step 4*   Have a retreat and discuss how ISP monitoring and evaluation is currently being done. The result will be heightened problem solving and creativity.

➤ *Action Step 5*   Evaluate the components that make up your individual planning process. Use Figure 5.1 as a model and see if there are any holes in your approach. If so, fill them.

SUMMARY AND IMPORTANT POINTS

Throughout this chapter, we have shared what we have learned about the conceptualization, measurement, and implementation of a system of supports since the supports paradigm was first introduced to the ID/DD field in the 1980s. Specifically, we have shown how individual support needs can be assessed; how a system of supports can be applied so as to enhance personal outcomes; the most important components of the development, implementation, monitoring, and evaluation of an individual plan; and how personal outcomes shape that process.

Important Points We Have Made in This Chapter

➤   Supports plans are not the same as achievement plans. The intent of supports plans is to obtain and provide those supports that enhance human functioning.

➤   The four prerequisites to employing a system of supports are the assessment of needed supports, the implementation of a system of supports, the use of a personal outcomes conceptualization and measurement model, and the availability of high-performance teams that use 21st century thinking styles.

➤   The six components of the ISP process are the assessment of support needs, the synthesis and alignment of that information with support strategies and sources of support, the actual development of the ISP, and then its implementation, monitoring, and evaluation.

➤   Implementation of a supports plan is a shared process among support staff, case management, and the client.

RESOURCES

Print

Bogenschutz, M., Hewitt, A., Hall-Lande, J., & LaLiberte, T. (2010). Status and trends in the direct support workforce in self-directed services. *Intellectual and Developmental Disabilities, 48*(5), 345–360.

McConkey, R., & Collins, S. (2010). The role of support staff in promoting the social inclusion of persons with an intellectual disability. *Journal of Intellectual Disability Research, 54*(8), 691–700.

McDonnell, J., & Hardman, M. (2010). *Successful transition programs: Pathways for students with intellectual and developmental disabilities.* Newbury Park, CA: Sage.

Electronic

Enhancing post-school outcomes. (2012) Retrieved from http://www.esu9.org

Case Management Society of Australia. (2012) Retrieved from http://www.cmsa.org.au/index.htm

Family Village: A global community of disability-related resources. (2012) Retrieved from http://www.familyvillage.wisc.edu

Status on the Prerequisites to Employing a System of Supports

Directions: This assessment will indicate whether the prerequisites for employing a system of supports are in place within your organization. If necessary, review Tables 5.2 and 5.3 for the components to the first two prerequisites. *In place* means that the respective component is an actual part of the organization's service/support delivery system. In reference to the five characteristics of high performance teams, *in place* means that these five characteristics (involved, informed, organized, accountable, and empowered) would be apparent to an external observer. Place a checkmark indicating the status for each prerequisite.

Prerequisite	Status (check)		
	In place	Not in place	Planned
Measurement of support needs			
System of support			
Organization framework (Table 5.3)			
Coordination framework (Table 5.4)			
Evaluation framework (Table 5.4)			
Personal outcomes conceptual and measurement model			
High-performance teams			
Involved			
Informed			
Organized			
Accountable			
Empowered			

6

Using Evidence-Based Practices to Enhance Decision Making

What You Can Expect in This Chapter

➤ Examples of how evidence-based practices assist in making good clinical, managerial, and policy decisions

➤ An evidence-based practices model that incorporates the multiple perspectives on evidence-based practices

➤ Specific steps to implement the evidence-based practices model

➤ Guidelines for interpreting the quality, robustness, and relevance of evidence

➤ Guidelines for implementing evidence-based practices and translating evidence into practice

Historically, services within the field of ID/DD reflected the concept of best practices based primarily on professional **ethics,** professional standards, and informed **clinical judgment.** In 2012, best practices are characterized as 1) incorporating current models of human functioning/disability; 2) emphasizing human potential, social inclusion, empowerment, equity, and self-determination; 3) using individualized supports to enhance personal outcomes; and 4) evaluating the impact of interventions, services, and supports on personal outcomes and using that information for multiple purposes that include reporting, monitoring, evaluation, and continuous quality improvement.

During the first decade of the 21st century, complementary standards or criteria in the form of evidence-based practices emerged throughout human services. We define *evidence-based practices* as practices that are based on current best evidence that is obtained from credible sources that used reliable and valid methods and is based on a clearly articulated, empirically supported theory or rationale. Furthermore, we suggest that there are three valid uses of evidence-based practices (Schalock et al., 2011). These purposes are to make

- **Clinical decisions** about the interventions, services, or supports that service recipients receive in specific situations; such decisions should be consistent with the individual's values and beliefs

- **Managerial decisions** about the strategies used by an organization to increase its effectiveness, efficiency, and sustainability

- **Policy decisions** regarding strategies for enhancing an organization or system's effectiveness, efficiency, and sustainability

The emergence of evidence-based practices stems from the same five contextual factors discussed in Chapter 4 related to the need for high-performance teams. By way of review, these five contextual factors relate to the transformation of professional services, the emergence of a new public management, the increased person and family-centered provision of individualized supports, a mind-set that the provision of supports should focus on reducing the discrepancy between a person's capability and the requirements of his or her environment, and the continuing need for well-trained and stable organization staff. To these five we would now add a sixth: the impact of social media. Online databases, chat rooms, and suggested interventions, remedies, and cures reinforce the need for empirical evidence as a basis for making good decisions. These six contextual factors have coalesced around the need for an evidence base that fills the void of traditional professionalism and, at the same time, meets the need for key stakeholders to have access to validated information as a basis for their decisions.

Some readers of this chapter will find the concept of evidence-based practices straightforward, rational, and doable; others will grapple with answering "What, how, and why?" The issue is not best practices versus evidence-based practices but, rather, best practices and evidence-based practices. The ID/DD field, as with most other human service fields, is just beginning to embrace the notion and application of evidence-based practices. In that regard, best practices and evidence-based practices will always involve professional judgment. Professional practices in assessment, diagnosis, interventions, and evaluation only deserve the qualification of "professional" if they are well validated and based on sound knowledge. Knowledge from scientific/empirical evidence is the best knowledge for professional practice. However, because empirically validated knowledge is not 100% complete (in any field), practices must carefully use other sound knowledge such as that provided by program and quality assurance standards. Furthermore, in practices concerning individual decisions, the application of knowledge in a particular case will require tacit knowledge rooted in the person's experiences, explicit knowledge based on empirically based best practices, and informed clinical judgment.

This chapter contains four sections. In the first section, we summarize three perspectives on evidence-based practices and introduce the reader to four models (including our own) that help understand the who, what, and how of evidence-based practices. In the second section, we explain how to operationalize our proposed model. In the third section, we discuss guidelines for interpreting the quality, robustness, and relevance of evidence. The chapter concludes with guidelines for translating evidence into practice and examples of the application of evidence-based practices at the organization and systems levels.

PERSPECTIVES ON AND
APPROACHES TO EVIDENCE-BASED PRACTICES

The concept and application of evidence-based practices, which originated in medicine in the 1990s, subsequently spread to many social and behavioral disciplines including education and special education, aging, criminal justice, nursing, public health, mental and behavioral health, and ID/DD. Across these broad areas, *evidence-based practices* generally means using current best evidence in making clinical decisions about the interventions and/or supports that service recipients receive in specific situations.

Perspectives on Evidence-Based Practices

Despite the widespread advocacy and use of evidence-based practices, there are at least three different perspectives on the subject: the empirical-analytical, the phenomenological-existential, and the poststructural (Broekaert, Autreque, Vanderplasschen, & Colpaert, 2010). These three perspectives relate to different approaches to intervention and the conceptualization, measurement, and application of evidence-based practices. The empirical-analytical perspective places a premium on experimental or scientific evidence as the basis for evidence-based practices. The phenomenological-existential perspective approaches treatment or intervention success according to reported experiences of well-being concerning the intervention. From the poststructural perspective, treatment or intervention decisions and intervention success are based on an understanding of public policy principles such as inclusion, self-determination, participation, and empowerment.

Approaches to Evidence-Based Practices

Four types of models have been formulated to address the complexity of evidence-based practices. We refer to these models as sequential, developmental, transdisciplinary, and systems.

Sequential Model Cooley, Jones, Imig, and Villarruel (2009) have developed a five-step, sequential model that involves the following steps: 1) determine question(s) to be answered to inform the client-specific decision; 2) search for research evidence related to the question(s); 3) evaluate the research evidence for its validity, relevance, and clinical applicability; 4) integrate the research evidence with clinical experience and client preferences to answer the question; and 5) assess performance of the previous steps as well as outcomes to improve future decisions.

Developmental Model Veerman and van Yperen (2007) have suggested a four-stage developmental model with the following steps: 1) specify the core elements of an intervention; 2) explicate the rationale and theory underlying an intervention; 3) obtain preliminary evidence that the intervention works in actual practice; and 4) present clear evidence that the intervention is responsible for the observed effect(s) and involves randomized control trials and well-designed, repeated case studies.

Transdisciplinary Model Satterfield, Spring, and Brownson (2009) have developed a transdisciplinary model that incorporates an ecological framework. Their model emphasizes shared decision making and focuses on the environmental and organization context, best available scientific evidence, practitioner's expertise, clinical expertise, decision making, and client preferences.

Systems Model The evidence-based practices conceptual and measurement model discussed in this chapter has been developed by an international workgroup (Schalock et al., 2011). It incorporates aspects of each of the models just described as well as the systems perspective that includes the individual, organization, and society. As shown in Figure 6.1 (p. 104), the first step of the model involves a clear understanding from a systems perspective of the practices in question. Such practices typically relate to assessment, intervention, and the provision of individualized supports and/or the organization's use of quality strategies. Each of these practices has intended effects at the level of the individual (e.g., enhanced personal outcomes), the organization (e.g., enhanced effectiveness and efficiency, improved service quality), and society (e.g., people with disabilities achieving higher social-economic status, more positive community attitudes toward people with ID/DD, changes in education and

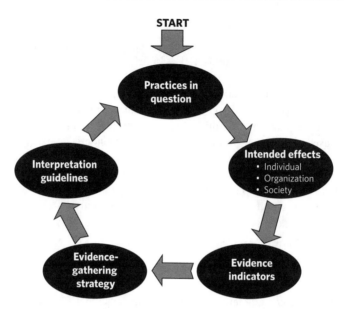

Figure 6.1. Evidence-based practices model. (Reprinted from *Evaluation and Program Planning, 34(3)*, Robert L. Schalock, Miguel Ángel Verdugo, Laura E. Gomez, Evidence-based practices in the field of intellectual and developmental disabilities: An international consensus approach, 273–282, Copyright 2011, with permission from Elsevier.)

training programs, changes in resource allocation patterns, changes in public policies). These intended effects are evaluated on the basis of **evidence indicators** that capture changes in personal outcomes, organization outputs, and societal-level indicators. As discussed later in reference to Figure 6.2, a number of **evidence-gathering strategies** can be used to evaluate evidence indicators and, thus, produce evidence. This model component, which emphasizes multiple evidence gathering strategies, is essential because it underscores the value of different research designs that can be used to address a problem that has long plagued the field of human services: Even though one might not be able to do experimental/control or randomized controlled trials, one can still evaluate the effectiveness of specific support strategies and policies. The final stage of the proposed model is the use of **interpretation guidelines** to evaluate the quality, robustness, and relevance of evidence.

OPERATIONALIZING THE AUTHORS' EVIDENCE-BASED PRACTICES MODEL

Figure 6.2 summarizes the major components (left column) and multiple perspectives (individual, organization, society) of the evidence-based conceptual model presented in Figure 6.1. This systems perspective is responsive to the drivers of evidence-based practices that Scott and McSherry (2008) identify as professional (e.g., specific practices that lead to better outcomes), organizational (i.e., increasing an organization's effectiveness and efficiency), and societal (i.e., the public's demand for best practices). We describe next how to operationalize the model's components.

Components 1 and 2: Practices in Question and Intended Effects

At the individual level, the practices in question typically relate to assessment, diagnosis, and interventions that can vary from medical treatment to the person-centered support

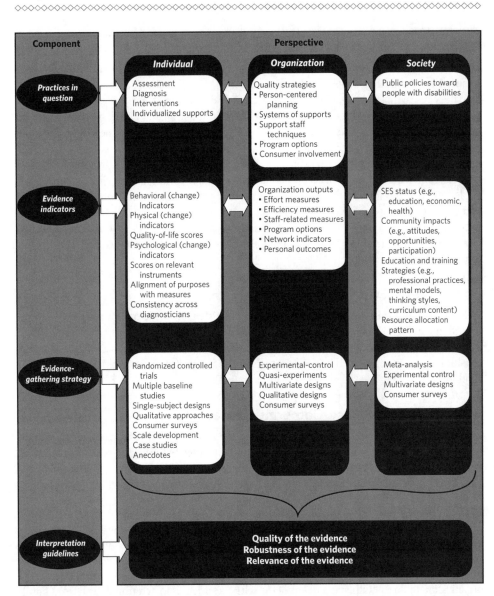

Figure 6.2. Evidence-based practices measurement framework. (Reprinted from *Evaluation and Program Planning, 34(3),* Robert L. Schalock, Miguel Ángel Verdugo, Laura E. Gomez, Evidence-based practices in the field of intellectual and developmental disabilities: An international consensus approach, 273–282, Copyright 2011, with permission from Elsevier.)

strategies discussed in Chapter 5. Regardless of the practices in question, objective and measurable indicators such as those summarized in Tables 3.1 and 3.2 need to be developed. Once developed and measured, they can be used to determine whether the practice in question leads to the intended outcomes.

The organization-level practices in question typically focus on determining the effectiveness of the five quality strategies listed in Figure 6.2 and how examining these strategies and specific organization management practices (e.g., high-performance teams) influence organization outputs. A listing of potential organization outputs is found in Table 3.4.

The goals and purposes of public policy and public service systems for people with disabilities have significantly changed over time in response to changes in both ideology and increased knowledge regarding the nature of disability. These changes have been influenced significantly by social and political movements, attitudinal changes, judicial decisions, statutory changes, participatory research and evaluation frameworks, and advances in research regarding the nature of disability. In that regard, 21st century national and international disability policy is premised on a number of concepts and principles that are 1) person-referenced (e.g., self-determination, inclusion, empowerment, individual and appropriate services, productivity and contribution, family integrity and unity) and 2) organization- and system-referenced (e.g., antidiscrimination, coordination and collaboration, accountability) (Shogren & Turnbull, 2010; Stowe, Turnbull, & Sublet, 2006). Over time, as understandings of disability and human functioning have deepened and become more progressive, these evolving core concepts and principles have increased the need to generate outcome data that can be used to establish societal-level evidence indicators (e.g., those summarized in Figure 6.2) and dependent variables that can be used in evidence-based practices research.

Component 3: Evidence Indicators

The evidence indicators listed in Figure 6.2 are consistent with the outcome categories presented in Chapter 3 (Tables 3.1 and 3.2) and the organization output indicators (Table 3.4). The only exceptions are 1) in reference to the individual (other indicators are listed that correspond to questions related to assessment, diagnosis, and interventions) and 2) societal-level indicators that expand on those presented in Table 3.1.

Component 4: Evidence-Gathering Strategy

As shown in Figure 6.2, evidence is gathered through various types of research designs. Table 6.1 provides examples of the four major types of designs being used in the first two decades of the 21st century. A thorough discussion of the research designs listed Table 6.1 is beyond the scope of this chapter; the interested reader is referred to the references found beneath the table.

➤ Tool for Application

The evidence-based practices model presented in Figure 6.2 provides the parameters for Organization Self-Assessment 6.1 (p. 117). The intent of this self-assessment is not to suggest that your organization engage in its own in evidence-based research—although, depending on your organization's level of evaluability, you may have already partnered with a university or research organization to do so. Rather, the intent of the self-assessment is to determine the level of familiarity with each evidence-based measurement component and the potential use of these components in your organization's performance-based evaluation and management system. Use the listings in Figure 6.2 to explain the factors involved in each measurement component.

When we use this self-assessment with organizations, a typical response pattern emerges. Most organization personnel can describe their individual and/or organization practices in question, but they are less familiar with the intended effects of these practices, the indicators they would use to evaluate the intended effects, and how they would go about gathering evidence. Addressing this lack of familiarity is one of the reasons we wrote Chapter 7. In reference to potential use, the response pattern is organization specific, with those organizations that exhibit a learning organization culture and those that employ high-performance teams much more likely to incorporate evidence-based practices into their service delivery systems. However, regardless of level of familiarity or degree of intended use, all respondents want to know how they should interpret evidence. We answer this question next.

Table 6.1.   Types of research designs used to gather evidence

Research design		Examples
Quantitative	Experimental (randomized or true experiment)	Between-subjects designs (equivalent groups) Randomized trials Within-subjects designs (repeated-measures designs) Mixed designs
	Quasi-experimental	Time series design Equivalent time series samples Equivalent samples design Nonequivalent control group Counterbalanced designs Separate sample: 1) controlled for history; 2) controlled for secular trends Separate sample pretest/posttest control group design Multiple time series design Institutional cycle design Regression-discontinuity design
	Nonexperimental	Descriptive research Relationships: 1) comparative; 2) correlational Causal-comparative: 1) ex post facto; 2) correlational causal-comparative studies Using surveys in nonexperimental designs: 1) cross-sectional designs; 2) longitudinal designs
Qualitative		Grounded theory Ethnography Participatory research Case study

Resources for the interested reader

Print

Neutens, J.J., & Rubinson, L. (2010). *Research techniques for the health sciences*. San Francisco, CA: Benjamin Cummings.

Norwood, S.L. (2010). *Research essentials: Foundations for evidence-based practice*. Boston, MA: Pearson.

Electronic

Belli, G. (2009). Nonexperimental quantitative research. In S.D. Lapan & M.T. Quartaroli (Eds.), *Research essentials: An introduction to designs and practices* (p. 59–77). Retrieved from http://media.wiley.com/product_data/excerpt/95/04701810/0470181095-1.pdf

Qual Page: Resources for qualitative research. (2012) Retrieved from http://www.qualitativeresearch.uga.edu/QualPage/

GUIDELINES FOR INTERPRETING EVIDENCE

The multiple perspectives on evidence and evidence-based practices necessitate multidimensional interpretation guidelines. The interpretation guidelines discussed in this section of the chapter need to be understood within the context of evidence-based practices being used to make clinical decisions about the interventions, services, or supports that clients receive in specific situations, managerial decisions about the strategies used by an organization to increase its effectiveness and efficiency, and public policy decisions regarding the provision of supports and services to people with disabilities and the promulgation of strategies that enhance an organization or system's effectiveness, efficiency, and sustainability.

Three interpretation guidelines are generally used to help determine whether the evidence produced regarding a particular policy or practice is strong enough to warrant the designation of an evidence-based practice (Schalock et al., 2011). Two of these interpretation guidelines—the quality of evidence and the robustness of evidence—are based on the empirical-analytical perspective discussed earlier in the chapter. The third—the relevance of evidence—is based on the emphasis within the phenomenological-existential perspective on reported experiences of well-being concerning the intervention, and the emphasis within the poststructural perspective on understanding the impact of public policy concepts and principles.

The Quality of the Evidence

The quality of evidence is related to the type of research design (see Table 6.1). Based on the methodology used, the quality of evidence can be ranked from high to low (Sackett, Richardson, Rosenberg, & Haynes, 2005):

- Randomized trials and experimental/control designs are ranked higher than quasi-experiments.

- Quasi-experiments are ranked higher than pre–post comparisons.

- Pre–post comparisons are ranked higher than correlational studies.

- Correlational studies are ranked higher than case studies.

- Case studies are ranked higher than anecdotes, satisfaction surveys, or opinions of respected authorities.

The Robustness of the Evidence

Robustness refers to the magnitude of the observed effects. The magnitude of the observed effects can be determined from 1) probability statements (e.g., the probability that the results are due to chance is less than 1 time in 100, $p < .01$); 2) the percent of variance explained in the dependent variable by variation in the independent variable; and/or 3) the statistically derived effect size. For the interested reader, more specific techniques for determining the robustness in qualitative approaches are found in Cesario, Morin, and Santa-Domato (2002) and Cohen and Crabtree (2008), and for quantitative approaches in Ferguson (2009), Lipsey (1998), and Wilkinson and the APA Task Force on Statistical Inference (1999).

The Relevance of the Evidence

Relevance is related to purpose. As discussed previously in the chapter, the purpose of evidence-based practices is to enhance clinical, managerial, and policy decisions. Determining the relevance of evidence requires three cognitive skills: analysis, evaluation, and interpretation.

- Analysis involves examining the evidence and its component parts and reducing the complexity of the evidence into simpler or more basic components or elements. The focus of the analysis should be on determining the degree of alignment among the practices in question, the evidence indicators, and the evidence-gathering strategy used (see Figures 6.1 and 6.2).

- Evaluation involves determining the precision, accuracy, and integrity of the evidence through careful appraisal of the results of the evidence-gathering strategy. An essential part of this evaluation involves determining the level of confidence that one has in the evidence as reflected in the previously discussed guidelines regarding the quality and robustness of evidence.

- Interpretation involves evaluating the evidence in light of the practices in question, the intended application purpose(s), and the intended effect(s). Such interpretation should be guided by the person's perception of benefit versus cost, field congruence models (e.g., United Nations, 2006), and clinical judgment (Schalock & Luckasson, 2005).

Specific guidelines for evaluating the relevance of evidence are just emerging in the ID/DD field. The following three guidelines are based on our reading of the evidence-based literature as it relates to making clinical, managerial, and policy decisions.

1. For those making clinical decisions related to diagnosis, classification, and planning supports, relevant evidence is that which enhances the congruence between the specific problem or issue and the available evidence. Such congruence will facilitate more accurate diagnoses, the development of more functional and useful classification systems, and the provision of a system of supports based on the person's assessed support needs. From the service recipient's perspective, information regarding specific, evidence-based practices should also assist the person in making personal decisions that are consistent with his or her values and beliefs. Examples include decisions regarding informed consent, placement options, selection of service/support providers, agreeing to interventions such as medication, and/or opinions regarding the intensity and duration of individualized supports.

2. For those making managerial decisions, relevant evidence identifies those practices that enhance a program's effectiveness and efficiency. In general, these practices relate to implementing quality support strategies that have been shown to significantly affect personal outcomes and organizational outputs.

3. For those making policy decisions, relevant evidence is that which 1) supports and enables organizations to be effective, efficient, and sustainable; 2) influences public attitudes toward people with disabilities; 3) enhances long-term outcomes for people with disabilities; 4) changes education and training strategies; and 5) encourages efficient resource allocation patterns.

In summary, these three interpretation guidelines facilitate knowing when evidence is strong and relevant enough to provide the basis for—in whole or in part—good decision making. Table 6.2 (p. 110) provides a summary of the interpretation guidelines regarding the robustness, quality, and relevance of evidence.

GUIDELINES FOR TRANSLATING EVIDENCE INTO PRACTICE

We recognize that changing educational and human service programs to include evidence-based practices is complex and requires many simultaneous changes in service and support strategies, organization structures and practices, and public policy. We feel that translating evidence into practice is most successful when the adapted practices are targeted to the three systems that affect human functioning: the microsystem (the individual), the mesosystem (the organization), and the macrosystem (the larger system including society). Regardless of which systems are targeted, organizations involved in implementing evidence-based practices need to apply a number of implementation guidelines that synthesize the critical elements involved in translating evidence into practice, be informed about the status of current evidence-based research, and learn from others as to how evidence can be translated into practice.

◇◇

Table 6.2. Summary of interpretation guidelines regarding evidence

Focus	Key guidelines
Quality	The quality of the evidence increases by using experimental or quasi-experimental research designs.
Robustness	The robustness of the evidence increases when studies report statistically significant results, a greater percentage of variance explained, and/or a statistically significant effect size.
Relevance	The relevance of evidence increases when it 1) enhances the congruence between the specific problem or issue and the available evidence; 2) assists individuals to make personal decisions that are consistent with their values and beliefs; 3) identifies those practices that enhance a program's effectiveness and efficiency; 4) supports or enables organizations to be effective, efficient, and sustainable; and/or 5) affects public attitudes toward people with disabilities.

Implementation Guidelines

The evidence-based practices implementation guidelines presented in Exhibit 6.1 are based on the critical elements involved in the translation of evidence into practice (Pronovost et al., 2008; Scott & McSherry, 2008) and an international consensus approach to the conceptualization and measurement of evidence-based practices in the ID/DD field (Schalock et al., 2011). These eight guidelines will be useful to organization leaders and managers, clinicians, and policy makers who want to enhance clinical, managerial, and policy decisions.

Examples of Translating Evidence into Practice

The information found in Exhibit 6.2 (p. 112) is based on the Ask Me! Survey that is conducted annually by The Arc of Maryland. People supported by the Maryland Developmental Disabilities Administration (DDA) are interviewed by peers on their quality of life in the eight domains summarized in Table 3.2. Starting in 2002, samples of adults at all community agencies supporting 10 or more individuals have been interviewed every 1, 2, or 4 years. Agencies receive their data each year to guide program enhancement, and the Maryland DDA puts the findings on its web site to help families and individuals make decisions about service providers.

Exhibit 6.3 (p. 114) is also based on information obtained from the Ask Me! Survey. This survey developed out of a consent decree between the Maryland Disability Law Center and the Maryland DDA. During the survey's pilot years, the Maryland state government began implementing Managing for Results, a strategic planning, performance measurement, and budgeting process that emphasizes the use of resources to achieve measurable results, accountability, efficiency, and continuous improvement in state government programs. The Maryland DDA has incorporated the Ask Me! Survey results in its Managing for Results submission. The data guide the agency in setting goals, identifying potential ways of reaching the goals, and measuring whether the goals were achieved.

Even though evidence-based practices are just emerging in the ID/DD field, it is not too early for organizations to begin the implementation process. To that end, the authors suggest the following three action steps.

➤ ACTION STEPS YOU CAN TAKE NOW

➤ *Action Step 1* Begin using the terminology of evidence-based practices. Language drives thinking and action, and, in that regard, organization personnel need to begin

---

EXHIBIT 6.1

Evidence-Based Practices Implementation Guidelines

1. Define the aim of the practice. There is no sense in collecting evidence unless the aim of the practice is decided beforehand. The first question is not "What works?" but "What is the most desirable way of action?" This procedure (described in the literature as value judgment) precedes the evaluation of evidence and, therefore, precedes the identification of a potential best practice.

2. Identify a potential best practice. One should search for relevant practices that are described systematically (i.e., organized, sequential, and logical), formally (i.e., explicit and reasoned), and transparently (i.e., apparent and communicated clearly).

3. Use practices whose documented effectiveness has been established. Table 6.2 summarizes relevant guidelines for interpreting evidence.

4. Evidence-based practices should be consistent with an ecological perspective. This guideline allows for a broader range of targets for intervention and encourages the design of interventions that are minimally intrusive.

5. The practice in question should be applicable across all stakeholders and relevant to the perspective of the individual, organization, or society.

6. The practice in question should be easy to teach via consultation and learning teams but within the constraints of resources (time, money, expertise). A potential useful model to implement this guideline involves what Pronovost et al. (2008, p. 963) refer to as the four Es: engage (i.e., explain why the intervention[s] is important), educate (i.e., share the evidence supporting the intervention), execute (i.e., design an intervention tool kit targeted at barriers, standardization, independent checks, reminders, and learning from mistakes), and evaluate (i.e., regularly assess for performance impacts and unintended consequences).

7. It should be possible to evaluate the practice in question by reliable, valid, and practical methods. This requires clear alignment among the components shown in Figures 6.1 and 6.2. Implementing this guideline also requires clearly stated outcomes targeted to concrete, observable behavior that can be objectively measured over time.

8. Be aware of organization receptivity. Implementing evidence-based practices is successful only within an organization or system context that is receptive to change, with strong facilitators, strong leadership, systems of monitoring and feedback, and appropriate resources.

For more information, contact Claudia Claes (Claudia.claes@hogent.be) or Stijn Vandevelde (Stijn.vandevelde@hogent.be).

---

using and understanding the terms *best practices, evidence-based practices, intended results, evidence, evidence-gathering strategies,* and *translating evidence into practice.* These terms are basic to 21st century mind-sets and mental models.

EXHIBIT 6.2

Organization-Level Application

Agencies submitted quality assurance plans to the state around the time the survey began in 2002. Goals on improving quality-of-life scores were generally associated with increases in quality of life during the subsequent 2–3 years.

- Physical well-being goals—increases in four domains
- Rights goals—increases in three domains
- Self-determination goals—increases in two domains
- Personal development goals—increases in two domains
- Interpersonal relations goals—increases in one domain
- Social inclusion goals—no change
- Material well-being goals—no change
- Emotional well-being goals—decreases in five domains

Goals on improving processes generally had no positive relation to quality-of-life change.

- Agency process goals—increase in one domain
- Staff process goals—no change
- Consumer process goals—no change
- Consumer satisfaction goals—decreases in three domains
- Staff satisfaction goals—decreases in five domains

One third of the agencies returned a survey in 2008 and indicated who was given the data: 83% top management; 71% midlevel supervisors; 49% board members; 43% direct support staff. Their verbatim responses on how the data were most useful fall into four general areas:

Planning and targeting

- Has helped to target more specific areas that we would not normally address
- Has helped to establish Q&A goals; focus on weaknesses and build on strengths
- Created new agency goals for our annual QA plan
- Since the score was low (in physical well-being), we instituted an aerobics program—have become progressively more involved in the Special Olympics
- Identified areas challenging people's lives and addressing those areas, strengthening skills to create more independence
- Helped to establish goals to improve our services; to see how we compare to state averages; to understand how our clients feel about these issues
- Facilitation communicating our strengths and weaknesses, which allows us to focus on our critical needs
- Results have been used in presentations and total performance management

(continued)

EXHIBIT 6.2 *(continued)*

Training, sensitizing, own evaluation

- For staff meetings and quality-of-life training and for parents' needs
- Reminder to consider opinions of consumers when making decisions
- Utilized in continuous quality control/quality assurance reviews
- Gave us a better idea about individuals' concerns

Comparison and confirmation

- Information about rights has aligned with information from other surveys (it is helpful to have that comparison)
- Validates internal and external reports by others and promotes self-advocacy for individuals

Information

- Consumer satisfaction data
- Identified trends both agency- and statewide
- Seeing where our strengths and weaknesses are as a provider
- The results assist with the agency quality assurance

For more information, contact Gordon Scott Bonham (gbonham@bonhamresearch.com).

➤ *Action Step 2* Incorporate into the thinking of your high-performance teams interpretation guidelines regarding the quality, robustness, and relevance of evidence. High-performance teams are the catalysts for change and need to use the guidelines summarized in Table 6.2 and Exhibit 6.1 in making decisions about incorporating specific strategies into their clients' individual supports plans. When addressing management decisions, these same interpretation guidelines are equally important.

➤ *Action Step 3* Begin using evidence-based practices. Start by studying carefully the examples presented in Exhibits 6.2 and 6.3. Extend outward from there to current research studies. That extension in and of itself will be informative and transitional. Ask yourself a basic question: Do your high-performance teams have access to current literature, and if they do have access, do they use the information?

SUMMARY AND IMPORTANT POINTS

Historically, the empirical-analytical perspective on evidence-based practices has been the basis for understanding and applying such practices. This perspective is reflected in our evidence-based conceptual model and measurement model (Figures 6.1 and 6.2) and evidence interpretation guidelines (Table 6.2). However, one should also incorporate the perspectives of the individual's well-being, the role of organization-based services and supports, and the impact of public policies on personal outcomes and organization outputs. One should also be sensitive to the drivers of evidence-based practices (including political, professional, and societal factors). On the basis of these concerns and the contextual

EXHIBIT 6.3

Systems-Level Application

In July 2001, Ask Me! provided the Maryland Developmental Disabilities Administration (DDA) with the percentage reporting positive quality of life and the average quality of life for each of eight domains. It recommended increasing the average quality of life in the domain of personal development while at least maintaining the average quality of life in the other seven domains and maintaining the percentages with positive quality of life in all eight domains. The DDA accepted the recommendations and established the goal that "individuals receiving community services are satisfied with their personal growth, independence and productivity." Two goal-related objectives were also established: 1) By the end of fiscal year _____, the percentage of respondents on the Ask Me! Survey expressing satisfaction in the following domains will remain the same or improve; and 2) By the end of fiscal year _____, the average score on the domain of personal development will increase by 5% from the previous year, and the average score on the other seven domains will remain the same or improve. The DDA met the first objective in three domains in 2006, four domains in 2007, six domains in 2008, and all eight domains in 2009. It met the second objective in four domains in 2006 and 2007 and in all eight domains in 2008 and 2009.

Earlier analysis of the 2004 data showed that increases had occurred since 2002 in six domains, and the 2004 Ask Me! annual report recommended, "Physical and emotional well-being are foundational to a life of quality and should be maintained, but attention should now turn to increasing self-determination and rights." The 2005 Ask Me! annual report further recommended, "Providers should focus on enhancing rights through enhancing self-determination and personal development." Although the DDA did not change its official goal, it increased its training on self-determination and rights. The Arc of Maryland also increased its efforts to promote self-determination and rights. Apparently, many community agencies followed the recommendations. As a result, quality of life increased more, and more consistently, during the second 4-year cycle in self-determination and rights than in the other six domains. The increases between 2002 and 2009 in the quality of life of adults in Maryland with developmental disabilities suggest that the Ask Me! Survey has been effective in giving a voice to people supported by Maryland community provider agencies and that DDA, community agencies, and advocates are listening.

For more information, contact Gordon Scott Bonham (gbonham@bonhamresearch.com).

factors discussed at the beginning of this chapter, we suggest that the best way to integrate these multiple perspectives is to use a systems perspective to conceptualize and measure evidence, and to use multiple judgment guidelines that incorporate the quality, robustness, and relevance of the evidence.

Throughout the chapter, we have also referred to the impact of using evidence-based practices and the results of doing so on organization effectiveness and efficiency. With regard to impact, using evidence-based practices produces changes in services and supports, approaches to assessment and evaluation, and the role of personnel. With regard to results, using evidence-based practices enables organizations to better explain the basis for the services and supports provided, increases the organizations' accountability (because the practices used have been demonstrated to produce positive changes in personal outcomes and organization outputs), and provides the basis for continuous quality improvement.

Important Points We Have Made in This Chapter

➤ Evidence-based practices provide information to make better clinical, managerial, and policy decisions.

➤ There are multiple perspectives on evidence-based practices that require a systems approach to their development and application, and multiple guidelines exist regarding the quality, robustness, and relevance of evidence.

➤ A sequential approach to developing evidence-based practices begins with the practices in question and their intended effects, progressing to developing evidence indicators that are evaluated through a number of evidence-gathering strategies, and ending with guidelines that frame evidence-based practices interpretation and implementation.

RESOURCES

Print

Kazdin, A.E. (2008). Evidence-based treatment and practice: New opportunities to bridge clinical research and practice, enhance the knowledge base, and improve patient care. *American Psychologist, 63,* 146–159.

Melnyk, B.M., & Fineout-Overholt, E. (2005). *Making the case for evidence-based practice.* Philadelphia, PA: Lippincott Williams & Wilkins.

Rathvon, N. (2008). *Effective school interventions: Evidence-based strategies for improving student outcomes* (2nd ed.). New York, NY: Guilford Press.

Roberts-DeGennaro, M., & Fogel, S.J. (2010). *Using evidence to inform practice for community and organizational change.* Chicago, IL: Lyceum Books.

Rugs, D., Hills, H.A., Moore, K.A., & Peters, R.H. (2011). A community planning process for the implementation of evidence-based practices. *Evaluation and Program Planning, 34*(1), 29–36.

Electronic

Center for Evidence Based Practices. (2012) Retrieved from http://www.evidencebasedpractices.org

HealthLinks, University of Washington. Evidence-based practice. (2012) Retrieved from http://healthlinks.washington.edu/ebp

National Health and Medical Research Council. A guide to the development, implementation, and evaluation of clinical practice guidelines. (2012) Retrieved from http://nhmrc.gov.au/_files_nhmrc/file/publications/synopses/cp30.pdf

University of Minnesota Libraries. Welcome to evidence-based practice: An interprofessional tutorial. (2012) Retrieved from http://www.biomed.lib.umn.edu/learn/ebp

Familiarity and Potential Use of Evidence-Based Practices Components

Directions: For each of the four measurement components listed below, indicate your level of familiarity (very, somewhat, or not familiar) and potential use (high, medium, or low). Note that the self-assessment can be based on either the individual or organization perspective.

Basis of assessment: Individual: _____   **Organization:** _____

	Familiarity			Potential use		
Measurement component	**Very**	**Somewhat**	**Not**	**High**	**Medium**	**Low**
Practices in question						
Intended effects						
Evidence indicators						
Evidence-gathering strategies						

7

Implementing a Performance-Based Evaluation and Management System

What You Can Expect in This Chapter

➤ A description of how performance indicators can be used in performance evaluation and management

➤ A discussion of the conceptualization and measurement of two performance-related indices (effectiveness and efficiency) that are basic to a performance-based evaluation and management system

➤ A performance-based evaluation and management model and the steps involved in its implementation

➤ A scale to assess an organization's effectiveness and efficiency

➤ Quality improvement strategies that focus on organization services and performance-related managerial strategies

A performance-based evaluation and management system builds on the measurement and use of personal outcomes and organization outputs discussed in Chapter 3. It reflects a systematic approach to measuring **performance-related indices** and using that information for performance evaluation and management. Such a system is based on the assessment of two performance-related indices:

- **Effectiveness indices** are measures of the processes implemented by an organization to produce organization outputs from the perspectives of the customer and the organization's growth.

- **Efficiency indices** are measures of the processes implemented by an organization to produce organization outputs from the perspective of the organization's financial and internal processes.

For many organizations that provide services and supports to people with ID/DD, the challenge that they and their leadership often face regarding performance evaluation and management is that they are data rich but information poor. Our observation is that organizations commonly face this challenge because they have not developed and implemented performance-based evaluation and management systems based on 1) cognitive and conceptual tools that involve an easy-to-understand program logic model showing the organization's major program components and their causal links; 2) empirical measures of the two previously listed performance-related indices; and 3) clear procedures on how to use the obtained information. As a result, performance evaluation and management is beyond the capability of many ID/DD organizations that grapple with data overload, data clutter, cognitive fog, and being data rich but information poor.

Our approach to performance-based evaluation and management is based primarily on two factors. The first is the concept of performance management as operationalized by the Centers for Medicare and Medicaid Services (U.S. Department of Health and Human Services, 2010), the U.S. Department of Education (Individuals with Disabilities Education Improvement Act, 2004; 2006), and the Urban Institute (Hatry, 2000). The second is the set of principles that emerge from personal and organization transformation (Zaffron & Logan, 2009). Our approach incorporates the following pillars that provide a clear focus for the organization's efforts and the resources necessary to develop and implement a system that is functional, relevant, and outcome oriented.

1. A commitment to the personal well-being of the organization's clientele, the enhanced effectiveness and efficiency of the organization, and the improvement of the organization's evaluation capability

2. A systems perspective that aligns input, throughput, and outcome/output variables and articulates causal linkages among the various components of the organization's service delivery program

3. A set of clearly articulated and measured organization effectiveness and efficiency indices

4. A performance-based evaluation and management model with specific implementation steps

5. An understanding of the multiple uses of performance-related information for reporting and continuous quality improvement

6. An integrated management information system that has four major parameters: data collection and storage; data analysis that includes the ability to relate data sets across input, throughput/process, and outcome/output variables; data retrieval; and data reporting options

This chapter is not about computerization or the development of a management information system. That can be left to the information technology professionals. However, the conceptualization and measurement framework discussed in the chapter is compatible with information processing models and systems engineering. We view information technology in the broader context of assisting organization change and redefinition by facilitating evaluation and research efforts through collecting, analyzing, reporting, and using empirical data for multiple purposes. There is a plethora of systems analysts and information technology specialists who will provide the technology once the components and content areas are in place.

This chapter begins with an organizing framework that involves a **systems approach** to performance-based evaluation and management. This framework depicts the factors that affect the two performance-related indices that are operationally defined in the second section. The third section presents a performance-based evaluation and management model and its specific implementation steps. The chapter concludes with several examples of how program-related indices can be used for reporting and continuous quality improvement.

A SYSTEMS APPROACH TO
PERFORMANCE-BASED EVALUATION AND MANAGEMENT

One way to cope with information overload is to use systems thinking and alignment as cognitive and conceptual tools to approach and use performance-based information. As originally discussed in Chapter 2, systems thinking focuses on the multiple factors that affect human functioning and organization performance, and alignment allows one to position the service delivery components into a logical sequence for the purposes of reporting, monitoring, evaluation, and continuous quality improvement.

These two 21st century thinking styles (i.e., systems thinking and alignment) are incorporated into program logic models that we also first discussed in Chapter 2 (see Figure 2.2, page 29) and are discussed further in Fielden, Rusch, Masinda, Sands, Frankish, and Evoy (2007). Figure 7.1, which is an extension of Figure 2.2, depicts the major components of a systems approach to performance-based evaluation and management. Figure 7.1 shows a program logic model that 1) depicts the underlying program theory; 2) articulates the operative relationships among a program's inputs, throughputs, and outcome/outputs; 3) aligns essential input, throughput/process, and outcome/output variables to enhance an organization's effectiveness and efficiency; 4) identifies critical indicators to monitor and use for multiple purposes; 5) specifies the core processes that can become the target of continuous quality improvement; and 6) reduces the complexity of the organization to a workable conceptual and measurement framework and, thus, clarifies for stakeholders the sequence of events from inputs through personal outcomes and organization outputs to allow for a fuller understanding of the factors that affect an organization's performance.

Input Variables

As depicted in Figure 7.1, at the individual level, one focuses primarily on the identification of personal goals and the pattern and intensity of the individual's assessed support needs. At the organization level, input focuses on the availability of resources related to tacit and explicit knowledge, time, social and financial capital, and technology. From the perspective of evaluation and continuous quality improvement, two other sets of input variables will affect an organization's performance: the characteristics of an organization's clientele and

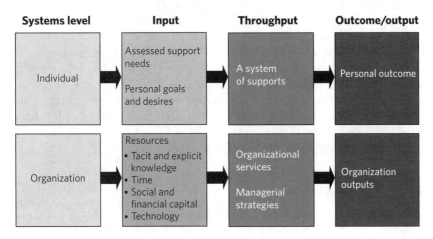

Figure 7.1.   A systems approach to performance management.

a number of contextual variables that can directly or indirectly affect the organization's throughput and outcome/output components. Chief among these two sets of variables are:

- Client characteristics: diagnosis, intellectual functioning level, adaptive behavior level, age, gender, pattern and intensity of support needs, mental health status, mobility, and marital status

- Contextual variables: organization culture (as reflected in historical and future-oriented mental models—see Table 1.4), community factors (e.g., attitudes toward the program and people with ID/DD), political environment (e.g., civil rights legislation), economic situation, geographical location (urban versus rural), family variables (e.g., level of family support for the program and involvement with the client and/or program), phase of program development (e.g., planning, initial stage, stable stage, ongoing stage), and formal linkages (e.g., consortium membership and/or interagency agreements)

Throughput/Process Variables

At the individual level, the primary throughput variable is the amount and types of supports the individual receives. As discussed more fully in Chapter 5, a system of supports should be aligned with the individual's assessed support needs and integrated into the development and implementation of an individual supports plan. As described in Tables 5.3 and 5.4, a system of supports includes incentives, cognitive supports such as assistive and information technology, environmental accommodation, skills training, positive behavior supports, use of natural supports, the involvement of professionals, and organization- and societal-level policies and practices.

At the organization level, the major throughput/process variables relate to organization services and **managerial strategies.** These are summarized in Table 7.1. The services listed in Table 7.1 should be based on the resources available to the organization; they should be aligned horizontally with the organization outputs and aligned vertically with the system of supports provided at the individual level (see Figure 7.1).

Personal Outcomes and Organization Outputs

Chapter 3 discusses the conceptualization and measurement of personal outcomes and organization outputs. As summarized in Tables 3.1 and 3.2, personal outcomes typically involve the measurement of person-referenced quality-of-life domains or social indicators such as socio-economic position (education, occupation, income), health (longevity, wellness), and/or subjective well-being (e.g., life satisfaction, positive affect such as happiness and contentment, and/or absence of negative affect such as sadness, worry, and helplessness). As summarized in Table 3.4, organization outputs typically involve the measurement of indicators related to personal outcomes, effort, efficiency, staff-related measures, program options, and network indicators.

Table 7.1.   Organization services and managerial strategies

Term	Definition
Organization services	A system of supports, community living alternatives, employment and education opportunities, community-based activities, transportation, and generic professional services
Managerial strategies	Leadership styles and 21st century thinking styles (Chapters 1 and 2), high-performance teams (Chapter 4), the development and use of evidence-based practices (Chapter 6), and the implementation of a performance-based evaluation and management system

Table 7.2. Organization-referenced effectiveness indices

Customer perspective

1. Aligns services and supports to assessed and/or requested support needs
2. Reports the number of clients placed into more independent, productive, and community-integrated environments
3. Evaluates personal outcomes
4. Reports aggregated personal outcomes
5. Demonstrates that the technology used enhances personal outcomes and/or organization outputs

Growth perspective

6. Articulates its mission and intended results
7. Allocates available resources to intended results
8. Develops program options (employment opportunities, community living alternatives, and educational opportunities)
9. Develops and uses high-performance teams
10. Monitors job satisfaction and develops job enrichment programs

PERFORMANCE-RELATED INDICES

A performance-based evaluation and management system is a systematic approach to evaluating an organization's performance based on the assessment of two performance-related indices: those related to an organization's effectiveness and those related to its efficiency.

Effectiveness Indices

Effectiveness indices are measures of the processes implemented by an organization to produce outputs from the perspectives of the customer and the organization's growth. These processes are operationalized in Table 7.2. Assessed scores on these measures can be summed to produce an effectiveness index (see Exhibit 7.1).

Efficiency Indices

Efficiency indices are measures of the processes implemented by an organization to produce organization outputs from the perspective of the organization's financial and internal processes. These processes are operationalized in Table 7.3. Assessed scores on these measures can be summed to produce an efficiency index (see Exhibit 7.1).

Table 7.3. Organization-referenced efficiency indices

Financial perspective

1. Compares unit costs (cost per hour, day, month) across different locations and platforms (e.g., employment programs, residential types, education programs)
2. Reports percentage of budget allocated to client-referenced supports
3. Monitors the relationship between social capital and agency-based fiscal capital
4. Uses fixed and variable (i.e., direct and indirect) cost data to establish a baseline cost rate to develop an economy of scale
5. Enters into partnerships and/or consortia

Internal processes perspective

6. Aligns input, throughput, and outcome/output components
7. Employs an integrated management system that goes across different geographical locations and program types
8. Demonstrates relationships between units of service and assessed support need
9. Uses effectiveness and efficiency indices as a basis for continuous quality improvement
10. Uses data for multiple purposes (e.g. reporting, monitoring, evaluation, continuous quality improvement)

➤ *Tool for Application*

The performance-related indices summarized in Tables 7.2 and 7.3 provide the basis of a performance-based evaluation and management system. Some of the indicators are person specific, some are service delivery specific, and some are outcome- or output specific. Collectively, they represent the throughput/process and outcome/output components of an organization's service delivery system. Information obtained from their assessment can be used for multiple purposes, such as reporting and continuous quality improvement, that will be discussed later in the chapter. The challenge for an organization's leadership is to choose well and invest in collecting, analyzing, and using only those indices for which there is a clearly defined purpose. Having said that, we realize that any ID/DD organization has multiple demands for data from different funding, regulatory, and accreditation agencies. Part of the duplication and inefficiency that this may engender is related to various entities and jurisdictions not being clear regarding the questions they are asking of the organization and the anticipated uses for the data provided. We trust that a careful reading of this chapter will facilitate clearer thinking.

In that regard, Organization Self-Assessment 7.1 (p. 137) provides a baseline on where your organization currently is in reference to effectiveness and efficiency indices. The self-assessment is straightforward and is based on the indices operationalized in Tables 7.2 and 7.3. In completing the assessment, place a check beneath the column that best reflects your current status on the respective indices. The resulting profile can be used for multiple purposes but primarily to establish a baseline or benchmark for subsequent reporting and continuous quality improvement activities.

A PERFORMANCE-BASED EVALUATION AND MANAGEMENT MODEL AND ITS IMPLEMENTATION

A multidimensional approach to performance evaluation and management is an emerging characteristic among ID/DD organizations that are attempting to redefine themselves. Although challenging, this change strategy is consistent with those strategies discussed in Chapters 2–6 and with the need for organizations to address the challenges identified in Chapter 1. Our intent in this section of the chapter is to discuss the parameters of a performance-based evaluation and management model and to outline the five specific steps required for its implementation. It is not our intent to suggest that all organizations need to embrace all of the specific indices listed in Tables 7.2 and 7.3; rather, as we suggested in reference to Organization Self-Assessment 7.1, organizations need to choose well and invest in collecting, analyzing, and using only those indices for which there is both feasibility regarding data collection and analysis and utility regarding data use.

Model

The primary purpose of a performance-based evaluation and management model is to provide ID/DD organization leadership with a framework to conceptualize, measure, and use performance-related information. A critical mind-set regarding this purpose is that ID/DD organizations need to see themselves as actively involved in evaluation and knowledge production.

Figure 7.2 shows graphically the parameters of our proposed performance-based evaluation and management model. The reader has already been introduced to each of these parameters with the exception of the **balanced scorecard** concept, which is explained in more detail later in the chapter.

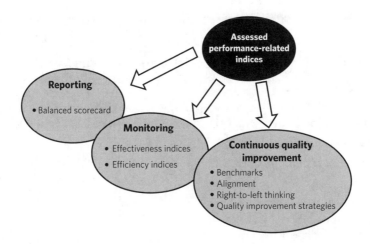

Figure 7.2.   A performance-based evaluation and management model.

Implementation Steps

Step 1: Select Performance-Related Indices   The selection of specific indices such as those presented in Tables 7.2 and 7.3 is based on the organization's evaluation capacity, which includes the data elements in its management information system and the profile that emerged from Organization Self-Assessment 7.1. We offer three important guidelines for the selection of specific indices: 1) Their collection and analysis should be feasible; 2) They should have utility—that is, they should provide meaningful information to organization stakeholders (including leaders and managers); and 3) They should be balanced—that is, the set selected should include indices that reflect the organization's effectiveness and efficiency.

Step 2: Operationally Define Each of the Selected Indices   Tables 7.2 and 7.3 will be helpful in operationally defining the performance-related indices that have been selected. If other indices are used, the definitions found in these two tables will provide a useful definitional guide.

Step 3: Measure the Indices   Exhibit 7.1 presents the Organization Effectiveness and Efficiency Indices Scale, which can be used to measure the 20 performance-related indices summarized in Tables 7.2 and 7.3 and assessed on Organization Self-Assessment 7.1. The scale has been developed and validated by the authors and their colleagues, who are members of an international research partnership (see Exhibit 8.2). The rationale for the scale is to provide empirically based effectiveness- and efficiency-related information that can be used for multiple purposes including self-evaluation, reporting, establishing benchmarks, and continuous quality improvement. The scale's development and content reflect the synthesis of 21st century thinking styles; published management literature; explicit, research-based knowledge; tacit knowledge (through the extensive use of focus groups); and organization-level, evidence-based practices. Note that in Exhibit 7.1, there are seven potential scores: 1) customer perspective and 2) growth perspective, which sum to 3) an effectiveness index; 4) financial perspective and 5) internal process perspective, which sum to 6) an efficiency index; and 7) a **sustainability index,** which indicates the organization's overall strength in reference to these effectiveness and efficiency indices.

EXHIBIT 7.1

Organization Effectiveness and Efficiency Indices Scale

Effectiveness indices:

Directions: Circle 2 if there is considerable evidence, 1 if there is some evidence, and 0 if there is no evidence for each of the 10 effectiveness indices.

Customer perspective

There is evidence that the organization

1. Aligns services and supports to   2   1   0
   assessed and/or requested support needs

2. Reports the number of clients placed into   2   1   0
   more independent, productive, and
   community-integrated environments

3. Evaluates personal outcomes   2   1   0

4. Reports aggregated personal outcomes   2   1   0

5. Demonstrates that the technology used   2   1   0
   enhances personal outcomes and organization
   outputs

                                           Customer perspective score _____

Growth perspective

6. Articulates its mission and intended results   2   1   0

7. Allocates available resources to intended results   2   1   0

8. Develops program options (employment   2   1   0
   opportunities, community living alternatives,
   and educational opportunities)

9. Develops and uses high-performance teams   2   1   0
   (high-performance teams characterized by
   trust, constructive conflict, commitment, mutual
   accountability, and focus on goals)

10. Monitors job satisfaction and develops job   2   1   0
    enrichment programs based on that information
    (job satisfaction is related to engagement,
    empowerment, personal development, and putting
    team members' abilities to use)

                                             Growth perspective score _____

Effectiveness index

   Customer perspective score + Growth perspective score   _____

(continued)

EXHIBIT 7.1 *(continued)*

Efficiency indices:

Directions: Circle 2 if there is considerable evidence, 1 if there is some evidence, and 0 if there is no evidence for each of the 10 efficiency indices.

Financial perspective

There is evidence that the organization

11. Compares unit costs (cost per hour, day, month) across different locations and platforms (e.g., employment programs, residential types, education programs)	2	1	0
12. Reports percentage of budget allocated to client-referenced supports	2	1	0
13. Monitors the relationship between social capital and agency-based fiscal capital	2	1	0
14. Uses fixed and variable (i.e., direct and indirect) cost data to establish a baseline cost rate to develop an economy of scale	2	1	0
15. Enters into partnerships (e.g., data sharing and case management) and/or consortia	2	1	0

Financial perspective score _____

Internal process perspective

16. Aligns input, throughout, and output components	2	1	0
17. Employs an integrated management system that goes across different geographical locations and program types	2	1	0
18. Demonstrates relationship between units of service and assessed support need	2	1	0
19. Uses effectiveness and efficiency indices as bases for quality improvement	2	1	0
20. Uses data for multiple purposes that include reporting, monitoring, evaluation, and quality improvement	2	1	0

Internal process score _____

Efficiency index

Financial perspective score + Internal process score _____

Sustainability index

Effectiveness index + efficiency index _____

Step 4: Monitor the Indices   Once the selected indices are operationally defined and measured, management needs to monitor them to ensure that the data collected, analyzed, and reported are current and accurate. In this regard, monitoring should be viewed as both an oversight and interactive process. This process involves the leadership roles of mentoring, directing, coaching, and instructing regarding the value and potential use of the selected indices. The monitoring template shown in Organization Self-Assessment 1.4 can be easily modified and used as an example.

Step 5: Use the Information for Performance Management   As depicted in Figure 7.2 and described more fully in the following section, the information that is obtained from the assessed performance-related indices can be used for two primary performance management purposes: reporting and continuous quality improvement.

USING PERFORMANCE-RELATED INDICES FOR REPORTING AND CONTINUOUS QUALITY IMPROVEMENT

The balanced scorecard concept was first introduced by Kaplan and Norton in 1996 to replace the traditional performance system that typically focused on assessing only financial performance. Using multiple perspectives on performance evaluation allows for a more balanced perspective on an organization's performance, thus providing more useful information to organization leaders and managers for reporting and continuous quality improvement (Niven, 2008; Tsai, Chou, & Hsu, 2009; Wu, Lin, & Chang, 2011).

Reporting

The results obtained from the measurement of the performance-related indices can be reported in a number of ways. Exhibit 7.2 provides one approach to how the various indices assessed on the Organization Effectiveness and Efficiency Indices Scale can be reported using the concept of a balanced scorecard.

EXHIBIT 7.2

A Balanced Scorecard Approach to Reporting Performance-Related Indices

Index	Scores
Effectiveness	Customer perspective score
	Growth perspective score
	Effectiveness index
Efficiency	Financial perspective score
	Internal process score
	Efficiency index
Sustainability index	Effectiveness + efficiency indices

The scorecard presented in Exhibit 7.2 is balanced in that it allows managers and other key stakeholders to understand the multidimensionality of an organization's performance. It also allows the respective stakeholders to understand the different perspectives on effectiveness and efficiency and demonstrates how these two evaluation categories relate to an organization's sustainability, which involves more than just the financial perspective. An organization's sustainability is also determined significantly by processes related to the customer, organization growth, and internal processes. Finally, for some organizations, the balanced scorecard will point out the need to develop key quality improvement strategies and performance indicators to achieve the strategic objectives for each balanced scorecard perspective (Fuller, 1997).

Continuous Quality Improvement

The reader is familiar with numerous quality improvement–related terms and systems such as **quality management,** total quality management, continuous quality improvement, and quality assurance. Whereas the intent of each of these strategies is to improve the quality of services and outcomes, the information used varies considerably. Our approach to quality improvement involves the use of tacit and explicit knowledge to enhance an organization's effectiveness, efficiency, and sustainability. Thus, quality improvement and organization change are intricately related. As discussed in Chapter 3 (see Exhibit 3.4), quality improvement requires a targeted area (personal outcomes and/or organization outputs); a goal (to enhance an organization's effectiveness, efficiency, and sustainability); one or more quality improvement strategies; a rationale; a responsibility center; a clear understanding of the role of leadership; an empirical base (e.g., benchmarks); and a clear description of the values governing the process.

We have discussed throughout the previous chapters the roles that supports, tacit and explicit knowledge, evidence-based practices, and high-performance teams play in enhancing an organization's effectiveness and efficiency. In Table 7.4, we synthesize this information along with the concepts of performance-related indices and a balanced scorecard to summarize 10 quality improvement strategies that focus on either person-centered services and supports or performance-related managerial strategies. The specific quality improvement strategies employed should be implemented and evaluated within the context of benchmarks established for each performance-related index and within the framework of a balanced scorecard. Consistent with our discussion in Chapter 3 of continuous quality improvement, we would also emphasize the essential roles of values and right-to-left thinking.

Many of these 10 quality improvement strategies and action steps are reflected in Exhibits 7.3, 7.4, and 7.5. Exhibit 7.3 (p. 131) presents an exemplary quality improvement plan based on the components discussed initially in Chapter 3 (Exhibit 3.4) and developed further in this chapter. The targeted area in the plan is quality of life–related personal outcomes, and the goal of the plan is to implement a system of supports within the organization. The rationale is that such a system of supports will enhance human functioning and, thus, quality of life. Exhibit 7.4 (p. 132–133), which is based on the Personal Outcome Measures developed by the Council on Quality and Leadership (Gardner & Mathis, 2009), shows how one organization (Adirondack Arc) uses outcome data for continuous quality improvement. Exhibit 7.5 (p. 134), which is based on the National Core Indicators (Bradley & Moseley, 2007), discusses how a number of states use outcome data for continuous quality improvement.

Table 7.4. Quality improvement strategies and action steps

Person-centered services and supports

Reduce mismatches between an individual's capabilities and his or her environmental demands by provid-ing a system of supports. Specific individualized supports should be targeted to the significant predictors of personal outcomes, and managerial strategies should be targeted to the significant predictors of organization outputs.

Involve consumers and families in the development and implementation of organization policies and practices.

Increase community activities and access and contacts with family members, friends, and people in one's social network.

Provide more normalized community living arrangements.

Have support staff provide facilitative assistance by providing assistive technology, fostering consumer empowerment, and ensuring a sense of basic security.

Performance-related managerial strategies

Incorporate into the organization's policies and practices future-oriented mental models that reflect 1) the value of social inclusion, self-determination, personal development, and community inclusion, and 2) the organization as a self-organizing system that reinforces thinking and doing, creativity, coordination, prior-ity setting, and communication patterns.

Develop an organization culture that encourages and reinforces innovation by 1) scanning the environment continuously for new and effective strategies related to skill training, assistive technology, and prosthet-ics; 2) employing cross-functional learning teams that increase skills and knowledge by synthesizing as-sessment information into individualized support programs, participating in data collection and program evaluation, understanding how to use organization input and person-referenced outcome data for quality improvement and data-based decision making, and interacting with one another to prevent siloism; and 3) encouraging the organization personnel to view the organization as a self-organizing system that rein-forces thinking and doing, creativity, coordination, knowledge production, and being committed to self-evaluation and using the information that results from such evaluation for quality improvement purposes.

Increase job satisfaction by increasing personal involvement at all levels and employing high-performance teams.

Assess relevant effectiveness and efficiency indicators such as those shown in Exhibit 7.1. Consider the initial assessed level as a benchmark and use right-to-left thinking to determine what needs to be in place for the respective indices to be implemented or improved on.

Implement a balanced scorecard approach to evaluating and reporting performance-related indices such as those listed in Tables 7.2 and 7.3. Consider the initial assessment as a benchmark and use right-to-left thinking as suggested above.

▶ ACTION STEPS YOU CAN TAKE NOW

So, how does an organization begin to implement or modify a performance-based evalua-tion and management system that can be used for multiple purposes? It might be viewed as a daunting task and, perhaps, not worth the effort required to reduce the organization's data overload, data clutter, and cognitive fog. However, from any perspective it is a necessary task in redefining ID/DD organizations. To facilitate the redefinition process, we suggest the following three action steps.

▶ *Action Step 1*   Develop a program logic model that reflects your organization's input, throughput, and outcome/output components. You might want to model it after the prototypic program logic model presented in Figure 2.2 or the systems-level/alignment model shown in Figure 7.1. Four benefits will result from such a model. First, the col-laborative construction of the logic model ensures that all those involved share a common vision for the program. Second, building a visual model of how a program operates requires stakeholders to state explicitly how they think program activities and resources will lead to

EXHIBIT 7.3

Exemplary Quality Improvement Plan

Targeted area: personal outcomes as measured by the GENCAT (Exhibit 3.1)

Goal: Implement a system of supports and integrate specific components of the system into the client's individual supports plan (ISP).

Strategies

1. Evaluate the pattern and intensity of each client's support needs using the Supports Intensity Scale.

2. Align within the new ISP format the needed supports with the eight core quality-of-life domains.

3. Implement a new ISP format that a) involves the client in a key role; b) identifies the individual's desired life experiences and goals; and c) specifies specific support strategies to enhance individual functioning and, thereby, improve the person's assessed quality-of-life scores.

4. Monitor the ISP every 3 months and evaluate yearly the impact of the supports provided on the person-referenced quality-of-life scores.

Rationale: The use of a system of supports reflects both best practices and evidence-based practices that result in enhanced human functioning and improvements in one's subjective and objective assessed quality-of-life indicators and domains.

Responsibility centers

1. Assessment team: Administer the GENCAT and the Supports Intensity Scale.

2. ISP team: Develop, implement, and monitor the ISP.

3. Information systems team: Coordinate the data input, statistical analyses, and quality improvement reports.

4. Evaluation team: Identify the specific supports implemented in the ISP and relate the supports to the obtained personal outcome measures.

Role of leadership: mentoring and directing, inspiring and empowering, collaborating and partnering

Empirical base: benchmarks comparing baseline levels of quality-of-life domain scores and those obtained 1 year after implementation of the individualized system of supports

Values governing the process: empowerment, self-direction, equality, and inclusion

EXHIBIT 7.4

Use of Personal Outcomes for Continuous Quality Improvement at the Organization Level

The Adirondack Arc uses the 25 items contained in Quality Measures 2005. These 25 outcomes contain items related to dignity and respect, friendships, community participation, and social roles. In each of these areas, people identify their own definition for each of the outcomes. For example, the personal outcomes include such items as people are respected and people participate in the life of the community. These definitions will vary from person to person. Each person receiving supports will have a unique definition of each of the Personal Outcome Measures that fits his or her own life situation. There are no norms for these personal quality-of-life measures. Each person is a unique sample of 1 with his or her very own unique meanings of the outcome.

The Adirondack Arc provides an opportunity for the person, family, and supporters to identify the individualized meaning of the outcome, determine whether it is present for the person, and then determine the connection between services and the presence or absence of the outcome. Our measurement answers the following questions: 1) What is important to the person?, 2) Is he or she getting what is important to him or her and getting the outcome as he or she has defined it?, and 3) Does the Arc or the community offer supports that facilitate that personal outcome?

Because the Personal Outcome Measures can provide a very large amount of information and data, we needed a way to condense it down into a few metrics that would be easily understandable and could be simply and cleanly charted. We regrouped the six categories (Identity, Autonomy, Affiliation, Attainment rights, Health, and Safeguards) into four major personal outcome indicators and a fifth indicator that tracks supports for each of the outcomes. A sixth indicator addresses the outcome interviews completed each year: 1) Self-Direction (Autonomy); 2) Community Focus (Affiliation); 3) Personal Well-Being (Safeguards, Rights, Health); 4) Person-Centered Planning (Identify and Attainment); and 5) Supports Present.

We do detailed outcome interviews for approximately half of the people we support each year. We have opened up the interview process to a wide number of A personnel and volunteers. Our intent is to expand the interview and learning process to a wide leadership including some direct support professionals. Everyone doing interviews has another "day job" in the agency.

We have elected to provide our staff training through continuous quality improvement. This adds to the cost, but it contributes to the reliability of our data and increases the frequency of in-house contact with continuous quality improvement. We developed a simple database in which we post all of the interview results, including the two items for each of the 25 outcome measures (whether the outcome, as defined by the person, is present and whether there is a support in place that facilitates the outcome) as well as internal demographic information, which allows us to perform data extractions using numerous parameters. The data now go back for more than a decade. We use items condensed from 50 data points for tracking growth, comparing programs with each other, comparing Arc performance with national performance standards, and informing our strategic planning process.

(continued)

EXHIBIT 7.4   *(continued)*

As shown below, we have built in charting of the six summary key indicators, which includes at least 5 years of data for the agency overall, with home-based and residential services broken out, as well as national performance averages and our internal targets.

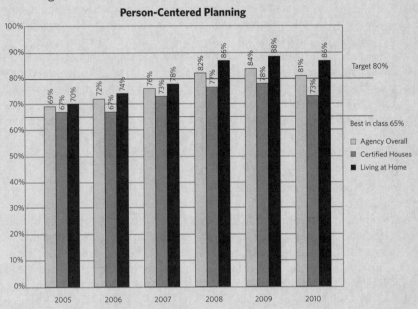

It is easy to track our aggregate progress. The demographics allow us to drill down to any level of microscopic focus (e.g., by program site, by service coordinator) to look for particulars. It is also easy to communicate with various internal and external constituencies about the performance of the organization.

A recent example of what we do with the information occurred with the release of our second-quarter data for 2010. The data showed a very recent decline (from 84% to 81%) in the scores of our Person-Centered Planning indicator, which had steadily improved during the prior 5-year period. By examining this in closer focus, program by program, we found that the deflection was concentrated in a few program sites, and we designed an intervention to provide resources to improve the performance of those sites.

The Person-Centered Planning measure is usually a leading indicator. We would expect that a lack of success in that endeavor would inevitably lead to future deterioration of the quality of supports provided. And we found that, in this case, the Community Focus indicator had already declined as well in at least one of the identified sites. Although an individual decline in community focus might be discovered incidentally, none of these system-level effects would be easily observable through anecdotal or normal quality assurance channels until the downstream resulting program failure became much more pronounced.

For more information, contact Lester Parker (arcmtnman@mac.com) or Jim Gardner (jfgardner@thecouncil.org).

EXHIBIT 7.5

Use of Personal Outcomes for Continuous Quality Improvement at the Systems Level

National Core Indicators (NCI), a joint venture between the National Association of State Directors of Developmental Disabilities Services (NASDDDS) and the Human Services Research Institute, has been in operation since 1997. To initiate the effort, 15 states initially stepped forward to work on the Core Indicators Project, as it was originally known, and pooled their resources to develop key performance benchmarks and methodologies for measurement. This pioneering work has led to the development and application of a common set of data-collection protocols to gather information about the outcomes of state service delivery systems for people with intellectual and developmental disabilities. These protocols include an adult consumer survey administered to a random sample of individuals in each participating state; three family surveys; and additional formats that are used to aggregate data about staff turnover, consumer participation on boards, and health and safety statistics.

Data from NCI are aggregated and used to support state efforts to strengthen long-term care policy, inform the conduct of quality assurance and quality management activities, and support comparisons with national norms. In addition, NCI data have been used as the basis of data briefs on specific areas of interest such as employment, health disparities, and autism spectrum disorders. NCI states and project partners continue to work toward the vision of using NCI data not only to improve practice at the state level but also to add knowledge to the field, to influence state and national policy, and to inform strategic planning initiatives for NASDDDS. As of October 2010, the NCI collaboration included 25 participating states and several substate entities.

Some of the ways in which states have used NCI data for continuous quality improvement are listed below.

- In Arizona and Washington, the statewide People First organizations are both working on addressing the findings related to high numbers of people reporting feelings of loneliness.

- The Texas Department of Aging and Disability Services publishes reports annually using NCI data to benchmark the quality of its programs for long-term services and supports. Over time, the data are used to identify opportunities for program improvements and to measure the impact of those improvements. The reports are posted online (http://www.dads.state.tx.us/news_info/publications/legislative/).

- Several states (e.g., Alabama, Oklahoma, Washington, Wyoming) are using NCI data as part of their Home and Community-Based Services (HCBS) waiver quality improvement strategies.

- Other states have used NCI data to improve the performance of individual providers.

- Finally, states have used NCI to identify particular issues in their service systems including the lack of community participation among young families with disabilities, the poor level of access for women with intellectual and development to gynecological exams, and the need for increased access among families to crisis services.

For more information, contact Val Bradley (vbradley@hsri.org).

predicted outcomes. Third, developing the model will facilitate a dialogue among stakeholders regarding the assumed linkages among conditions, services, and outcomes. Fourth, the process establishes a mind-set regarding the potential for organization change.

➤ *Action Step 2*   Develop an initial list of performance indicators associated with each program component box in your program logic model. The organization-referenced effectiveness and efficiency indices listed in Tables 7.2 and 7.3 (and assessed via Exhibit 7.1) will help you here. Once this is done, align these performance indicators with data sets in your current management information system. Depending on the organization, there may be small discrepancies, but aligning these elements should be very easy. If the discrepancy is very large, then it is time to ask a series of questions such as "What data sets are currently being measured, how retrievable are they, and for what purposes are they being used?" Referring back to the organization profile obtained in Organization Self-Assessment 7.1 will facilitate this alignment and allow the organization to begin thinking—if it hasn't already—"What are performance indicators and indices?"

➤ *Action Step 3*   Have some creative problem-solving sessions with the agencies responsible for certification, licensing, and/or accreditation. Explain 1) the importance of a systems approach to performance evaluation and management (Figure 7.1); 2) the development, evaluation, and use of performance-related indices (Tables 7.2, 7.3, and Exhibit 7.1); 3) what a performance-based evaluation and management model might look like in your jurisdiction (Figure 7.2); and 4) how those agencies can support performance-based quality improvement strategies that focus on person-centered services and supports and performance-related managerial strategies (see Table 7.4).

SUMMARY AND IMPORTANT POINTS

Throughout this chapter, we have focused on the necessary components for—and uses of—a performance-based evaluation and management system, which we define as a systematic approach to measuring performance-related indices and using that information for performance evaluation and management. We also have: 1) shown how data from such a system can be used for reporting and continuous quality improvement; and 2) discussed the prerequisites required to fully implement such as system that involve systems thinking, program logic models, and empirical measures of two performance-related indices.

Important Points We Have Made in This Chapter

➤ A performance-based evaluation and management system is a systematic approach to measuring performance-related indices and using that information for multiple purposes that fulfill accountability requirements and performance management needs.

➤ A program logic model provides a useful framework for articulating the operative relationships among a program's input, throughput, and output components and clarifying the sequence of factors that affect an organization's performance.

➤ An organization's performance can be evaluated and managed using a balanced scorecard composed of effectiveness, efficiency, and sustainability indices.

➤ A performance-based evaluation and management model focuses on the use of assessed performance-related indices for reporting and continuous quality.

➤ Quality improvement strategies can focus on person-centered service and supports and performance-related managerial strategies.

RESOURCES

Print

Baker, S.L., Beitsch, L., Landrum, L.B., & Head, R. (2007). The role of performance management and quality improvement in a national voluntary public health accreditation system. *Journal of Public Health Management & Practice, 13*(4), 427–429.

Cheng, M.I., Dainty, A., & Moore, D. (2007). Implementing a new performance management system within a project-based organization: A case study. International *Journal of Productivity and Performance Management, 56*(1), 60–75.

de Lancer Julnes, P. (2008). *Performance-based management systems: Effective implementation and maintenance.* New York, NY: Auerbach Publications.

van den Heuvel, J., Bogers, A.J., Does, R.J., van Dijk, S.L., & Berg, M. (2006). Quality management: Does it pay off? *Quality Management in Health Care, 15*(3), 137–149.

Electronic

Agency for Healthcare Research and Quality. (2012) Retrieved from http://www.ahrq.gov

Management Systems International. (2012) *Strategic management and performance improvement.* Retrieved from http://www.msiworldwide.com/index.cfm

Performance management collaborative. (2012) Retrieved from http://www.turningpointprogram.org/Pages/perfmgt.html

World Health Organization. (2012) *Performance assessment tool for quality improvement in hospitals.* Retrieved from http://www.pathqualityproject.eu

Current Status on the Four
Perspectives of Performance-Related Indices

Indices	Current status (check)		
	In place	Being developed	Needs to be done
Effectiveness (see Table 7.2)			
Customer perspective			
Aligns services and supports...			
Reports numbers...			
Evaluates...			
Demonstrates...			
Growth perspective			
Articulates...			
Allocates...			
Develops program...			
Develops and uses...			
Monitors...			
Efficiency (see Table 7.3)			
Financial perspective			
Compares...			
Reports...			
Monitors...			
Uses fixed...			
Enters into...			
Internal process perspective			
Aligns...			
Employs...			
Demonstrates...			
Uses...			
Uses data...			

8

Creating Value and Enhanced Sustainability Through Innovation

What You Can Expect in This Chapter

➤ A framework for creating value and enhancing sustainability

➤ Six promising innovation areas that create value through innovation

➤ Specific strategies to enhance an organization's sustainability

Some people believe that organizations that provide services and supports to people with ID/DD are an endangered species. Although we don't agree with this prognosis, we have stressed throughout the book that organizations need to be increasingly concerned about their effectiveness, efficiency, and sustainability. Indeed, ID/DD organizations need to redefine themselves in terms of how they operate and approach innovation. A big part of the redefinition process requires developing new approaches to organizational services and managerial strategies. Both involve creating value through innovation and thereby increasing the organization's sustainability.

It is important to understand three perspectives on the concept of sustainability. The first is definitional: Sustainability means to keep up and prolong, to buoy up, and to nourish. The second relates to an interesting concept in ecology referred to as *sustainability intelligence*: the ability to adapt to change and learn from experience to deal with one's environment (Goleman, 2009). The third perspective is strategic. Senge (2006), for example, indicates that integrating the concept of sustainability into an organization's strategy creates a range of sound service delivery opportunities and practices.

Our experiences indicate that ID/DD organizations need a road map to help maneuver through the challenges of innovation so that they can overcome resistance to change (a topic we discuss in Chapter 9). Thus, creating value and enhancing an organization's sustainability through innovation requires a clear understanding of what's involved as reflected in and examples from those organizations that have done so. In the first section of the chapter, we provide a framework for creating value and enhancing sustainability through innovation. In the second section, we discuss and provide examples of the key components involved in implementing the framework. In the third section, we present six examples of promising innovation areas that can positively affect an organization's sustainability. In the fourth section, we outline a number of specific strategies to enhance an organization's sustainability. Our intent in this chapter is not to suggest that ID/DD organizations need to completely scrap their current service delivery systems to be sustainable; rather, 21st century organizations need to redefine themselves by using the six change strategies outlined in the previous chapters, develop new organization services and managerial strategies, and reconfigure their current services and supports.

A CONCEPTUAL FRAMEWORK FOR CREATING VALUE AND ENHANCING SUSTAINABILITY

Figure 8.1 outlines the components of our conceptual framework for creating value and sustainability through innovation. The intent of this framework is to provide the context for innovation (i.e., the need for innovation and the values guiding innovation), the ingredients of innovation (i.e., creativity and a learning culture), and the sequential innovation steps related to developing new approaches and reconfiguring current approaches. As noted in Figure 8.1, the desired end result of these processes is the enhancement of an organization's sustainability. Although most of the factors composing the conceptual framework have been discussed in previous chapters, we discuss more fully here the five components involved in implementing the framework.

Component 1: Need for Innovation

Chapter 1 discusses the challenges facing ID/DD organizations. The four challenges listed in Figure 8.1 (see the "Need for innovation" box) reflect those that most directly influence the need for innovation. You might also want to review your organization's profile from Organization Self-Assessment 1.1. As we mentioned in reference to that self-assessment, organizations and systems have the potential to grow and develop. Most likely, you have already begun to address these challenges and have developed either new approaches or reconfigured your current approaches. The examples presented in the third section of this chapter will either augment what you have already begun or provide models you can use to develop new approaches or reconfigure your current approaches.

Component 2: Ingredients for Innovation

Listing only two ingredients for innovation may appear overly simplistic, but our experience with innovative organizations indicates strongly that the two most important ingredients for innovation are using creativity among personnel and developing a learning culture that is embedded within the organization.

Creativity   Creativity is not a solitary process. It happens when talented people get together and when ideas merge with future-oriented mental models. A critical factor in innovation is that creativity needs "hubs" such as the three paradigms that inform services and supports for people with ID/DD: the social-ecological model of disability, the quality-of-life concept, and the supports paradigm. In addition to hubs, creativity needs networks through which it can be implemented. Sustainable organizations provide these hubs and networks.

More specifically, creativity involves the generation of ideas that are original, novel, and useful. Creativity, which is based on divergent thinking, is fresh and inventive. Many organizations are characterized by reinforcing convergent thinking whereby personnel try to reduce a list of alternatives to a single correct answer. Although problem solving is frequently relevant, it is not the type of thinking you want to encourage and reinforce when innovating. Creativity requires divergent thinking whereby organization personnel try to expand the range of alternatives and new approaches by "standing outside the box" and generating many possible alternatives.

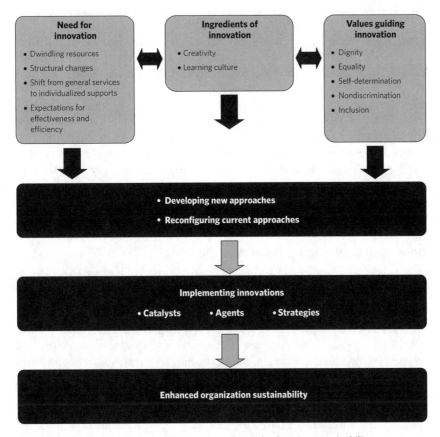

Figure 8.1. Conceptual framework for creating value and enhancing sustainability.

Every organization has a number of creative people who can lead the innovation efforts. Creative people exhibit the full range of personality traits. Research on creativity has generally reported modest correlations between certain personality characteristics and creativity. For example, Feist (1998) found that highly creative people are more autonomous, introverted, open to new experiences, norm doubting, self-confident, self-accepting, driven, ambitious, dominant, hostile, and compulsive. At the core of this set of personality characteristics are the related traits of independence and nonconformity, which suggests that creative people tend to think of themselves as less easily influenced by the opinions of others than the average person.

Learning Culture　The concept of a learning organization was discussed in Chapter 4 in reference to high-performance teams. Some of the characteristics discussed there relate to mentoring, some to the use of tacit and explicit knowledge, and some to encouraging learning and doing among all personnel. Three clusters of characteristics are most contributory to a learning culture:

- Scanning the environment continuously for new and effective strategies related to skill training, assistive technology, facilitating staff-directed activities, environmental accommodation, prosthetics, positive behavior supports, and new support practices

- Reinforcing creativity and trying new approaches

- Taking risks and rewarding risk taking and team efforts

Component 3: Values Guiding Innovation

Innovation cannot occur in a vacuum, nor is innovation value free. Values related to dignity, equality, self-determination, nondiscrimination, and inclusion reflect not only best practices but also most of the future-oriented mental models discussed in Chapter 1 (see Table 1.4 and Organization Self-Assessment 1.3). These values and mental models not only form the vision and culture of an organization but also provide a framework for guiding innovation. New approaches and/or reconfigured approaches should be consistent with the following three values-based trends in the field: 1) models of disablement that focus on human potential and the ameliorating effects of environmental factors; 2) an emphasis on quality of life that focuses on social inclusion, self-determination, personal development, community inclusion, and the provision of individualized supports; and 3) organizations viewing themselves as self-organizing entities that focus on quality improvement and as open systems that reinforce thinking and doing, creativity, and coordination.

Component 4: Developing and Reconfiguring

The groundwork has already been laid in the previous six chapters for either developing new approaches or reconfiguring current approaches. A review follows:

- In Chapter 2, we encouraged organization personnel to expand their thinking and incorporate a systems perspective, synthesize and integrate extensive information, and align their organization's service delivery components into a logical sequence for the purposes of reporting, monitoring, evaluation, and continuous quality improvement.

- In Chapter 3, we described the measurement and use of personal outcomes and organization outputs and their use for multiple purposes.

- In Chapter 4, we discussed the characteristics of high-performance teams and the key role they play in enhancing an organization's effectiveness and efficiency.

- In Chapter 5, we described a person-centered approach to supports provision and stressed the importance of assessing a person's support needs and aligning those needs with the provision of a system of supports.

- In Chapter 6, we discussed how organization personnel can use evidence-based practices to make better clinical, managerial, and policy decisions.

- In Chapter 7, we described the components of a performance-based evaluation and management system and show how data sets from such a system can be used for multiple purposes.

Throughout these six chapters, we also have offered real-life examples that reflect how ID/DD organizations nationally and internationally are using these six change strategies to either develop new approaches or reconfigure their current approaches. We expand on those examples later in this chapter in our discussion of six additional promising innovative areas related to social capital, networking, consortia membership, knowledge production, horizontal and vertical alignment, and values-based businesses.

Component 5: Implementing Innovation

Heraclites reminds us that there is nothing permanent except change—or, according to the English translation, "the only constant is change." Innovation is meaningless unless it leads to change and transformation. Thus, we have included in our framework (Figure 8.1) the three critical elements in implementing innovation and bringing about change: catalysts, agents, and strategies.

Change Catalysts

- Values that include dignity, equality, self-determination, nondiscrimination, and inclusion

- Leadership that supports change by mentoring and directing, coaching and instructing, inspiring and empowering, and collaborating and partnering

- Empowerment that involves organization personnel feeling a sense of competence, relatedness, and autonomy

- Technology that focuses on reducing the discrepancies between people's competencies/abilities and the requirements of their environments.

Change Agents   Changing the organization through innovation will not happen without two key change agents: leaders and high-performance teams. As discussed in Chapter 1, innovative leadership involves communicating a shared vision, encouraging and supporting the power of personal mastery, stressing a systems perspective, promoting a community life context, viewing one's organization as a bridge to the community, monitoring personal outcomes and organization outputs, ensuring the transfer of knowledge throughout the entire organization, and promoting and monitoring the transformation/redefinition process. The second critical change agent is the organization's high-performance teams and the protocols they establish. Creativity leads to innovation; innovation involves change; and change can result in disorganization and conflict. This disorganization and conflict can be significantly reduced via high-performance teams who follow the six protocols summarized in Exhibit 4.1.

Change Strategies   Implementing innovations involves the same concepts and processes as described in Chapters 3 (see Exhibit 3.4, p. 53) and 7 (see Exhibit 7.3, p. 131) regarding continuous quality improvement strategies and plans. By way of review, continuous quality improvement involves the use of tacit knowledge, evaluation data, and evidence-based practices to enhance an organization's effectiveness, efficiency, and sustainability. Thus, innovation needs to be couched within the context of the wisdom that comes from experience, knowledge that comes from research-based information, and good decisions based on evidence-based practices.

➤ Tool for Application

In summary, enhanced sustainability is a goal that should guide the redefinition of ID/DD organizations and the new or reconfigured approaches they develop to adapt to a rapidly changing social and political environment. Innovation is key to fulfilling the goal of enhanced sustainability. So, who does the innovation? The simple answer is *everyone*. Creative people are everywhere in most organizations. Frequently, all they need is encouragement and a vehicle such as a high-performance team through which the processes depicted in Figure 8.1 can be accomplished. Organization Self-Assessment 8.1 (p. 158) provides a structure to begin developing your own framework for creating value and enhancing sustainability through innovation.

Organizations often need a road map to help maneuver through the challenges of innovation. The results of Organization Self-Assessment 8.1 will provide such a road map. Specifically, on the basis of your answers, you will be in a better position to encourage and reinforce creativity and innovation within the context of your organization's culture. The profile will also reflect whether the innovation/change catalysts are there to make it happen.

Without these catalysts, innovation will go nowhere. Finally, the response profile can serve as a baseline for organization transformation and a benchmark to evaluate change over time.

We turn next to six promising innovative areas that contain elements of the processes depicted in Figure 8.1 and Organization Self-Assessment 8.1. We conclude the chapter with specific strategies to enhance an organization's sustainability.

SIX PROMISING AREAS THAT CREATE VALUE THROUGH INNOVATION

In the 1960s, Marc Gold revolutionized education and training strategies in the ID/DD field when he taught individuals with significant sensory and motor impairments to assemble bicycle brakes. His strategy was to use the verbal prompt "try another way" and a physical cue that provided minimum assistance. We may be at a comparable period in the ID/DD system in that many organizations need to develop new or reconfigured approaches to their service delivery systems.

Innovation requires thought and action. With regard to thought, Pinker (2005, p. 148) reminds us that "language is a window into human nature, exposing deep and universal features of our thoughts and feelings." Innovation requires a "language of thought" that includes the path and manner of operation (e.g., vertical and horizontal); acting relationships (e.g., networking); increased focus on individualization and flexibility (e.g., individual supports plans and horizontally aligned, high-performance teams); a definition of places and paths (e.g., organizations being bridges to the community and the provision of in-home supports); causal relationships (e.g., outcomes-based research); a focus on personal and family-related goals; and an awareness of the distinction between processes and outcomes.

Regarding action, Pinker (2009) provides a useful way to think about what innovation needs to involve as we move from the information age to the conceptual age.

- Design: The product must be more than functional; it must also be beautiful, whimsical, and emotionally engaging.

- Story: A compelling narrative is essential for persuasion.

- Symphony: The ability to piece elements together into a winning combination. What is in greatest demand today is not analysis but synthesis.

- Empathy: the need to move beyond logic and toward understanding what makes people forge relationships and care for others

- Play: the need to work and play

- Meaning: People need to be free to pursue purpose, fulfillment, and personal mastery.

The purpose of this section of the chapter is to describe six promising innovative areas that incorporate thought and action, are based on a synthesis of published management literature, and are augmented by real-life examples. Hopefully, they will provide organization personnel with a verbal prompt and a physical cue. The key aspects of each of the six areas are summarized in Table 8.1.

Maximize Social Capital

Social capital plays an important role in strengthening community capacity and participation. Social capital refers to the connections among individuals related to social networks

Table 8.1. Key aspects of promising innovative areas

Area	Key aspects
Social capital	Social networks and norms of reciprocity and trust
	Connecting people to social capital networks in their communities
Networking	Governments partnering with private companies and nonprofits
	Models include third-party government and joined-up government
Consortia	Identify core values and desired outcomes
	Share expertise and resources
Knowledge producers	Knowledge generation (e.g., demonstration projects, research)
	Knowledge generation throughout the organization
Horizontal and vertical alignment	Horizontally aligns essential input variables and throughput processes to desired policy outcomes
	Vertically aligns the three systems that affect human functioning and organizational performance: microsystem, mesosystem, macrosystem
Values-based business	Culture that is consumer directed, fosters creativity, change thinking, fosters learning, and focuses on outcomes
	Views "profits" as the enhancement of personal outcomes and "loss" as lost opportunities for personal growth and development

and the norms of reciprocity and trust that arise from them. An international body of literature indicates that social capital increases neighborhood stability, helps mitigate the insidious effects of socioeconomic disadvantage, provides for happiness and being connected to others, decreases the rates of illness and death, rivals marriage and affluence as a predictor of life happiness, and reduces the instances of crime and abuse (Bradley & Kimmich, 2003; Putnam & Feldstein, 2003).

In reference to people with ID/DD, the theory and practice of social capital become manifest when people form mutual support systems, personal futures planning sessions, circles of support, communities, and social networks. Social capital serves as a catalyst in our thinking and innovation, because it brings together and emphasizes the following (Schalock et al., 2007):

- Systems thinking and synthesis: Social capital is about networks and trusting relationships among networks and webs of people. A community of many trusting, knowledgeable, but isolated people is not rich in social capital.

- Organic growth and emergence: Social capital exists not in people but in the relationships between and among people. We can promote and encourage the development of social capital, but we cannot plan or control the nature of the resulting relationships. Networks and webs of interaction emerge.

- Engagement and learning through knowledge exchange. Social capital grows when people develop trusting and reciprocal relationships. Trust, mutual understanding, and shared values are often initially communicated through the exchange of tacit information. The converse corollary may also prove true: that social capital is a necessary condition for us to successfully transfer knowledge. Only when people trust us can we pass on innovative ideas and transfer knowledge to them.

ID/DD organizations cannot create social capital. Instead, they can develop innovative practices that help individuals find and nurture social networks within their own communities based on trust and reciprocity. Strategies for doing so include web-based chat rooms, online social networks, mobile support teams, self-advocacy groups, employment, and volunteerism.

Engage in Networking

We now live in the age of the network: Public and private boundaries are becoming increasingly blurred as governments partner with private companies and nonprofit organizations to do more and more of the government's work. Governance by network represents the confluence of four important trends that are altering the shape of public sectors worldwide. These four are as follows:

- Third-party government: the increasing use of private firms and nonprofit organizations to deliver services and fulfill policy goals (Kettl, 2002)

- Joined-up government: the increasing tendency for multiple government agencies to join together to provide integrated services that dismantle stovepipes/silos; examples include one-stop vocational rehabilitation services and school-to-work transition programs (Downs & Carlon, 2009)

- The digital revolution: the recent technological advances that enable organizations to collaborate in real time with external partners. The level of collaboration technology ranges from web portals, to shared databases, to common data (Goldsmith & Eggers, 2004). This aspect of networking provides key information that changes consumers' choices, thus creating new incentives for organizations to be innovative in aligning their practices with the public's priorities (Goleman, 2009). A maxim in economics holds that healthy markets communicate information openly.

- Consumer demand: the increased citizen demand for more transparent information, control over one's own life, and choice and variety in government services to match the customized service provision that technology has spawned in the private sector. This trend provides heightened potential for innovation. As stated by Goleman (2009),

> For organizations, radical transparency can create a vibrant new competitive playing ground, one where doing the right thing also means doing better. Rewards will go to organizations that innovate most quickly, upgrading qualities such as sustainability that consumers are using to compare agencies. The greatest penalties in "lost sales" will go to organizations that dig in their heels and resist change, even as customers insist upon it. (p. 95)

> This quote strengthens the relevance of the provider profiles discussed in Chapter 3 (see Exhibit 3.3).

Despite the potential advantages and benefits that accrue with networking, there are challenges related to aligning processes with outcomes, providing insight and averting communication meltdown by developing effective knowledge-sharing practices across a number of organizations, coordinating multiple partners and activities, managing the tension between competition and collaboration, overcoming data deficits, and creating strategies for capacity building. To help overcome these challenges, Goldsmith and Eggers (2004) suggest the importance of knowing your inputs, favoring improvements, and sharing what you learn. Furthermore, through their extensive research on networking, they have found the following factors to be the most important in developing sustainable networks: clear communication, flexibility, diverse skills, multiple partners, clear desired outcome or outputs, leveraging assets, and using technology (p. 51).

Participate in Consortia

A consortium is a combination of agencies working together toward a common purpose or goal. Consortia are not the same as the third-party government or joined-up government networks just discussed. Rather, consortia tend to be composed of ID/DD organizations that, either formally (through interagency agreements) or informally (through mutual respect), focus their combined efforts on specific goals. Logan, King, and Fischer-Wright (2008) discuss a four-component model that is useful in consortium development. The process is built on the tangible benefits of core values and noble causes. Once these are identified, the participants agree on specific outcomes that flow logically from the core values. At this point, members address a basic question: "Are our assets sufficient for the outcomes?" They then undertake efforts to share expertise, resources (e.g., facilities, assessment teams, data management, advocacy activities, the translation of evidence into practice), and research efforts. In addition, they develop specific action steps to achieve the desired outcomes. Logan et al., 2008 have found that, during these four stages, membership will evolve from a more singular, "my organization" emphasis to an interrelated network with increasingly common values, increased problem solving and innovation, heightened collaboration, reduced silos, and more compatible organization cultures.

Exhibit 8.1 (p. 148) presents an overview of the Taiwan Consortium on Community Living, which has brought about significant changes in Taiwan's service delivery system for people with ID/DD. The consortium's development and dynamics are quite consistent with the four-component model just discussed; this example also reflects the importance of a clearly defined, desired outcome of which all consortia members are aware (Ryback, 2010).

From an organization's perspective, engaging in networking and participating in consortia are easier said than done. Both involve building connections and strategic relationships. Strategic alliances can be used to increase resources in such areas as physical facilities, technological systems, information sharing, and human resources, advocacy, access to funding sources, and more efficient resource allocation. Such alliances also allow organizations to address broader issues that might otherwise be outside the scope of an organization's skill or capabilities. Alliances can provide safety in numbers; stimulate new creative ideas for service delivery (including colocation of services); encourage innovation, quality, and access; and facilitate enhanced personal outcomes and organization outputs.

The literature on strategic alliances cautions that organizations and their leaders need to consider the process as a continuum of possible arrangements that moves from lesser to greater intensity based on the outcomes sought. Thus, organization leaders need to approach the task of strategic relationship building analytically and with deliberation. Strimling (2006), for example, discusses the following four activities, which range from low intensity, greater autonomy, and less formalization (in the case of communication) to higher intensity, less autonomy, and greater formalization (in the case of integration).

- Communication: affiliations in which information and ideas are shared

- Coordination: federations, associations, or coalitions in which resources are shared

- Collaboration: consortia or networks that engage in joint design and/or implementation of specific activities

- Integration: joint ventures or projects that entail strategic integration of personnel, resources, strategies, and/or operations

EXHIBIT 8.1

Uniting for a Cause

In August 2007, the Taiwan Community Living Consortium was formed to accomplish the following goals: 1) increase the quality of living for the marginalized through the advocacy and promotion of community-based living concepts and services; 2) secure the rights of the marginalized to quality, community-based social housing by changing government housing policies and services; 3) assist individuals experiencing discrimination in the area of housing and independent living rights; 4) promote the sharing of knowledge, experience, and resources by building a network of individuals and organizations passionate about housing rights and independent living; and 5) grow in knowledge and expertise through training, conferences, book publications, and exchanges with international experts.

The genesis for the consortium began in 2002 with three members: a research scholar, a social worker/activist, and a practitioner. As the number of consortium members has grown (there are now 50 member organizations), their influence and voice in society has also become more influential. As a result, the consortium has been able to gather enough support to effect changes in government policies and programs supportive of the consortium's goals.

One major contributing factor that sparked the rapid change is expertise from other countries regarding future-oriented mental models and specific ways to implement the ecological model of disability, the supports paradigm, and the concept of quality of life and personal outcomes. The change in mind-set, from giving care to providing support, and quality focused on right-to-left thinking instead of process focused left-to-right thinking, profoundly shaped people's approaches to providing services and supports.

The consortium will continue to refine community-based living service quality standards and to provide training to service providers so that the process of deinstitutionalization and community living will advance more rapidly. The consortium will also work hard to influence Taiwan's housing laws to include an implementable housing policy. The consortium is working with universities in mainland China as well as many service providers there to transfer and implement the valuable concepts, models, and know-how learned. The dream of the consortium is not only to change Taiwan but also to impact mainland China.

For more information, contact Chun-Shin Lee (chunshin.lee@vtcidd.org).

Becoming Knowledge Producers

One of the hallmarks of ID/DD organizations that create value through innovation is that they become knowledge producers and share that knowledge across public and private audiences. Much of this knowledge is produced by engaging in pilot studies whose successful results can be generalized across similar organizations or service delivery systems, incorporating both implicit and explicit knowledge into organization policies and practices through knowledge exchange, determining the significant predictors of personal outcomes and organization outputs and sharing that information in publications and web-based reports, and implementing high-performance teams and describing their impact on an organization's effectiveness and efficiency. Each of these sources of knowledge can serve as an innovation example or model for knowledge production.

In addition to these activities, there are three areas within the ID/DD field that provide excellent opportunities for organizations to demonstrate their creativity and innovation. These three areas pertain to developing better time management strategies within organizations, forming research partnerships, and exploring an outcomes-based approach to accountability.

Time Management   Time is a precious commodity for ID/DD organizations and should be viewed as a major resource that, when used productively, enhances an organization's effectiveness, efficiency, and sustainability. A number of time aphorisms have been offered in Chapter 4 (see Exhibit 4.2) to help high-performance teams develop innovative time management strategies. Despite the wisdom contained in these aphorisms, the field needs creative and innovative approaches to meet the challenges stemming from the following commonly accepted future-time scenario (Robinson & Godbey, 2005). In the future, more flexible work schedules and 24-hour services will allow people to customize their daily and weekly use of time, and technologies will reduce the time involved in any one activity. In addition, workers will insist on flextime and part-time schedules, fewer people will have to travel long distances for essential goods and services, services will be more customized and personalized, and technology operating in real time will allow more people to work outside of the traditional 9–5 workday.

Research Partnerships   Twenty-first century ID/DD organizations will increasingly become involved in research partnerships. Many factors discussed in previous chapters will foster this involvement: the shift toward self-management, the measurement and use of personal outcomes and organization outputs, the development of high-performance teams who want to evaluate the results of employing a system of supports, the implementation of a performance-based evaluation and management system, and the development of quality improvement strategies based on research findings and evidence-based practices. The need for innovation emerges in reference to demonstrating the best use of these partnerships in knowledge production and knowledge translation. Exhibit 8.2 provides an example of a research partnership that meets these criteria.

Outcomes-Based Approach to Accountability   Traditional accountability mechanisms that rely on process and compliance standards typically clash with the standards of high-performance organizations and teams that stress flexibility, creativity, and measurable outcomes. This is especially true in organizations that focus exclusively on quality assurance rather than focusing on both quality assurance and quality improvement based on the assessment of personal outcomes and organization outputs. As public policy moves more to an outcomes-based approach to accountability, there are a number of important guidelines for developing this approach. Chief among these are tying incentives to results rather than activities, developing the mindset of a values- and performance-based organization, seeking reasonable performance guarantees to ensure that all stakeholders will be accountable for their actions, not suffocating flexibility in a false chase for perfection, and sharing the savings gained from operating more efficiently. Each of these guidelines provides the focus for innovative approaches. Sharing the knowledge gained from such endeavors is equally important.

Horizontal and Vertical Alignment

As 21st century thinking styles, alignment and systems thinking can be used to create value and innovation by aligning the service delivery system both vertically and horizontally. Horizontally,

EXHIBIT 8.2

Example of a Research Partnership on Quality of Life and Systems Change

Partners include the University of Salamanca (Spain), Ghent University (Belgium), Hastings College (Hastings, Nebraska), the Arduin service delivery program in the Netherlands, and the research coordinator of the Ask Me! project in Maryland (United States). Activities have included scale development and validation (see Exhibits 3.1, 3.2, and 7.1); conducting empirical studies determining significant predictors of personal outcomes; developing an international consensus document on evidence-based practices in the field of intellectual and developmental disabilities (ID/DD); working with policy makers in strategies to manage for results; counseling ID/DD organizations to apply the quality-of-life model; teaching university graduate students and organization personnel the principles of evidence-based practices, the importance of outcomes research, and specific quality improvement strategies; organizing meetings and symposia for promoting organization- and systems-level change; and developing user-friendly, staff-directed approaches to understanding data and applying best practices.

For more information, contact Robert L. Schalock (rschalock@ultraplix.com).

the essential input and throughput variables are aligned with desired policy outcomes such as enhanced personal outcomes, organization outputs, and societal outcomes. Vertically, the input, throughput, and outcome/output components of the microsystem (the individual), the mesosystem (the organization), and the macrosystem (the larger service delivery system such as state, regional, provincial, or national) are aligned so that all levels of the service delivery system are organized for maximum effectiveness and efficiency. Figure 8.2 shows graphically the concept and components of vertical and horizontal alignment.

Being aligned horizontally and vertically affects an organization and system's sustainability. Horizontal alignment positions the service delivery components into a logical sequence for the purposes of reporting, monitoring, evaluation, and continuous quality improvement. Vertical alignment results in 1) macrosystem-level values-based policies and resources aligned with individual- and organization-level resources; 2) the **service delivery framework** and **administrative principles** aligned with managerial strategies; and 3) organization services, societal outcomes, organization outputs, and systems change indicators being available for reporting, monitoring, evaluation, and continuous quality improvement.

Key components to horizontally aligning the microsystem and mesosystem are discussed in Chapter 7 (in reference to Figure 7.1). Table 8.2 summarizes the key components involved in horizontal alignment at the macrosystem level.

Be a Values-Based Business

The traditional definition of business is a commercial or mercantile activity producing a means of livelihood. The term also denotes a movement or action, a personal concern, or a serious activity requiring time and effort. For ID/DD organizations, a successful values-based business is one that has a consumer-directed culture, fosters creativity and innovation, captures change thinking, fosters learning, focuses on outcomes, orients itself horizontally, and

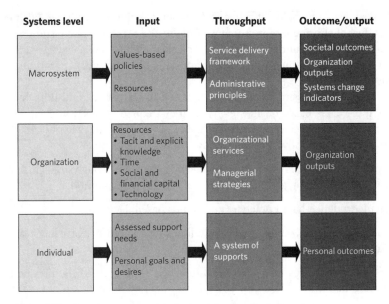

Figure 8.2. A systems approach to horizontal and vertical alignment.

Table 8.2. Key macrosystem components

Input
Value-based policies: dignity, equality, self-determination, nondiscrimination, inclusion
Resources: tacit and explicit knowledge, social and financial capital, technology

Throughput
Service delivery framework: Two frameworks are increasingly being used to provide a macrosystem-level policy delivery framework. One is the International Classification of Functioning, Disability, and Health (ICF) model of human functioning (World Health Organization, 2001) that is used to provide an ecological model of disability framework that is implemented via the supports paradigm (see Chapter 5). The ICF framework, which is based on a social-ecological model of disability, shows the influence of one's health condition and body functions and structures on activities and participation, which in turn are influenced by personal and environmental factors. The second framework is the concept of quality of life, which provides a vehicle to implement the paradigm shift in services and supports, a model for the development and implementation of individual support plans, and a framework for outcomes evaluation and continuous quality improvement. As a service delivery framework, the concept is attractive to a number of jurisdictions because the eight quality-of-life domains summarized in Table 3.2 align closely with the 34 articles composing the 2006 United Nations *Declaration on the Rights of Persons with Disabilities* (Buntinx & Schalock, 2010).
Administrative principles: individualization, collaboration and coordination, capacity building (e.g., high-performance teams, learning organizations, increased evaluability), program options, cultural responsiveness, person- and family centeredness, accountability (Shogren & Turnbull, 2010)

Outcome/output
Societal outcomes (social-economic position, health, personal well-being, inclusive living, education, employment environments)
Organization outputs: personal outcomes, effort and efficiency indicators, staff-related indicators, program options, network indicators
System change indicators: 1) trends in spending related to intellectual and developmental disabilities (community services and individual and family support); 2) trends in increased program options (residential, employment, and education); 3) access to services (e.g., transportation, waiting lists); and 4) availability of specific services across geographical areas

is socially responsible by being effective and efficient. Such a values-based business views "profits" as the enhancement of personal well-being and increases in consumers' independence, productivity, community integration, and satisfaction. "Loss" is viewed in terms of lost opportunities, suboptimal functioning, and lack of independence, productivity, and community integration.

Most ID/DD leaders and managers have the vision, attitudes, and skills to foster the development of values-based businesses. What they frequently lack, however, are specifics regarding how to develop and foster a values-based culture. Thus, we offer the following guidelines to stimulate innovation and creative thinking.

- Create a culture that is community based and enhanced through strategic thinking, quality improvement, and the principles of a learning organization.

- Execute evidence-based practices and values-based decisions.

- Structure the organization horizontally, focusing on high-performance teams and feedback mechanisms.

- Implement strategies related to individualized supports and the production of desired outcomes.

- Involve clients and their families in the development and implementation of organization policies and practices.

In summary, although the six promising areas that create value through innovation are not exhaustive, they do reflect the future of redefined ID/DD organizations and their sustainability. They also reflect a number of core concepts found in the organization change and development literature: sustainability, values-based businesses, action-centered leadership and management, mindful learning, knowledge creation, working knowledge, performance measurement, managing for results, organization learning, quality improvement, product and process design, and horizontally oriented performance teams. Central to these concepts—and to the ongoing necessity for organizations to create value through innovation—is the need for leaders and managers to embrace the best methods and sound science, give decision-making responsibilities to frontline personnel, avoid unnecessary routines, make outcomes measurement constant and pervasive, communicate values and expectations, incorporate a systems perspective that involves action feedback, and promote a community life context. Collectively, these innovative areas and the challenges posed by change and development needs provide the opportunity for ID/DD organizations to enhance their sustainability. Specific strategies for doing so are discussed next.

SPECIFIC STRATEGIES TO ENHANCE AN ORGANIZATION'S SUSTAINABILITY

In this section of the chapter, we present three specific strategies that can be used to enhance an organization's sustainability. These are to 1) develop new approaches based on the promising areas just discussed, 2) reconfigure your current approaches, and 3) use performance-based indices as benchmarks to guide organization change and to evaluate whether the organization has developed a range of sound service delivery opportunities and practices. The section concludes with a discussion of the key role of leadership in enhancing sustainability.

Develop New Approaches

Table 8.1 summarizes the key aspects of the six promising areas discussed in this section. Of the six, we have seen that the following four new approaches are both feasible and easy to communicate.

- Develop social capital. It is not hard to set up web-based chat rooms, mobile support teams, self-advocacy groups, online social network accounts, and volunteer programs.

- Increase networking and consortia membership. We truly live in the age of the network wherein partnerships are being developed in response to governmental outsourcing, ever-increasing digital connectivity, and increased consumer demands.

- Become a knowledge producer and enter into research and development partnerships to develop information, innovation, solutions, tools, techniques, and products that can be marketed and either sold or used as a basis for technical assistance.

- Work with policy makers, funders, and regulators to align the service delivery system vertically. Governments and funding sources are searching for ways to enhance the effectiveness and efficiency of the services and supports they provide to people with ID/DD. The common language and conceptual framework depicted in Figure 8.2 has received wide acceptance across a number of jurisdictions.

Reconfigure Your Current Approach

Chapter 1 discusses 10 challenges that reflect the need for innovation among ID/DD organizations. How organizations respond to these challenges also reflects the organizations' sustainability. Table 8.3 summarizes a number of ways to think about reconfiguring your current approach on the basis of material presented in the preceding chapters. For expository purposes, we have organized the table around four sustainability areas: maximize resources, provide an individualized system of support, measure personal outcomes and organization outputs, and demonstrate effectiveness and efficiency.

Use Performance-Related Indices as Benchmarks

The concept of a sustainability index was introduced in Chapter 7 in reference to using the Organization Effectiveness and Efficiency Indices Scale (Exhibit 7.1) and obtaining a sustainability index based on the sum of the organization's effectiveness index (composed of scores reflecting the customer and growth perspectives) and the efficiency index (composed of scores reflecting the financial and internal process perspectives). These two performance-related indices and their factor scores can be used to develop benchmarks to guide the enhancement of an organization's sustainability and evaluate whether the organization has developed a range of sound service delivery opportunities and practices. Strategies to enhance each of the four perspectives are summarized in Table 8.4.

The Role of Leadership in Creating Sustainable Organizations

Sustainable organizations are those that have the ability to adapt to change and, thus, provide a range of sound service delivery opportunities and practices. There are four components to their creation: how we look to the future, how we think about services, how we think about staff, and how we provide a system of supports. As described in Exhibit 8.3, leadership plays a critical role in creating a sustainable organization.

Table 8.3. Exemplary sustainability solutions to the challenges facing intellectual and developmental disability (ID/DD) organizations

Sustainability area	Exemplary sustainability solutions
Maximize resources	Bundle critical functions
	Engage in networking and consortia
	Gain access to social capital and natural supports
	Rethink the multiple nature of resources
	Base resource allocation on assessed support needs
Provide an individualized system of supports	Engage in person-centered planning
	Implement individual supports plans based on assessed support needs and personal goals
	Focus on support objectives
	Engage in right-to-left thinking
	Commit to evidence-based practices
Measure personal outcomes and organization outputs	Operationally define outcome and output categories and indicators of quality of life
	Implement a real-time, performance-based evaluation and management system
	Use outcome and output information for multiple purposes including reporting, monitoring, evaluation, and continuous quality improvement
Demonstrate effectiveness and efficiency	Develop high-performance teams
	Focus on continuous quality improvement
	Become knowledge producers and values-based businesses
	Stress vertical and horizontal alignment
	Use an outcomes approach to accountability

Table 8.4. Benchmark-related strategies to enhance an organization's sustainability

Perspective	Benchmark-related strategies
Customer	Align services and supports to assessed support needs
	Assess personal outcomes and use the information for continuous quality improvement
	Demonstrate the impact of assistive technology on personal outcomes
Growth	Clearly state organization goals and objectives and allocate resources to their achievement
	Develop program options
	Use high-performance teams
	Implement job enrichment programs
Financial	Compute and compare unit costs across programs and locations
	Report percentage of budget allocated to client-referenced supports
	Develop an economy of scale based on fixed and variable costs
	Enter into partnerships
Internal process	Align organization horizontally
	Employ an integrated management information system
	Demonstrate the relationship between units of services/supports to assessed support needs and personal outcomes
	Use data for multiple purposes

EXHIBIT 8.3

The Role of Leadership in Creating Sustainable Intellectual and Developmental Disability Organizations

1. How we look to the future

   Leaders need to create the future: Creating the future is about both implementing innovation and creating vision.

   Increased technology: Organizations need to invest the staff and volunteer time required to learn and implement technology for people served by the agency. This further involves assisting people with intellectual and developmental disabilities in using the Internet for employment, social networking, and learning.

2. How we think about services

   Values-based businesses: Being values based involves how we operate our organizations, how we teach staff, and how we serve people. It is not about what we say but, rather, about actual implementation. This means translating values into the everyday work of everyone at the organization.

   Targeted supports: Targeting supports requires personalization of each service based on how each person says he or she wants to live his or her life. Needs are met according to each person's service delivery preferences. People's time is not wasted in services that meet this criterion.

   Active thinking about implementation: Plans are only developed because someone needs to have the supports and services detailed in them. Plans are only worthwhile if they are translated into action. Problem solving is an essential component of implementing each person's supports and services.

3. How we think about staff

   Active teaching models: The organization views itself as having an obligation to help staff grow. Administrators actively teach, provide technical assistance, and problem-solve with other staff.

   Encouraging staff to think, problem-solve, lead, and continually translate values, research, and theories into practice: Leaders have a key role in designing organizations in which staff want to learn. Implementing this knowledge is a vital component of how organizations operate on a daily basis. Telling stories that are values based and helping everyone think about successes and failures provide key avenues for learning.

4. How we provide a system of supports

   Systems advocacy: Leaders should think about and then act on how their organizations need to be involved in systems advocacy to create an overarching system that truly works for each person receiving services or awaiting services.

   Reducing the burden of work that creates nonwork: Paperwork is only one such burden. Others include unresponsive systems and rules that serve little purpose and waste valuable time.

   Creating a sustainable and flexible system: Systems should be designed so that people receive the supports and services they need when they require them and in ways that they prefer. Finding a balance in which the provision of services is not

(continued)

EXHIBIT 8.3   *(continued)*

burdensome to people and their families and the cost of services is not burdensome to the funding system is a challenge that can be solved through creativity and
innovation.

Service coordinators versus support brokers: Systems should be designed to be
simple and provide the assistance people need to navigate their options. Service
coordinators play this navigation role as people think about the various individual
services and providers they wish to use. Support brokers play a navigation role as
part of agencies that act as providers without walls, providing individual services
and personalized supports for people. Both service coordinators and support
brokers should advocate in a way that not only increases the power of people and
their families but also creates services that are sustainable over the long term. To
be sustainable, these supports and services must be provided according to each
person's preferences and in ways that are sufficient to meet each person's needs.

For more information, contact Joanna Pierson (jpierson@arcfc.org).

▶ ACTION STEPS YOU CAN TAKE NOW

Creativity and innovation can be both fun and productive. They also require ongoing support
and perseverance. To that end, we suggest the following five action steps that you can take
now to create value and enhance sustainability through innovation.

➤ *Action Step 1*   Carefully review Organization Self-Assessment 8.1 and the status of
the ingredients for innovation. Address the *no* responses regarding the four change catalysts and
the two change agents.

➤ *Action Step 2*   Shift the focus in high-performance team meetings from problem
solving, which uses convergent thinking, to creating and innovating, which use divergent thinking. Initially select one or two of the six promising innovative areas discussed in this chapter
and use them as a basis for developing either new practices or reconfiguring existing programs,
services, or supports.

➤ *Action Step 3*   If you have not already done so, begin to explore networking possibilities and/or consortium development. It is a safe bet that other organizations are facing
the same challenges as you are and are willing to collaborate, network, or become consortium
members. Exhibit 8.1 provides an example of a successful consortium.

➤ *Action Step 4*   Add an *innovation* component to your strategic planning process.
Share Figure 8.1 and Table 8.1 with board members and others involved in developing mission
statements and implementing strategic plans. Use the specific strategies discussed in the last section of this chapter to develop talking points and action plan documents.

➤ *Action Step 5*   Consider innovation as a significant component of continuous quality improvement. The intent of both is to enhance an organization's effectiveness, efficiency, and
sustainability.

SUMMARY AND IMPORTANT POINTS

Substantive and transformational decisions are always made in difficult times. Organizations need to be concerned about their sustainability, but they should view it from the three perspectives discussed in this chapter: as the need to keep up and buoy up, as the ability to adapt to change and learn from experience, and as a concept to be integrated into an organization's strategy so as to create a range of sound service delivery opportunities and practices.

Creating value through innovation and, thereby, increasing an organization's sustainability depends on three critical factors: a language of thought that is compatible with innovation, progressive mental models that are values based, and an organization culture that encourages and reinforces creativity and innovation.

Important Points We Have Made in This Chapter

➤ Redefinition involves developing new approaches or reconfiguring current approaches. Innovation is basic to both.

➤ The ingredients of innovation involve creativity and an organization-based learning culture.

➤ Values should guide the innovation process.

➤ All members of an organization should be involved in the process of creating value through innovation.

➤ Implementing innovations involves change catalysts, change agents, and change strategies.

RESOURCES

Print

Dringoli, A. (2009). *Creating value through innovation.* Cheltenham, UK: Edward Elgar.

Johnson, S. (2010). *Where good ideas come from: The natural history of innovation.* New York, NY: Riverhead.

Nambisan, P., & Nambisan, S. (2009). Models of consumer value co-creation in health care. *Health Care Management Review, 34*(4), 344–354.

Viens, C., Lavoie-Tremblay, M., Leclerc, M.M., & Brabant, L.H. (2005). New approaches to organizing care and work: Giving way to participation, mobilization, and innovation. *Health Care Manager, 24*(2), 150–158.

Electronic

Center for Innovation and Change. *Creating Value through Excellence in Financial Management (exinfm).* Retrieved from http://www.exinfm.com/board/index.html

Virginia Commonwealth University-Rehabilitation Research and Training Center. Retrieved from http://www.worksupport.com

Status of Prerequisites for Creating Value Through Innovation

Directions: Answer each question related to the self-assessment activities listed below.

Element and self-assessment activities

Ingredients for innovation

- List the five most creative people in your organization. Look beyond the leadership and management level and focus on high-performance team members.
  Names: _____, _____,
  _____, _____, _____.

- Evaluate the learning culture of your organization. The three key areas regarding innovation are

  ➤ Environmental scanning: Yes___ No___

  ➤ Reinforcing creativity: Yes___ No___

  ➤ Taking risks and rewarding risk taking: Yes___ No___

Implementing innovation

- Evaluate the presence/absence of these four change catalysts:

  ➤ Values such as those listed in Figure 8.1: Yes___ No___

  ➤ Leadership that supports innovation: Yes ___ No___

  ➤ Degree of perceived empowerment among organization personnel:
  High___ Medium___ Low___

  ➤ Technology that focuses on reducing discrepancies between people and their environments: Yes___ No___

- Evaluate the presence or absence of these two change agents:

  ➤ Facilitating and innovative leadership: Yes___ No___

  ➤ High-performance teams: Yes___ No___

- Are change strategies viewed as quality improvement strategies within your organization? Yes ___ No___

9

Overcoming Resistance to Change

What You Can Expect in This Chapter

➤ Principles of behavioral change and attitude formation

➤ Effective strategies for overcoming resistance to change

➤ A five-stage approach to bringing about permanent change

➤ Lessons learned and key catalysts in organization change

We approach change and overcoming resistance to change within the context of innovation. By approaching change as part of the innovation process, one proactively addresses issues related to the need for change; the ingredients of change; values guiding the change process; and the catalysts, agents, and strategies involved in change. Furthermore, change does not have to be draconian. When approached as a necessary component of innovation and sustainability, change is viewed more positively as a process of rewriting the future of one's organization.

Despite this optimism, we realize that change is hard and easier to talk about than do. Because of the challenges involved in organization change, there is a plethora of literature related to change strategies and the need to consider change as a multistage process. Where appropriate, we incorporate that literature into this chapter. We also recognize that some changes are easier than others and that, frequently, a very small innovation can have a profound impact. Take, for example, the concept of *choice architecture* (Thaler & Sunstein, 2008), which has been used by public and private entities to significantly boost donations and change people's behavior. By having to opt out of a donation or activity (e.g., organ donations on drivers' licenses), the opt-in default turns people's inertia-like tendency to stick with the default option into an advantage.

Throughout the preceding eight chapters, we have viewed change as a positive value and necessary activity in transforming how 21st century organizations approach the critical issues of measuring and using personal outcomes and organization outputs, developing high-performance teams, employing a system of supports, using evidence-based practices, and implementing a performance-based evaluation and management system. Although we have used the term *change strategies* throughout the preceding chapters, we have deferred to this chapter a more complete discussion of how specific and enduring change is brought about. To that end, this chapter has four sections. In the first section, we discuss why people resist change and emphasize the importance of understanding and addressing those reasons. The second section is based on the observation that significant change can occur through understanding some very basic principles of behavioral change and attitude formation (thus, that section is entitled "Change on the Back of an Envelope"). The third section outlines a more detailed, five-stage model for bringing about permanent change. The final section presents two examples of lessons learned and key catalysts in organization change.

WHY PEOPLE RESIST CHANGE

People resist change for a number of reasons. Some of those reasons involve the possible implications of change, the need to learn new skills, and not seeing the benefit of change. People also resist change that is perceived as inconsistent with their mental models and/or the perceived purpose of the organization providing services and supports. Resisting change can also be due to complacency. Kotter (1996), for example, suggests that each of the following sources of complacency can cause individuals to resist change: the absence of a major visible crisis, too many visible resources, low overall performance standards, organizational structures that focus employees on narrow functional goals, internal measurement systems that focus on the wrong performance indicators, a lack of sufficient performance feedback from external sources, a kill-the-messenger mentality, a low-candor and low-confrontation culture, and human nature's capacity for denial—especially if people are already busy or stressed.

One of the most insightful explanations for why people resist change relates to how they experience the future. As expressed by Zaffron and Logan,

> Everyone experiences a future in front of them, even though few could articulate it. It goes beyond what they expect to happen, hope will happen, or think might happen. This future lives at a gut level. We know it is what will happen, whether we can give words to it or not. We call this the default future, and everyone has one. So does every organization.(2009, p. xxxi)

An individual's default future significantly influences how willing he or she is to change and what he or she thinks will happen because of the change. According to Zaffron and Logan (2009), one lives one's default future unaware that, by doing so, he or she makes it happen. This notion is commonly referred to as the power of one's self-fulfilled prophecy. Zaffron and Logan suggest that the same dynamic exists at the organization level and that the reason most significant change efforts fail is that, regardless of the change strategies employed, the default future of employees and leaders is still in place.

The concept of a default future is critical to one's understanding of why people resist change and how to bring about enduring change. From a change management perspective, leaders and managers need to focus on rewriting the future in reference to what people know will happen. As Alexander Graham Bell reminded us, the mind must see before it can believe. Therefore, successful change—as with successfully implemented innovation—must have an empirical and/or demonstrable basis. People must see the benefits of change before they are willing to change.

CHANGE ON THE BACK OF AN ENVELOPE

This section is based on the premise that many potentially significant changes do not require draconian efforts and thus euphemistically can be done "on the back of an envelope." Our reading of change literature and personal experiences indicates that effective change can be accomplished if leaders and managers do three things: 1) address key questions that personnel have about the proposed change and what it means, 2) understand basic principles of behavioral change and attitude formation, and 3) implement one or more effective strategies to overcome resistance to change.

Addressing Key Questions

Before embracing change, people usually (and appropriately) ask a number of key questions. Goleman (2009) discusses some typical examples of such questions:

- Do we care about it, and what would we lose if we ignore this? This question raises the fundamental issue of a clear vision of the change and its impact, values, priorities, and ethics.

- How will we have to change our thinking and acting? This question raises the issue of mental models, default futures, and staff functions.

- What do I need to know, and what do we really need to know? This question raises the issue of the power of knowledge and stresses understanding the relevance and potential impact of the innovation/change.

- What are the logistics of change? This question indicates the need for a clear understanding of the change process, one's role in that process, and his or her status following the change.

- Are the changes worth it? This question underlies the importance of assisting staff to rewrite their future and showing them what can happen so that all personnel can see their future roles and, thus, reduce their anxiety about change.

Principles of Behavioral Change and Attitude Formation

Although we focus on people's behavior as they either embrace change or resist it, when discussing how best to overcome one's resistance to change, we cannot overlook the reciprocal relationship between behavior and attitudes (Petty & Wegener, 1998). Thus, innovation and change leaders need to consider the fundamental principles of behavioral change and attitude formation summarized in Table 9.1.

The principles regarding attitudinal formation listed in Table 9.1 are based on a growing body of scientific evidence that points to the significant role that thought and emotion play in people's attitudes and behaviors and, thus, cause people to either embrace or resist change. Because attitude formation is the key factor in embracing or resisting change, additional comments about these four principles are warranted.

Table 9.1. Principles of behavioral change and attitude formation

Behavioral change
Analyze where you are and where you want to go (*analysis* and *vision*).
Know how to get there (*strategy*).
Set specific, obtainable goals (*goal*).
Proceed in small, obtainable steps so that success is ensured and opportunities for reinforcement are provided (*small steps*).

Attitude formation
People perform according to how they think about a situation (*mental models*).
Language transforms how people think and how they respond to situations they encounter (*language*).
Understanding and emotional commitment facilitate change (*understanding*).
People are motivated more by the intrinsic value of anticipated change than by external rewards (*intrinsic motivation*).

Principle 1: Mental Models   How people behave is based on how and what they think about the situations they encounter. For example, if one accepts a defectology model of disability, the focus of intervention and support will be to fix the person's perceived defects. Conversely, if one approaches disability from a social-ecological perspective, the focus will be on environmentally based supports that facilitate human functioning and social inclusion. Analogously, people resist innovation and change when others throughout the organization use language such as conflict is bad, change cannot happen, success is leader dependent, and/ or personal and family outcomes cannot be measured (Pinker, 2005).

Principle 2: Language   Language transforms how people think and act. This principle rests on the fundamental distinction between descriptive language and future-based language. Descriptive language depicts or represents things as they are or have been; future-based language projects a new future for organizations and the clientele they serve (Zaffron & Logan, 2009). Future language reflects (and reinforces) future-oriented mental models.

Principle 3: Understanding   Behavioral change is facilitated through understanding and emotional commitment. Heath and Heath (2009), for example, suggest that the first lesson in getting people to embrace difficult changes is to tell them what you want them to do in a way that will make intuitive sense to them. In this process, one needs to engage with emotions, not just facts. This principle underlies the importance of recognizing that basic emotions such as hope and fear shape people's attitudes and expectations about the future. Hope fosters optimism, engagement, and creativity; fear inhibits thought, action, and innovation.

Principle 4: Intrinsic Motivation   People are more motivated by the intrinsic value of an innovation/change than they are by external rewards. This principle rests on the concept of internal locus of control (see Chapter 4) and the key roles that a sense of autonomy, mastery, and purpose play in human behavior (Pinker, 2009).

Implementing Effective Strategies to Overcome Resistance to Change

The 10 back-of-the-envelope strategies listed in Table 9.2 are based on principles that we have gleaned from both the organization change literature and our experiences with organizations that have successfully implemented new and innovative approaches to their service delivery system—despite some resistance to change. The strategies also suggest how one can address

Table 9.2.   Ten effective strategies for overcoming resistance to change

1. Identify the historically based mental models (see Table 1.4) that frequently limit change. Successful leaders have found that successful change requires identifying and changing the limiting factor(s) represented in non–future-oriented mental models, thereby increasing their leverage.
2. Reassure personnel that their futures will be secure.
3. Be clear as to the organization's vision for the future and how personnel can help in achieving it.
4. Tie in self-interest so that there are incentives to change and disincentives for clinging to old habits and mental models.
5. Demonstrate that change is possible (e.g., pilot studies).
6. Pace change to allow for understanding, absorption, and the asking of questions.
7. Recognize that people process information differently. Change is easier for people who are perceptive-intuitive than for those who are systematic-receptive.
8. Provide values training around those values guiding the change process.
9. Empower consumers and personnel to help implement the change.
10. Work continuously to change mind-sets regarding the organization's view of itself as one that reinforces future thinking and doing, creativity, taking risks, priority setting, and open communication.

the key questions asked by stakeholders and integrate the principles of behavioral change and attitude formation summarized in Table 9.1.

➤ *Tool for Application*

You can learn a lot from the back of an envelope. This will be apparent as you complete Organization Self-Assessment 9.1 (p. 173), which focuses on the approach you have taken thus far to implement change and deal effectively with any resistance to change that you have experienced. To complete the self-assessment, you must 1) have tried recently to implement innovation or change and 2) be familiar with the material presented in Tables 9.1 and 9.2.

Your analysis of this profile will be valuable and will identify the factors you should look for in the five-stage change model (discussed next) for bringing about permanent change. If your efforts were unsuccessful in the proposed innovation/change, see (by analyzing your *yes* and *no* patterns) whether you had overlooked important behavioral change and attitude formation principles as you interacted with the respective personnel. Also, you might want to consider becoming more *connected*. According to Ryback (2010), one needs to work jointly with individuals to bring about change through 1) knowing how one affects others, understanding the needs, concerns, and mind-sets of others, and appreciating the organization context within which the communication is taking place; 2) motivating people to listen to each other and reinforcing action; and 3) articulating clearly desired outcomes, identifying those involved in achieving those outcomes, and celebrating the successful attainment of personal outcomes and organization outputs.

If the change effort was successful, then pay close attention to three things. First, the discrepancy between the principles you used and those you checked *effective* in the self-assessment; second, the discrepancy between the principles you used and those you checked *ineffective*; and, third, the listing of the specific strategies you used. The success strategies should be built into your organization, and that knowledge should be shared.

A FIVE-STEP APPROACH TO BRINGING ABOUT PERMANENT CHANGE

Addressing change on the back of an envelope may not be sufficient to bring about permanent change in an organization and/or its service delivery system. The initial change strategies might not be implemented well, the process might lose steam because of a lack of short-term positive results, or the changes might not produce the desired results. Thus, a more detailed, multistage approach is often needed to either overcome the resistance to change or bring about permanent change. The purpose of this section is to describe a five-stage process for doing so.

There is a growing body of management literature directed at maximizing organization and systems change in human services agencies. This literature, which is generally based on theories of individual and organization development, indicates that bringing about permanent change is a multistage process that involves 1) creating a clear vision of the future, 2) using simple communication to enhance knowledge and understanding, 3) employing **constructive engagement** that involves leadership empowering others to implement the change, 4) generating short-term wins to provide immediate feedback and reinforcement, and 5) anchoring the new approaches in the organization's culture. These five stages are presented graphically in Figure 9.1.

Clear Vision

The eight change strategies discussed in this book, along with the organization-specific innovations discussed in Chapter 8, convey a picture of what the future will look like. Whether the changes relate to measuring and using personal outcomes and organization outputs, developing high-performance teams, employing a system of supports, using evidence-based

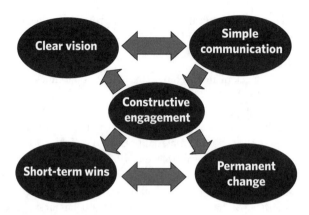

Figure 9.1.   Five-stage model for bringing about permanent change.

practices, or implementing a performance-based evaluation and management system, they need to appeal to the long-term interests of the organization's multiple stakeholders and to be viewed as realistic and obtainable. Furthermore, the proposed changes need to be operationalized succinctly so that they are clearly understood, can provide guidance for decision making, and are flexible enough to allow individual initiative and alternative responses in light of changing conditions. Finally, they need to be easy to communicate; it should be possible to explain the proposed changes within 5 minutes. As reflected in these criteria (and discussed more fully in Kotter, 1996), the characteristics of a clear, effective vision are that it is imaginable, desirable, feasible, focused, flexible, and communicable.

Simple Communication

Chapter 4 describes the essential aspects of communication as clarity, authenticity, accuracy, efficiency, completeness, timeliness, focus, and openness. In reference to bringing about permanent change, we would add simplicity. According to Kotter (1996, p. 89), the typical amount of communication regarding a change of vision is 13,400 words or numbers. This amount is the equivalent of one 30-minute speech, one hour-long meeting, one 600-word article in the organization's newspaper, or one 2,000-word memo. Thus, the reader should remember that the key elements in the effective communication of a vision are simplicity (eliminate all jargon and technobabble), examples, multiple forums, and repetition. Simple communication also allows leadership to articulate the connections between new behaviors and organization success.

Constructive Engagement

Constructive engagement involves leading by example and empowering personnel to implement the change. Ashbaugh (2008), for example, draws on his work with systems change and his familiarity with the change management literature to suggest three prerequisites for successful organization change: 1) the leadership and management necessary to implement and sustain the change, 2) the positive engagement of the parties responsible for implementing the change, and 3) a level of understanding and knowledge among those parties that is sufficient to implement the change. The roles and functions of leadership (see Organization Self-Assessment 1.4) are essential in fulfilling each of these three criteria.

Empowering others to implement change is the second part of the constructive engagement equation. Typically, that empowerment is manifest through the effects of high-performance teams. A high-performance team provides an effective mechanism to empower people to implement permanent change by (Ashbaugh, 2008; Kotter, 1996; Miner, 2005)

- Participating in planning and implementation efforts

- Providing values and managing change training sessions

- Communicating a sense of vision and making structural changes compatible with the vision

- Aligning information and personnel systems to the vision

- Explaining seeming inconsistencies

- Confronting supervisors who undercut needed change

Short-Term Wins

A fundamental principle of successful behavioral and organization change is to proceed in small, obtainable steps to ensure success. This success provides opportunities for self-reinforcement and celebration. Inherent in this change principle is the concept of a change threshold that can be lowered to reduce the organization's resistance to change. The work described in Exhibit 9.1 by the ITINERIS Foundation in South America reflects how the threshold can be lowered and what change indicators emerge as the resistance to change is reduced. Once the threshold is crossed, the role that short-term wins play in bringing about permanent change will be apparent because crossing the threshold 1) produces the opportunity to visibly recognize and reward people who made the win possible, 2) provides evidence that sacrifices are worth it, 3) helps fine-tune vision and strategies, 4) undermines cynics and self-serving resisters, and 5) builds momentum (Kotter, 1996, p. 123).

Anchoring the New Approach (Permanent Change)

The process of anchoring the new approach is the final stage of bringing about permanent change. Anchoring is based on the previous four stages: creating a clear vision, communicating simply and effectively, employing constructive engagement, and generating short-term wins. Real transformation takes time and occurs when four conditions are met: when the change becomes the established way of doing things; when sufficient time is taken to ensure leadership development and succession; when people are hired, promoted, and/or developed who can implement the innovations and changes; and when the change process is reinvigorated through conducting successful new projects that involve change agents such as networking and consortia membership.

➤ Tool for Application

Anchoring the new approach and bringing about permanent change is facilitated by monitoring the change process. Organization Self-Assessment 9.2 (p. 174) provides a framework and process for doing so.

The *yes* responses in the self-assessment provide the basis for celebration, and the *no* responses form the basis for action. Some of the most common errors to organization change efforts will be reflected in your *no* responses. According to Kotter (1996, p. 16), these common errors include allowing too much complacency; failing to create a sufficiently powerful, constructive engagement; underestimating the power of vision; failing to develop strategies for achieving the vision; permitting obstacles to block the new vision; failing to create short-term wins; declaring victory too soon; and neglecting to anchor changes firmly in the organization's culture.

EXHIBIT 9.1

Crossing the Threshold of Change

The ITINERIS Foundation (*itineris* means "journey" in Latin) is an Argentinian organization that, since 1999, has facilitated personal, organizational, and community change in Latin America. The theoretical framework employed during the organization change sessions is based on the quality-of-life concept, rights, self-determination, inclusion, and the supports paradigm. These sessions have involved professionals, self advocates, parents as presenters/reactors, and staff from all levels of organizations providing services and supports to people with intellectual and developmental disabilities and family members as participants. Key concepts incorporated into the workshops are that 1) change in mind-set is a nonlinear process; 2) change strategies must be based on local conditions but reflect international trends; 3) change involves resistance to change, but resistance to change is a sign that the process is genuine; 4) personal interactions and synergy sustain change; and 5) change is a transformation-of-practices process that involves active and thoughtful participation and empowerment.

During the 11 years of conducting change-focused workshops, we have 1) encountered multiple sources of resistance to change (e.g. verticality and the exercise of power from outside of each social actor, isolation, individualism, passivity and dependence, lack of initiative of social actors); 2) identified three sources that promote change (horizontality and empowerment, teamwork and networks, and activation and self-management); and 3) empirically studied nine thresholds of organization change that, when crossed, provide short-term wins for the organization.

Nine Thresholds of Organizational Change

➤ The organization reaches financial balance and becomes aware of its nonfinancial resources (mainly its social capital).

➤ The organization asks for integral training that is customized for its needs, interests, and context.

➤ At least one sector of the organization implements the quality-of-life and supports paradigms.

➤ Beneficiaries/clients are occasionally consulted about their interests.

➤ Some workers propose to do their jobs in a way that is innovative for the organization and that challenges the usual practices.

➤ Some organization services/programs are provided using both organization and community resources.

➤ All organization actors are reached by a long-term process of change and training, facilitated by the organization (not less than 2 years).

➤ The beneficiaries/clients, their families, professionals, and workers plan coordinated supports.

➤ The organization searches for and tests tools to orient its programs and services according to the new paradigms.

(continued)

EXHIBIT 9.1   *(continued)*

Having reached the threshold does not automatically mean that the organization has redefined itself. Some organizations take 2–3 years just to decide to
start a process, others take time to implement it, and still others have difficulty
maintaining it and fluctuate between classic and advanced practices. Even if
the organization has developed gradually to reach these thresholds, resistance
forces can be reactivated and prevent this evolution from continuing. However,
once one or more thresholds are crossed, the benefits of short-term wins come
into play.

For more information, contact Andrea S. Aznar or
Diego González Castañón (itineris@fibertel.com.ar).

LESSONS LEARNED AND KEY CATALYSTS IN ORGANIZATION CHANGE

Successfully implementing the factors involved in bringing about permanent change—clear
vision, simple communication, constructive engagement, and short-term wins—requires
strong leadership and an organization culture within which change is encouraged, reinforced,
and celebrated. It also requires learning from how others have put it all together. Exhibits 9.2
(p. 168) and 9.3 (p. 169) offer two useful examples.

Lessons Learned About Organization Change

The Training and Technical Assistance to Providers (T-TAP) project worked intensively
with 14 community rehabilitation providers and 10 mentor organizations between 2002 and
2007 to redirect resources and facilitate individual integrated and customized employment
outcomes. The organizations participating in T-TAP that were successful in implementing
change and expanding employment opportunities taught us the valuable lessons summarized
in Exhibit 9.2.

Key Catalysts in Organization Change

Arduin is a Dutch organization providing services for people with ID/DD. Established in
1969, Arduin was initially a residential institution providing what many by the early 1990s
considered poor services. In 1994, new management at the organization developed a course
of action based on the premise that people with ID/DD should be able to decide how to give
meaning to their own lives. This change required a completely different way of organizing
services and supports. The action plan developed to bring about the necessary changes was
based on the quality-of-life concept and the supports paradigm. Arduin was transformed
in the early 21st century from an institution to a new community-based organization that
focused on supporting each individual based on his or her personal goals and assessed
support needs. The separation of the three life spheres—living, work/daily activities, and
leisure—is fundamental in the process of deinstitutionalization and promoting a life of
quality. At present, the 600+ clients live in over 140 regular houses in the community, work
full-time in a variety of businesses or day centers, and are supported by support workers
according to the pattern and intensity of their assessed support needs.

EXHIBIT 9.2

Lessons Learned About Organizational Change from Community Rehabilitation Providers

Lesson 1: Establish clear and uncompromising goals. Organizations that were the most successful established a clear commitment to community employment. This commitment was reflected in restructuring resources, establishing a wide range of outreach and communication paths, investing heavily in finding jobs, and developing new partnerships. The goal made it clear that there could not be "business as usual."

Lesson 2: Communicate expectations to everyone and often. Expectations were communicated in a variety of ways including policy initiatives, outreach activities (e.g., newsletters, family meetings), the intake process, and celebrations.

Lesson 3: Reallocate and restructure resources. Allocating dedicated resources to community employment was a central part of the change process. Successful organizations redefined job positions and expectations to clearly focus on employment outcomes and insulated these positions from other responsibilities.

Lesson 4: Just do it! Successful agencies were aggressive about implementing career planning and job placement at the individual level. They also demonstrated urgency in career planning and job development, conducted outreach to families to engage members in the employment process, routinely used personal networks to identify job opportunities, and defined clear, short-term responsibilities for each team member.

Lesson 5: Develop partnerships. Successful organizations developed community partnerships that supported employment outcomes such as creation of a local business network that promoted access to jobs for people with intellectual and developmental disabilities or an agency partnership that focused on meeting the individualized support needs of a specific consumer.

Lesson 6: Consider the whole person. Involvement of all stakeholders in career planning and the 30-day placement plan ensures commitment to variation in schedules, arranging for transportation, scheduling nonwork appointments, and providing other work and nonwork activities and supports. For many individuals, entering employment also required giving up relationships and supports that may have been built up over an extended period of time. Successful organizations support the maintenance of personal relationships so that an individual gains more than he or she loses when entering an integrated job.

For more information, contact John Butterworth (john.butterworth@umb.edu).

EXHIBIT 9.3

Five Key Factors in One Organization's Permanent Change

1. A clear vision

   - A focus on quality of life and on the support paradigm was continuous during the program changes.

   - It was essential that the focus on quality of life be carried through consistently in all of the decisions made, at the organizational level as well as at the individual level.

   - In this process, creative thinking was necessary. For example, because of expanding costs of transport, Arduin started its own taxi company to reduce the costs of buying cars (a taxi company pays lower taxes when buying a car).

   - Regarding the focus on quality of life, there was no "yes, but...."

2. Simple communication that provides guidance, knowledge, and understanding

   - Good communication was very important for communicating the processes in the organization with clients, parents and legal representatives, and staff members.

   - A good system of communication was an important condition. In this regard, Arduin's web site was developed to provide continuous and actual information. The web site includes housing and employment opportunities, personal plans, and real-time staff notes.

3. Constructive engagement

   - All staff members got job and salary guarantees and were asked for their willingness to change job profiles if this would be necessary.

   - A lot of energy and time was invested in training focused on empowerment and self-determination. Workers had to learn to support people in community-based settings, with new roles and new responsibilities, because most of them were trained primarily in nursing. The emphasis was on values training and changing attitudes and habits of the staff.

   - Arduin developed, in cooperation with two training colleges and two other organizations working for people with intellectual and developmental disabilities, a new education program for support workers in the Netherlands. This huge effort resulted in the Arduin Academy on Quality of Life, in which the quality-of-life concept is the framework within which all courses are developed and offered to clients and staff.

4. Organizational changes that generated short-term gains

   - The coaching model was implemented along with the complete abolishment of middle management. Houses and employment or activity units work with self-directive autonomous teams, with their own responsibilities.

   - New job profiles were introduced such as that of support worker, who does the actual support in the house or at work, and personal assistant, who is the person engaged with the client in a continuous dialogue on wishes, goals, and support needs.

(continued)

◇◇

EXHIBIT 9.3   *(continued)*

- As many old jobs disappeared, we searched for all staff members' second talents to realize the promised job guarantees. For example, a former cook of the institutional kitchen now works on IT.

- A lot of bureaucracy was abolished because the focus had to be on direct support staff. Arduin has an administrative overhead of no more than 8%. Most regular meetings were abolished.

- The approach taken to health care was reorganized to involve generic health care professionals.

5. Anchoring the new approach in the organization's culture

- A system of supports was developed, incorporating consumers in the development and implementation of their individual supports plans.

- A program-wide quality management system was implemented that was based on the systematic measurement of personal outcomes and organization outputs.

For more information, contact Jos van Loon (Jloon@arduin.nl).

▶ *ACTION STEPS YOU CAN TAKE NOW*

▶ *Action Step 1*   Identify small changes that will have an impact on your organization. These changes might relate to piloting new approaches to service delivery or establishing a pilot project on developing and implementing one or more high-performance teams. The intent is to show that change can occur and to provide short-term wins that can be reinforced and celebrated.

▶ *Action Step 2*   If you are having trouble implementing change and overcoming resistance to change, study in detail the *no* responses from Organization Self-Assessment 9.2. Target these errors as the first step in using a more productive approach.

▶ *Action Step 3*   Share the principles of behavior change and attitude formation (Table 9.1) with staff, along with the concept of a default future. Discussing these ideas will provide the basis for demonstrating leadership skills related to mentoring and directing, coaching and instructing, inspiring and empowering, and collaborating and partnering.

▶ *Action Step 4*   Think about ways to effectively address people's default future. A number of suggestions are found in Table 9.2. Chief among these are being clear about your organization's future vision, reassuring people that their future will be secure, and tying in self-interest so that there are incentives for everyone to support the change.

▶ *Action Step 5*   Study Exhibits 9.1–9.3 very closely. What lessons can you learn, and what action plans can you develop to bring about permanent change?

SUMMARY AND IMPORTANT POINTS

Change is a positive value that leads to positive endeavors. Thinking about how to make changes is the first step after defining what you want. Furthermore, change is necessary to transform existing ID/DD organizations into effective and efficient 21st century organizations. Our intent in this chapter has been to integrate change principles from psychology, management literature, and personal experiences to provide readers with three skill clusters regarding how to overcome resistance to change. The first skill is understanding why people resist change so that these reasons can be addressed. The reasons can vary from fear of the unknown, to concern about how the change will affect them personally, to confusion about their role in the change process. The second skill is recognizing that change frequently can occur rather easily if one adequately addresses questions and implements the basic principles of behavioral change and attitude formation. The third skill is acknowledging that permanent change is frequently hard to implement and requires a multistage approach (see Figure 9.1).

In addition to the strategies discussed in this chapter regarding overcoming resistance to change, leaders also need to recognize the distinction between technical work and adaptive work. As discussed by Kagen, Sockalingam, Walker, and Zachik (2010), technical work involves managing the implementation of concrete strategies, whereas adaptive work involves changing how personnel think. In technical work, the tasks of leadership are to ensure that values, beliefs, and perspectives are aligned; to define problems and their solutions clearly; and to delegate work tasks and assign responsibility for implementation and evaluation. In adaptive work, in which the focus is on changing how people think so as to alter deeply imbedded mental models, the task of leadership is quite different. Here, leadership needs to create a meaningful context for learning to occur so that organization personnel can find new solutions for current challenges, reduce the gap between the values people stand for and the realities they face, reduce conflict through the conflict-resolution strategies discussed in Chapter 4, and encourage risk taking and experimentation. Throughout these adaptive work processes, leaders need to (Heifetz, Linsky, & Grashow, 2010)

- Understand the context of the resistance to change and the successful change strategies discussed in this chapter

- Regulate stress among personnel by drawing attention to tough questions, temporarily reclaiming responsibility for tough issues, bringing conflict to the surface, and not letting people explain away problems

- Establish a structure for problem solving by breaking problems down into parts and creating time frames, decision rules, and clear role assignments

- Maintain a focus on the issues at hand

- Give the workplace back to the people and protect all voices

---

Important Points We Have Made in This Chapter

➤ Change should be viewed as part of the innovation process.

➤ The concept of a default future is central to one's understanding of why people resist change and why leadership needs to focus on rewriting the future in reference to what people know will happen.

➤   Change requires implementing the change strategies discussed in this chapter.

➤   Permanent change relates to vision, communication, constructive engagement, short-term wins, and anchoring the new approaches in your organization's culture.

RESOURCES

Print

Hull, T.H., Miles, R.H., & Balka, D.S. (2010). Overcoming resistance to change. *Principal Leadership, 10*(8), 36.

Mills, A.J., Helm-Mills, J., & Dye, K. (2008). *Understanding organizational change.* New York, NY: Routledge/Taylor & Francis.

Electronic

Bacal, R. *Resistance to change—how and why people resist: Part I.* (2012) Retrieved from http://work911.com/managingchange/resistancetochange1.htm

Changing Minds. Change management. (2012) Retrieved from http://changing-minds.org/disciplines/change_management/change_management.htm

Toolpack Consulting. (2012) Retrieved from http://www.toolpack.com/change.html

Wynn, G. *Managing resistance to change.* (2012) Retrieved from http://www.managingchange.biz/manage_change_resistance.html

Approaches Taken to Overcoming Resistance to Change

Directions: Using a recently proposed or attempted innovation/change as your example, answer each of the questions below. Regarding to the principles used and their effectiveness, refer to Table 9.1.

1. Briefly describe the proposed innovation/change: _____

2. Were your change efforts successful?   Yes _____   No _____

   If not, why not?   _____

3. In reference to the successful process, please check the principles and strategies used and their effectiveness in the chart below.

Principles (Table 9.1)	Used		Effective	
Behavioral change				
Analysis and vision	Yes _____	No _____	Yes _____	No _____
Strategies	Yes _____	No _____	Yes _____	No _____
Goal	Yes _____	No _____	Yes _____	No _____
Small steps	Yes _____	No _____	Yes _____	No _____
Attitude formation				
Mental models	Yes _____	No _____	Yes _____	No _____
Language	Yes _____	No _____	Yes _____	No _____
Understanding	Yes _____	No _____	Yes _____	No _____
Intrinsic motivation	Yes _____	No _____	Yes _____	No _____

4. From Table 9.2, indicate the specific strategies you used to overcome any resistance to change:

Framework for Monitoring the Change Process

Directions: Summarize your status by checking *Yes* or *No* regarding each of the change processes listed below.

Stage question	Status evaluation	
1. Has a clear, effective vision regarding the proposed change been formulated?	Yes _____	No _____
2. Has the vision been communicated clearly and effectively?	Yes _____	No _____
If not, why not?_____		
3. Have personnel been constructively engaged in the change process?	Yes _____	No _____
If no, why not?_____		
4. Have there been short-term wins?	Yes _____	No _____
If no, why not?_____		
5. Have the short-term wins been acknowledged and celebrated?	Yes _____	No _____
6. Have the following requirements for permanent change occurred?		
a. Change has become the established way	Yes _____	No _____
b. Significant time for leadership development	Yes _____	No _____
c. People hired, promoted, and/or developed to implement the change	Yes _____	No _____
d. Change process reinvigorated through new projects	Yes _____	No _____

10

Redefining Organizations

Through the previous nine chapters, we have outlined and discussed the change strategies required to redefine organizations that provide services and supports to people with ID/DD. Those change strategies involve expanding the ways organization leaders think, measuring and using personal outcomes and organization outputs, developing high-performance teams, employing a system of supports, using evidence-based practices, implementing a performance-based evaluation and management system, increasing sustainability through innovation, and overcoming resistance to change. We also have provided real-life examples of how those proposed changes can be successfully planned and implemented. What is not explained fully in those chapters is what a redefined ID/DD organization would look like and, though implicated, the specific roles that wisdom and **future consciousness** play in the redefinition process. These two topics are the subjects of this final chapter.

Redefined ID/DD organizations are characterized as being community based, horizontally structured, support coordinators, evidence-based practitioners, knowledge producers, and quality improvement oriented. These characteristics describe an organization that can successfully address the challenges discussed in Chapter 1 and, at the same time, meet the accountability requirements for enhanced effectiveness, efficiency, and sustainability. Later in this chapter, we also discuss the role that wisdom and future consciousness play in the continued evolution of organizations. On the basis of Lombardo's (2008, 2010) work, we define *wisdom* as the continuously evolving understanding of what is important, ethical, and meaningful, and we define *future consciousness* as a person's capacity to appreciate and see the relevance of linking the past and future, engaging in goal-directed thinking, and experiencing self-efficacy and self-responsibility. Wisdom provides the rationale and strategies for change, and future consciousness provides the direction and parameters of the change.

What You Can Expect in This Chapter

➤ To gain an understanding of the role that wisdom, future consciousness, and critical thinking skills play in redefining organizations

➤ The six characteristics of redefined organizations providing services and supports to people with intellectual and developmental disabilities

➤ A resource guide that relates text material to the six characteristics of a redefined organization providing services and supports to people with intellectual and developmental disabilities, and the three needs of special education and human service organizations

➤ Ideas that propel organizations into the future

Although we have focused in this book almost exclusively on ID/DD organizations, we feel we would be remiss if we did not extend our change model to organizations serving other populations such as students with special needs, people of age, and those with mental and behavioral health impairments. As discussed later in the third section of this chapter, such organizations face the same challenges as ID/DD organizations, and thus we feel that leaders in those fields will see the relevance to their organizations of the eight change strategies.

This chapter has five sections. The first section expands on the role of wisdom and future consciousness in redefining organizations. The second section describes more fully the six characteristics of a redefined ID/DD organization. In the third section, we align these characteristics to our eight change strategies. In the fourth section, we apply the successful change strategies to special education and human service organizations as they increasingly provide individualized supports, engage in outcomes evaluation, and implement continuous quality improvement strategies. The chapter concludes by discussing the key role that ideas play in all of our futures.

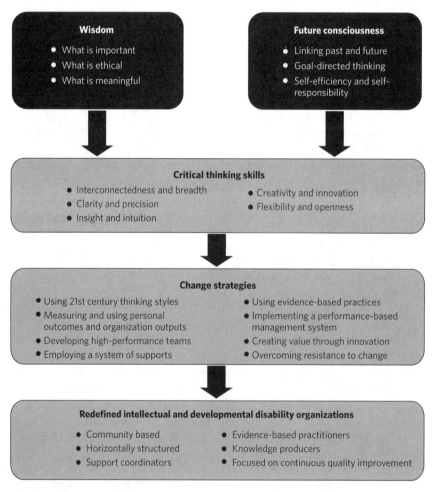

Figure 10.1. The role of wisdom and future consciousness in redefining organizations that provide services and supports to people with intellectual and developmental disabilities. (*Key:* ID/DD, intellectual and developmental disabilities.)

THE ROLE OF WISDOM AND FUTURE CONSCIOUSNESS IN REDEFINING ORGANIZATIONS

Figure 10.1 depicts the roles of wisdom and future consciousness in redefined ID/DD organizations. As noted in the figure, wisdom and future consciousness result in critical thinking skills, which we have used in synthesizing current literature and sharing real-life examples that serve as the basis for the eight change strategies discussed in Chapters 2–9. Although it is beyond the scope of this chapter to discuss wisdom, future consciousness, and critical thinking skills in detail, essential aspects of each are discussed next.

Wisdom

Wisdom allows people to understand and explain what is important, ethical, and meaningful. Wisdom is an evolving process of learning and transformation that allows us to understand today's challenges and to see how everything is interconnected. Furthermore, according to Lombardo (2010), wisdom—the ideal toward which we strive—is what allows for a holistic and integrative understanding of the world around us and combines knowledge with practical understanding.

Future Consciousness

Future consciousness allows people to appreciate the relevance of linking the past and future, engage in goal-directed thinking, and experience personal growth and purpose through self-efficacy and self-responsibility. A focus on the future allows for an awareness of the ever-moving wave of new theories, new techniques, and social and humanitarian issues (Slostak, 2010). As discussed more fully by Lombardo (2008, 2010; http://centerforfutureconsciousness.com), heightened future consciousness includes optimism about the future, an informed sense of contemporary trends and challenges, creativity, and curiosity regarding future possibilities.

Critical Thinking Skills

Cognitive psychologists have identified a number of critical thinking skills, with the specific skills varying by investigator and orientation. In general, these critical thinking skills involve clarity, precision, insight, relevance, creativity, flexibility, decision making, and breadth and depth of one's approach to a problem. We view the five critical thinking skills listed in Figure 10.1 as most relevant to organization leaders as they incorporate wisdom and future consciousness into their organizations' policies and practices. These five critical thinking skills have been exemplified in each change strategy proposed in this book and in the rationale, description, and examples given regarding their implementation.

CHARACTERISTICS OF A REDEFINED INTELLECTUAL AND DEVELOPMENTAL DISABILITY ORGANIZATION

Each organization must redefine itself regarding its mission and primary goals. Embedded within that redefinition, however, will be the mental models, concepts, and change strategies discussed throughout the preceding chapters. A redefined organization is more than a static list of characteristics; it is a dynamic, evolving entity that creates its own identity through innovation, an organization mind-set, a culture, and an attitude that there are no problems—only opportunities.

We do not want to be viewed as overly reductionistic, but we have found that the most sustainable redefined organizations possess the six characteristics that are listed at the bottom of Figure 10.1 and described more fully in Table 10.1, along with indicators of each. When the indicators

Table 10.1. Characteristics and indicators of redefined organizations providing services and supports to people with intellectual and developmental disabilities

Community based

Uses generic services

Maximizes social capital and social networks

Provides access to natural supports

Provides or procures inclusive education settings, normalized living environments, and typical work environments

Uses community-referenced comparisons to evaluate personal outcomes

Horizontally structured

Employs high-performance teams with clear responsibilities and accountability requirements

Empowers direct support staff

Includes clientele in organization planning and management

Exhibits leadership roles that involve mentoring and directing, coaching and instructing, inspiring and empowering, and collaborating and partnering

Support coordinators

Assesses the individual's support needs

Uses a system of supports in the development and implementation of the individual supports plan

Employs an organization-based supports coordinator to develop, implement, and evaluate an individual supports plan

Employs or procures a systems-level case manager to integrate support plan components across systems

Serves as a bridge to the community

Evidence-based practitioners

Bases intervention and habilitation practices on current best evidence that is obtained from credible sources

Bases clinical and managerial decisions on evidence-based practices

Measures personal outcomes and organization outputs

Interprets the quality, robustness, and relevance of the evidence

Implements evidence-based practices through engagement, education, execution, and further evaluation

Knowledge producers

Uses tacit and explicit knowledge

Employs systems thinking

Uses a program logic model to align input, throughput, and outcome/output program components

Monitors and evaluates the impact of services and supports on personal outcomes

Evaluates the effects of services and supports on personal outcomes through one or more evidence-gathering strategy

Focus on continuous quality improvement

Implements an internal information/data system that provides feedback

Uses assessed personal outcomes and organization outputs as a basis for continuous quality improvement

Determines the significant predictors of personal outcomes and organization outputs and uses this information to target resources and strategies

Encourages and reinforces learning and innovation among all staff

Employs a systematic approach to enhancing the organization's effectiveness, efficiency, and sustainability

associated with each characteristic are assessed, they can be used for multiple purposes that include **benchmarking**, reporting, monitoring, evaluation, and continuous quality improvement.

ALIGNING REDEFINED ORGANIZATION CHARACTERISTICS TO CHANGE STRATEGIES

Table 10.2 aligns the six characteristics of redefined ID/DD organizations with text-referenced materials that include tables, figures, exhibits, and organization self-assessments. The detail-

Table 10.2.   Characteristics of redefined organizations referenced to text materials

Characteristic	Key concepts	Text material
Community based	Future-oriented mental models	Table 1.4
	Change catalysts	Self-Assessments 1.3, 2.1
	Social capital and networking	
Horizontally structured	High-performance teams	Tables 4.1–4.3, 9.1
	Overcoming resistance to change	Figure 9.1
		Exhibits 4.3, 4.4, 9.1, 9.2, 9.3
		Self-Assessments 9.1, 9.2
Support coordinators	A system of supports	Tables 5.3–5.10
		Figure 5.1
		Exhibits 5.1–5.6
		Self-Assessment 5.1
Evidence-based practitioners	Evidence-based practices	Tables 6.1, 6.2
		Figures 6.1, 6.2
		Exhibits 6.1–6.3
		Self-Assessment 6.1
Knowledge producers	Performance-based evaluation and management system	Tables 3.1–3.4, and 7.1–7.3
		Figures 7.1, 7.2
	Evaluation	Exhibits 7.1, 7.2
		Self-Assessments 3.1, 7.1
Quality improvement	Program logic models	Tables 2.3, 5.6
	Quality improvement plans and strategies	Figures 2.2, 7.1, 8.2
	21st century thinking styles	Exhibits 3.4, 7.3
		Self-Assessments 2.5, 3.3

ed rationale and elaboration regarding these text-referenced materials are found on pages adjacent to each.

APPLICATION TO SPECIAL EDUCATION AND HUMAN SERVICE ORGANIZATIONS

At one point in its initial development, this book was entitled *Leading and Managing in Turbulent Times: A Leadership Guide for Special Education and Human Service Organizations.* For both editorial and practical considerations, we decided that a more singular focus on ID/DD organizations made better sense. However, during the last decade of the 20th century and the first of the 21st, our experience with organizations dealing with students with special needs, people of age, and those with mental and behavioral impairments has convinced us of related needs for a clear focus and redefinition. More specifically, two major trends have brought about the need for special education and human service organizations to provide individualized supports, engage in outcome evaluation, and implement continuous quality improvement processes. First, the landscape has changed regarding how special education and human service organizations see themselves and operate. Basic to this change has been the movement during these last two decades from easy-to-identify, easy-to-describe systems of public support and education to highly complex networks composed of widely varying levels and types of providers, settings, and structures. These changes have increased the need for information regarding contracting, reporting, and accountability. The changes have also brought about different approaches to how resources are deployed. Increasingly, we are seeing the use of vouchers, individual budgets, and resource allocation models that are typically based on the standardized assessment of the person's support needs across life domains as well as the person's exceptional medical and behavioral support needs.

The second trend is that during this same time period, a new model of disability has emerged globally. Historically, a person-centered deficit model was used to describe a person with ID/DD and provide services to fix the person's perceived deficits. During the last three decades, this perception of disability has shifted to an ecological model that explains human functioning as resulting from the interaction of the person with his or her environment and that focuses on providing individualized supports within community settings to enhance human functioning and promote positive personal outcomes.

These two trends are challenging special education and human service programs in the same way they are challenging ID/DD organizations. Across special education and human service programs, we have observed the need for these organizations to redefine themselves by providing individualized supports, engaging in outcomes evaluation, and implementing quality improvement strategies. Table 10.3 presents an easy-to-use resource for accessing the text-referenced material related to these three needs. The application of these change strategies to special education and human service programs is based on the values guiding innovation (Figure 8.1), future-oriented mental models (Table 1.4), and 21st century thinking styles (Table 2.1). The implementation of change strategies is brought about by the four change catalyst discussed in Chapter 1: values, leadership, technology, and empowerment. If you encounter resistance to change, then the material presented in Tables 9.1 and 9.2, Figure 9.1, Exhibits 9.1–9.3, and Organization Self-Assessments 9.1 and 9.2 will be of value.

THE KEY ROLE THAT IDEAS PLAY IN THE FUTURE

One cannot change the past; what one can change is the future. Two favorite quotes (referenced in Lombardo, 2010) provide the focus of this final section of the book. One is by Winston Churchill: "The empires of the future are the empires of the mind" (p. 37); the second is by John F. Kennedy: "Change is the law of life…and those who look only to the past or the present are certain to miss the future" (p. 38). These two quotes provide the context of Organization Self-Assessment 10.1 (p. 182) and the key ideas you should take away from this book.

Table 10.3. Special education and human service organizations' use of the eight change strategies

Characteristic	Change strategy	Text material
Individual supports	A system of support	Tables 4.1–4.3, 5.3–5.10, 6.1, 6.2
	Evidence-based practices	Figures 2.1, 4.1, 6.1, 6.2
	High-performance teams	Exhibits 4.1–4.4, 5.1–5.6, 6.1–6.3
		Self-Assessments 4.1, 5.1, 6.1
Outcomes evaluation	Measuring personal outcomes and organization outputs	Tables 2.2, 3.1–3.4, 7.2–7.3
		Exhibits 3.2, 7.1, 7.2
	Performance-based evaluation and management system	Self-Assessments 2.2, 3.1, 3.2, 7.1
		Figures 7.1, 7.2
Continuous quality improvement	Creating value through innovation	Tables 1.4, 1.5, 8.1, 8.2, 9.1, 9.2
	21st century thinking styles	Figures 2.2, 7.1, 8.1, 8.2, 9.1
	Overcoming resistance to change	Exhibits 8.1–8.3, 9.1–9.3
		Self-Assessments 2.5 , 8.1, 9.1, 9.2

➤ *Tool for Application*

In Organization Self-Assessment 10.1, we ask that you think about two relevant questions. First, after reading this book, are you better able to meet each of the 10 challenges introduced in Chapter 1? Second, if your answer is yes, what specific strategies will you use to address the challenges?

Key Ideas to Take Away

Louis Menand's (2001) far-reaching book on great thinkers discusses ideas and the role they play in people's futures. According to Menand, ideas are like tools that are devised by people to cope with the world. They are produced by groups of individuals, are social, and are dependent on their human character and the environment. Furthermore, ideas should never become ideologies, and therefore ideas represent compromises.

Throughout this book, we have shared fundamental ideas that provide a mind-set for redefining organizations. These ideas, which are based on the wisdom we have gained from our 30+ years of working with organizations and their clientele, our reading of management literature, and our future consciousness, are that organization redefinition 1) is possible because organizations and systems have the potential to change and become more effective and efficient; 2) involves innovation, wisdom, future consciousness, and 21st century thinking styles; 3) does not occur without the presence of change catalysts related to values, leadership, technology, and empowerment; 4) requires information regarding personal outcomes and organization outputs that is used for the multiple purposes discussed throughout the text; and 5) results in organizations becoming community based, horizontally structured, support coordinators, evidence-based practitioners, knowledge producers, and quality improvement oriented.

On the basis of these fundamental ideas, we conclude the book with the following key concepts that underlie organization redefinition.

1. Three thinking styles are essential to organization redefinition: systems, synthesis, and alignment.

2. Redefining organizations requires the measurement and use of personal outcomes and organization outputs.

3. Successful organizations are based on visionary leadership and high-performance teams.

4. The application of a system of supports enhances human functioning and a life of quality.

5. Using evidence-based practices leads to good clinical, managerial, and policy decisions.

6. Reporting and continuous quality improvement use information obtained from a performance-based evaluation and management system.

7. An organization's sustainability requires creating value through innovation.

8. Change is brought about through alignment, involvement, participation, networks, and innovation.

In the end, organization redefinition is about improving people's quality of life; it is not about overthrowing the established order. Redefinition is done for the good of society and to achieve group ends. Thus, this book is not the beginning of the end; rather, it is the end of the beginning.

Are You Ready to Meet the Challenges?

Directions: For each of the 10 challenges listed below, indicate whether, after having read this book, you are better able to meet the respective challenge. If your answer is yes, briefly specify the strategy or strategies you plan to use.

Challenge	Yes	No	Strategy if yes
Address dwindling resources	Yes	No	_____
Respond to increased demand for services and supports	Yes	No	_____
Move from vertical to horizontal structure	Yes	No	_____
Shift from general services to individualized supports	Yes	No	_____
Emphasize self-determination	Yes	No	_____
Focus more on personal outcomes	Yes	No	_____
Allocate resources based on the person's assessed support needs	Yes	No	_____
Increase use of social capital and natural supports	Yes	No	_____
Implement evidence-based practices	Yes	No	_____
Demonstrate increased effectiveness and efficiency	Yes	No	_____

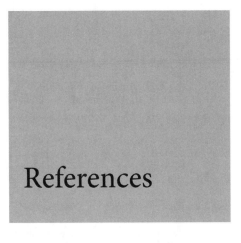

References

Ashbaugh, J. (2008). Managing systems change in human service agencies. *Intellectual and Developmental Disabilities, 46,* 480–483.

Bloom, B. (1956). *Taxonomies of educational goals.* New York, NY: College University.

Bonham, G.S., Basehart, S., Schalock, R.L., Marchand, C.B., Kirchner, N., & Rumenap, J.M. (2004). Consumer-based quality of life assessment: The Maryland Ask Me! Project. *Mental Retardation, 42*(5), 338–355.

Bradley, V.J., & Kimmich, M. (Eds.). (2003). *Quality enhancement in developmental disabilities: Challenges and opportunites in a changing world.* Baltimore, MD: Paul H. Brookes Publishing Co., Inc.

Bradley, V.J., & Moseley, C. (2007). National core indicators: Ten years of collaborative performance measurement. *Intellectual and Developmental Disabilities, 45,* 354–358.

Broekaert, E., Autreque, M., Vanderplasschen, W., & Colpaert, K. (2010). The human prerogative: A critical analysis of evidence-based and other paradigms of care in substance abuse treatment. *Psychiatric Quarterly, 81*(3), 227–238.

Brown, R.I., Schalock, R.L., & Brown, I. (2009). Quality of life: Its application to persons with intellectual disabilities and their families—Introduction and overview. *Journal of Policy and Practice in Intellectual Disabilities, 6,* 2–6.

Buntinx, W.H.E. (2008). The logic of relations and the logic of management. *Journal of Intellectual Disability Research, 52,* 558–597.

Buntinx, W.H.E., & Schalock, R.L. (2010). Models of disability, quality of life, and individualized supports: Implications for professional practice in intellectual disability. *Journal of Policy and Practice in Intellectual Disabilities, 7*(4), 283–294.

Cabrera, D., Colosi, L., & Lobdell, C. (2008). Systems thinking. *Evaluation and Program Planning, 3,* 317–321.

Cascio, J. (2009, July/August). Get smart. *The Atlantic,* 94–100.

Cesario, S., Morin, K., & Santa-Domato, A.S. (2002). Evaluating the level of evidence. *Qualitative Research, 31,* 708–714.

Claes, C., van Hove, G., van Loon, J., Vandevelde, S., & Schalock, R.L. (2010). Quality of life measurement in the field of intellectual disability: Eight principles for assessing quality of life-related outcomes. *Social Indicators Research, 98,* 61–75.

Cohen, D.J., & Crabtree, B.F. (2008). Evaluative criteria for qualitative research in health care: Controversies and recommendations. *Annals of Family Medicine, 6,* 331–339.

Cooley, H.M., Jones, R.S., Imig, D.R., & Villarruel, F.A. (2009). Using family paradigms to improve evidence-based practice. *American Journal of Speech-Language Pathology, 18,* 212–221.

Council on Quality and Leadership. (2010). *Personal outcome measures.* Towson, MD: Author.

Covey, S.R. (2004). *The 8th habit: From effectiveness to greatness.* New York, NY: Free Press.

Deci, E.L., & Ryan, R.M. (2002). Overview of self-determination theory: An organismic dialectical perspective. In E.L. Deci & R.M. Ryan (Eds.), *Handbook of self-determination research* (pp. 3–31). Rochester, NY: University of Rochester Press.

DiRita, P.A., Parmenter, T.R., & Stancliffe, R.J. (2008). Utility, economic rationalism and the circumscription of agency. *Journal of Intellectual Disability Research, 52,* 618–624.

Donaldson, S.I. (2007). *Program theory-driven evaluation science.* Mahwah, NJ: Lawrence Erlbaum Associates.

Downs, A., & Carlon, D.M. (2009). School-to-work transition programs within third-party government: A process-based organizational analysis. *Journal of Disability Policy Studies, 20,* 131–141.

Dyehouse, M., Bennett, D., Harbor, J., Childress, A., & Dark, M. (2009). A comparison of linear and systems thinking approaches for program evaluation illustrated using the Indiana Interdisciplinary GK-12. *Evaluation and Program Planning, 32,* 187–196.

Edmonton, P.D.D. (2011). *My life: Personal outcomes index.* Edmonton, Canada: Author.

Emerson, E., Graham, H., & Hatton, C. (2006). The measurement of poverty and socio-economic position involving people with intellectual disability. In L.M. Glidden (Ed.), *International review of research in mental retardation* (pp. 77–108). New York, NY: Academic Press.

Feist, G.J. (1998). A meta-analysis of personality in scientific and artistic creativity. *Personality and Social Psychology Review, 2,* 290–309.

Ferguson, C.F. (2009). An effect size primer: A guide for clinicians and researchers. *Professional Psychology: Research and Practice, 40,* 532–538.

Fielden, S.J., Rusch, M.L., Masinda, M.T., Sands, J., Frankish, J., & Evoy, B. (2007). Key considerations for logic model development in research partnerships: A Canadian case study. *Evaluation and Program Planning, 30,* 115–124.

Fuller, C.W. (1997). Key performance indicators for benchmarking health and safety management in intra- and inter-company comparisons. *Benchmarking for Quality Management and Technology, 4*(3), 165–180.

Gardner, J.F., & Caran, D. (2005). Attainment of personal outcomes by people with developmental disabilities. *Mental Retardation, 43*(3), 157–174.

Gardner, J.F., & Mathis, E.A. (2009). Inclusion: Progress and promises beyond the disability bubble. *International Journal of Leadership in Public Services, 43,* 157–173.

Gentry, R. (2009). Smart homes for people with neurological disability: State of the art. *NeuroRehabilitation, 25,* 209–217.

Gladwell, M. (2005). *Blink: The power of thinking without thinking.* New York, NY: Little, Brown.

Goldsmith, S., & Eggers, W.D. (2004). *Governing by network: The new shape of the public sector.* Washington, DC: Brookings Institute Press.

Goleman, D. (2009). *Ecological intelligence.* New York, NY: Broadway Books.

Grol, R., Baker, R., & Moss, F. (2008). *Quality improvement research.* London, UK: BMJ Books.

Gugiu, P.C., & Rodriguez-Campos, L. (2007). Semi-structured interview protocols for constructing logic models. *Evaluation and Program Planning, 30,* 339–350.

Guttman, H.M. (2008). *Great business teams: Cracking the code of standout performance.* Hoboken, NJ: John Wiley & Sons.

Hatry, H. (2000). *Performance measurement.* Washington, DC: The Urban Institute.

Heath, C., & Heath, D. (2005). *Made to stick: Why some ideas survive and others die.* New York, NY: Random House.

Heath, C., & Heath, D. (2009). *Switch: How to change things when change is hard.* New York, NY: Broadway Books.

Heifetz, R.A., Linsky, M., & Grashow, A. (2010). *Practices of adaptive leadership: Tools and tactics for changing your organization and the world.* Boston, MA: Harvard Business Publishing.

Helal, A., Mokhtari, M., & Abdulrazak, B. (2008). (Eds.). *The engineering handbook of smart technology for aging, disability, and independence.* Hoboken, NJ: Wiley Interscience.

Helitzer, D., Hollis, C., Hernandez, B.U., Sanders, M., Roybal, S., & van Deusen, I. (2010). Evaluation of community-based programs. The integration of logic models and factor analysis. *Evaluation and Program Planning, 33,* 223–233.

Hines, A. (2006, September/October). Strategic foresight: The state of the art. *The Futurist,* 18–22.

Individuals with Disabilities Education Improvement Act (IDEA) of 2004, PL 108-446, 20 U.S.C. §§ 1400 *et seq.*

Isaacs, B., Clark, C., Correia, S., & Flannery, J. (2009). Using quality of life to evaluate outcomes and measure effectiveness. *Journal of Policy and Practice in Intellectual Disabilities, 6*(1), 52–61.

Jenaro, C., Verdugo, M.A., Caballo, C., Balboni, G., Lachapelle, Y., & Otrebski, W. (2005). Cross-cultural study of person-centered quality of life domains and indicators. *Journal of Intellectual Disability Research, 49,* 734–739.

Kagen, E.B., Sockalingam, S., Walker, J.A., & Zachik, A. (2010). The work of leadership in systems change for human services and education: Addressing the adaptive challenge. In G.M. Blau & P.R. Magrab (Eds.), *The leadership equation: Strategies for individuals who are champions for children, youth, and families* (pp. 53–79). Baltimore, MD: Paul H. Brookes Publishing Co., Inc.

Kaplan, R.S., & Norton, D.P. (1996). *The balanced scorecard: Translating strategy into action*. Boston, MA: Harvard Business Press.

Kettl, D.F. (2002). *The transformation of governance: Public administration for the twenty-first century*. Baltimore, MD: John Hopkins University Press.

Kotter, J.P. (1996). *Leading change*. Boston, MA: Harvard Business Press.

Kuppens, S., Bossaert, G., Buntinx, W., Molleman, C., & Van-Abbeele, A. (2010). Factorial validity of the Supports Intensity Scale (SIS). *American Journal on Intellectual and Developmental Disabilities, 115,* 327–339.

Lakin, K.C., & Stancliffe, R.J. (2005). Expenditures and outcomes: Future directions in policy and research. In R.J. Stancliffe & K.C. Lakin (Eds.), *Cost and outcomes of community services for people with intellectual disabilities* (pp. 313–337). Baltimore, MD: Paul H. Brookes Publishing Co., Inc.

Lipsey, M.W. (1998). Design sensitivity: Statistical power for applied experimental research. In L. Bickman & D.J. Rog (Eds.), *Handbook of applied social research methods* (pp. 39–68). Thousand Oaks, CA: Sage Publications.

Logan, D., King, J., & Fischer-Wright, H. (2008). *Tribal leadership: Leveraging natural groups to build a thriving organization*. New York, NY: HarperCollins.

Lombardo, T. (2008). *The evaluation of future consciousness*. New York, NY: AuthorHouse.

Lombardo, T. (2010, September/October). Wisdom facing forward: What it means to have heightened future consciousness. *The Futurist,* 34–42.

Mackenbach, J.P., Stirbu, I., Roskam, A.R., Schapp, M.M., Menvielle, G., & Kunst, A.E. (2008). Socio-economic inequalities in health in 22 European countries. *The New England Journal of Medicine, 358,* 2468–2481.

Mauboussin, M.J. (2010, March/April). Smart people, dumb decisions. *The Futurist,* 24–30.

Menand, L. (2001). *The metaphysical club: A story of ideas in America*. New York, NY: Farrar, Straus and Giroux.

Millar, A., Simeone, R.S., & Carnevale, J.T. (2001). Logic models: A systems tool for performance management. *Evaluation and Program Planning, 24,* 73–81.

Miner, J. (2005). *Organizational behavior: Behavior I: Essential theories of motivation and leadership*. Armonk, NY: M.E. Sharpe.

Nelson, E.C., Batalden, P.B., & Godfrey, M.M. (Eds.). (2007). *Quality by design: A clinical microsystems approach*. Hoboken, NJ: John Wiley & Sons.

Niven, P.R. (2008). *Balanced scorecard step-by-step for government and non-profit agencies* (2nd ed.). Hoboken, NJ: John Wiley & Sons.

Noordegraaf, M. (2007). From "pure" to "hybrid" professionalism: Present-day professionalism in ambiguous public domains. *Administration and Society, 39,* 761–784.

Passig, D. (2003). A taxonomy of future thinking skills. *Informatics in Education, 2,* 79–92.

Passig, D. (2007). Melioration as a higher thinking skill of future intelligence. *Teachers College Record, 109,* 24–50.

Petty, R.E., & Wegener, D.T. (1998). Attitude change: Multiple roles for persuasion variables. In D.T. Gilbert, S.T. Fiske, & G. Lindsey (Eds.), *The handbook of social psychology* (pp. 50–75). New York, NY: McGraw-Hill.

Pinker, D. (2005). *A whole new mind: Moving from the information to the conceptual age*. New York, NY: Riverhead Books.

Pinker, D. (2009). *Drive: The surprising truth about what motivates us*. New York, NY: Riverhead Books.

Pronovost, P., Berenholtz, S., & Needham, D. (2008). Translating evidence into practice: A model for large scale knowledge translation. *British Medical Journal, 337,* 963–965.

Putnam, R.D., & Feldstein, L.M. (2003). *Better together: Restoring the American community*. New York, NY: Simon & Schuster.

Reinders, H. (2010). The importance of tacit knowledge in practices of care. *Journal of Intellectual Disability Research, 54,* 28–37.

Reinders, H. (2008). The transformation of human services. *Journal of Intellectual Disability Research, 52,* 564–571.

Robinson, J., & Godbey, G. (2005, September/October). Time on our hands. *The Futurist,* 22–32.

Ryback, D. (2010). *ConnectAbility: Eight keys to building strong partnerships with your colleagues and your customers*. New York, NY: McGraw-Hill.

Sackett, D.L., Richardson, W.S., Rosenberg, W., & Haynes, R.B. (2005). *Evidence-based medicine: How to practice and teach EBM*. Philadelphia, PA: Churchill Livingstone.

Satterfield, J.S., Spring, B., & Brownson, R.C. (2009). Toward a transdisciplinary model of evidence-based practice. *The Milbank Quarterly, 87,* 368–390.

Schalock, R.L. (2001). *Outcomes-based evaluation* (2nd ed.). New York, NY: Springer.

Schalock, R.L., & Bonham, G.S. (2003). Measuring outcomes and managing for results. *Evaluation and Program Planning, 26,* 229–235.

Schalock, R.L., Bonham, G.S., & Verdugo, M.A. (2008). The conceptualization and measurement of quality of life: Implications for program planning and evaluation in the field of intellectual disability. *Evaluation and Program Planning, 31*(2), 181–190.

Schalock, R.L., Borthwick-Duffy, S.A., Bradley, V.J., Buntinx, W.H.E., Coulter, D.L., Craig, E.M.,… Yeager, M.H. (2010). *Intellectual disability: Definition, classification, and systems of supports* (11th ed.). Washington, DC: American Association of Intellectual and Developmental Disabilities.

Schalock, R.L., Gardner, J.F., & Bradley, V.J. (2007). *Quality of life for persons with intellectual and other developmental disabilities: Applications across individuals, organizations, communities, and systems.* Washington, DC: American Association of Intellectual and Developmental Disabilities.

Schalock, R.L., Keith, K.D., Verdugo, M.A., & Gomez, L.E. (2010). Quality of life model development and use in the field of intellectual disability. In R. Kober (Ed.), *Enhancing the quality of life for people with intellectual disabilities: From theory to practice* (pp. 8–18). New York, NY: Springer.

Schalock, R.L., & Luckasson, R. (2005). *Clinical judgment.* Washington, DC: American Association on Mental Retardation.

Schalock, R.L., Verdugo, M.A., Bonham, G.S., Fantova, F., & van Loon, J. (2008). Enhancing personal outcomes: Organizational strategies, guidelines, and examples. *Journal of Policy and Practice in Intellectual Disability, 5,* 276–285.

Schalock, R.L., Verdugo, M.A., & Gomez, L.E. (2011). Evidence-based practices in the field of intellectual and developmental disabilities. *Evaluation and Program Planning, 34*(3), 273–282.

Schalock, R.L., Verdugo, M.A., Jenaro, C., Wang, W., Wehmeyer, M., Xu, J., & Lachapelle, Y. (2005). Cross-cultural study of quality of life indicators. *American Journal on Mental Retardation, 110,* 298–311.

Scott, K., & McSherry, R. (2008). Evidence-based nursing: Clarifying the concepts for nurses in practice. *Journal of Clinical Nursing, 18,* 1085–1095.

Senge, P.M. (2006). *The 5th discipline: The art and practice of the learning organization.* New York, NY: Doubleday.

Shogren, K.A., & Turnbull, H.R. (2010). Public policy and outcomes for persons with intellectual disability: Extending and expanding the public policy framework of the 11th edition of Intellectual disability: Definition, classification, and systems of supports. *Intellectual and Developmental Disability, 48*(5), 375–386.

Slostak, A.B. (2010). *Creating the school you want: Living at tomorrow's edge.* New York, NY: Rowman & Littlefield.

Storey, K. (2010). Smart houses and smart technology: Overview and implications for independent living and supported living services. *Intellectual and Developmental Disabilities, 48*(6), 464–469.

Stowe, M.J., Turnbull, H.R., & Sublet, C. (2006). The Supreme Court, "Our Town," and disability policy: Boardrooms and bedrooms, courtrooms, and cloakrooms. *Mental Retardation, 44,* 83–99.

Strimling, A. (2006). Stepping out of the tracks: Cooperation between official diplomats and private facilitators. *International Negotiation, 11,* 91–127.

Summers, J.A., Poston, D.J., Turnbull, A.P., Marquis, J., Hoffman, L., Mannan, H., & Wang, M. (2005). Conceptualizing and measuring family quality of life. *Journal of Intellectual Disability Research, 49*(10), 777–783.

Test, D.W., & Mazzotti, V.L. (2011). Transitioning from school to employment. In M.E. Snell & R. Brown (Eds.), *Instruction of students with severe disabilities* (7th ed., pp. 569–611). Upper Saddle River, NJ: Pearson Education.

Thaler, R., & Sunstein, C. (2008). *Nudge: Improving decisions about health, wealth, and happiness.* New Haven, CT: Yale University Press.

Thomas, K. (1976). Conflict and conflict management. In M. Dunnette (Ed.), *The handbook of industrial and organizational psychology* (pp. 125–148). Chicago, IL: Rand McNally.

Thompson, J.R., Bradley, V.J., Buntinx, W.H.E., Schalock, R.L., Shogren, K., Snell, M.E.,…Yeager, M.H. (2009). Conceptualizing supports and the support needs of people with intellectual disability. *Intellectual and Developmental Disabilities, 47,* 135–146.

Thompson, J.R., Bryant, B., Campbell, E.M., Craig, E.M., Hughes, C., Rotholz, D.A. & Wehmeyer, M.L. (2004). *The Supports Intensity Scale (SIS): User's manual.* Washington, DC: American Association on Mental Retardation.

Thompson, J.R., Tasse, M.J., & McLaughlin, C.A. (2008). Interrater reliability of the Supports Intensity Scale (SIS). *American Journal on Mental Retardation, 113,* 231–237.

Tow, B.L., & Gilliam, D.A. (2009, May/June). Synthesis: An interdisciplinary discipline. *The Futurist,* 43–47.

Tsai, W.H., Chou, W.C., & Hsu, W. (2009). The sustainability balanced scorecard as a framework for selecting socially responsible investment: An effective MCDM model. *Journal of Operational Research Society, 60*(10), 1396–1410.

United Nations. (2006). *Convention on the rights of persons with disabilities.* Retrieved from www.un.org/disabilities/convention

U.S. Department of Education. (2006). *A test of leadership: Charting the future of U.S. higher education.* Washington, DC: Author.

U.S. Department of Health and Human Services, Centers for Medicare and Medicaid Services. (2010). Quality letters (1–9). Retrieved from https://cms.hhs.gov/medicaid/waiversqcomm.asp

U.S. General Accounting Office. (1999). *Managing for results: Opportunities for continual improvements in agencies' performance plans* (GAO/GGD/AIMD-99-215). Washington, DC: Author.

van Loon, J., van Hove, G., Schalock, R.L., & Claes, C. (2010). *Personal outcomes scale: A scale to assess an individual's quality of life.* Middleburg, The Netherlands: Stichting Arduin.

Veerman, J.W., & van Yperen, T.A. (2007). Degrees of freedom and degrees of certainty: A developmental model for the establishment of evidence-based youth care. *Evaluation and Program Planning, 30,* 212–221.

Verdugo, M.A., Arias, B., Gomez, L.E., & Schalock, R.L. (2010). Development of an objective instrument to assess quality of life in social services reliably and validly in Spain. *International Journal of Clinical and Health Psychology, 10*(1), 105–123.

Verdugo, M.A., Arias, B., Ibanez, A., & Schalock, R.L. (2010). Adaptation and psychometric properties of the Spanish version of the Supports Intensity Scale (SIS). *American Journal of Intellectual and Developmental Disabilities, 115*(6), 496–503.

Verdugo, M.A., Schalock, R.L., Keith, K.D., & Stancliffe, R. (2005). Quality of life and its measurement: Important principles and guidelines. *Journal of Intellectual Disability Research, 49,* 707–717.

Walsh, P.N., Emerson, E., Lobb, C., Hatton, C., Bradley, V., Schalock, R.L., & Moseley, C. (2010). Supported accommodation for people with intellectual disabilities and quality of life: An overview. *Journal of Policy and Practice in Intellectual Disabilities, 7,* 137–142.

Wang, M., Schalock, R.L., Verdugo, M.A., & Jenaro, C. (2010). Examining the factor structure and hierarchical nature of the quality of life construct. *American Journal on Intellectual and Developmental Disabilities, 115,* 218–233.

Wasserman, D.L. (2010). Using a systems orientation and foundation theory to enhance theory-driven human service program evaluations. *Evaluation and Program Planning, 33,* 67–80.

West, M.R., & Markiewicz, L. (2004). *Building team-based working: A practical guide to organization performance.* Oxford, United Kingdom: Blackwell Publishing Co.

Wilkinson, L., & APA Task Force on Statistical Inference. (1999). Statistical methods in psychology journals: Guidelines and explanations. *American Psychologist, 54,* 594–604.

World Health Organization. (2001). *International classification of functioning, disability, and health (ICF).* Geneva, Switzerland: Author.

Wu, H.-Y., Lin, Y.-K., & Chang, C.-H. (2011). Performance evaluation of extension education centers in universities based on the balanced scorecard. *Evaluation and Program Planning, 34*(1), 37–50.

Zaffron, S., & Logan, D. (2009). *The three laws of performance: Rewriting the future of your organization and your life.* San Francisco, CA: Jossey-Bass.

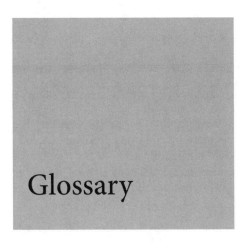

Glossary

accountability   Being responsible for one's actions and ensuring that resources are used effectively and efficiently. Effective use of resources leads to enhanced personal outcomes; efficient use of resources leads to enhanced organizational outputs that are consistent with anticipated or planned results.

adaptive behavior   The collection of conceptual, social, and practical skills that have been learned and are performed by people in their everyday lives.

administrative principles   Systems-level administrative principles that support a redefined and horizontally and vertically aligned service delivery framework. These principles include individualization, collaboration and coordination, capacity building (e.g., high-performance teams, learning organization, increased organization evaluation capacity), program options, cultural responsiveness, person- and family-centered planning, and accountability.

alignment   Placing or bringing critical organization functions into line. Alignment positions the service delivery components of an organization into a logical sequence for the purposes of reporting, monitoring, evaluation, and continuous quality improvement. Critical thinking skills used in alignment are serial thinking, linear thinking, and convergent reasoning.

assistive technology (AT)   Use of mechanical or electronic devices that reduce the mismatch between a person's competency and the cognitive, social, and practical demands of his or her environment.

balanced scorecard   Using multiple perspectives to evaluate an organization's performance. The behavioral scorecard approach used in the text is based on four performance-related indices: organization outputs, effectiveness, efficiency, and sustainability.

benchmark   A standard against which to evaluate current organization performance and a goal that directs future continuous quality improvement efforts.

benchmarking   A process of comparison.

best practices   Research-based knowledge, professional ethics, professional standards, and clinical judgment applied to people with intellectual and closely related developmental disabilities. Best practices can be characterized by 1) basing services and supports on an ecological model of disability; 2) emphasizing human potential, social inclusion, empowerment, equity, and self-determination; 3) incorporating a systems perspective into an organization's policies and practices; 4) using a system of supports to enhance personal outcomes; and 5) evaluating the impact of services and supports on personal outcomes.

change catalysts   Individuals or processes that bring about change or transformation. The four change catalysts discussed in the text are values, leadership, empowerment, and technology.

change strategies   Techniques that transform and redefine an organization to increase its effectiveness, efficiency, and sustainability. The eight change strategies discussed in the text are using 21st century thinking skills, measuring and using personal outcomes and organization outputs, developing high-performance teams, employing a system of supports, using evidence-based practices, implementing a performance-based evaluation and management system, creating value through innovation, and overcoming resistance to change.

clinical decisions   Decisions about the interventions, services, or supports that clientele receive in specific situations.

clinical judgment   A special type of judgment rooted in a high level of clinical expertise and experience. Clinical judgment emerges directly from extensive data and is based on training, experience, and specific knowledge of the person and his or her environment.

conflict   State of incompatible or opposing attitudes, behaviors, objectives, or goals. As discussed in the text, assertive accommodation is the most effective approach to conflict resolution.

consortia   A combination of agencies working together toward a common purpose and goal. Consortia tend to be composed of disability-related organizations that either formally (through interagency agreements) or informally (through mutual respect) focus their combined efforts on special goals.

construct   An abstract or general idea based on observed phenomena and formed by arranging parts of elements.

constructive engagement   A key component in creating permanent change. Constructive engagement involves both leading by example and empowering personnel to implement innovation or change.

contextual factors   Trends or changes that affect an organization and its service delivery system. Six contextual factors are discussed in the text: a transformation in the culture of professional services, the emergence of new public management, the focus on consumer-driven services and supports, an emphasis on meeting clients' support needs, the continuing need for a stable supply of support staff, and the impact of social media.

continuous quality improvement   Using tacit and explicit knowledge to enhance an organization's effectiveness and efficiency. Tacit knowledge involves the wisdom that comes from personal experience. Explicit knowledge is based on research findings and empirically based information. This knowledge is incorporated into an organization's quality improvement plan, which focuses on changing organization policies, practices, training, and use of technology within the context of the values guiding innovation: dignity, equality, self-determination, nondiscrimination, and inclusion.

critical thinking skills   Cognitive skills that facilitate good decision making and the successful implementation of change strategies. These skills include making distinctions, seeing perspectives and relationships, conducting analysis, evaluation and interpretation, seeing sequential relations and linear relationships, and demonstrating convergent thinking.

developmental disability   A severe, chronic disability of an individual that is attributable to a mental or physical impairment or a combination of mental and physical impairment. A useful way to group individuals with developmental disabilities is based upon 1) cognitive impairments such as metabolic and immune deficiency disorders and chromosomal abnormalities, 2) sensory-neurological impairments such as epilepsy and spina bifida, 3) physical impairments such as cerebral palsy, and 4) emotional-behavioral impairments such as autism or dual diagnosis.

disability   The expression of limitations in individual functioning due to personal and environmental factors. A person's disability occurs within a social context and represents a substantial disadvantage to the individual.

ecological model   A model that explains human functioning as resulting from the interaction of the person with his or her environment. Ecological models focus on providing individualized supports within community settings to enhance human functioning and promote personal outcomes.

effectiveness   The degree to which an organization's intended results are achieved. An organization's effectiveness can be evaluated on the basis of effectiveness indices.

effectiveness indices   Measures of the processes implemented by an organization to produce organization outputs from the perspectives of the customer and the organization's growth (see Table 7.2 and Exhibit 7.1).

efficiency   Producing an organization's planned results in relation to the expenditure of resources. An organization's efficiency can be evaluated on the basis of efficiency indices.

efficiency indices   Measures of the processes implemented by an organization to produce organization outputs from the perspective of the organization's financial and internal processes (see Table 7.3 and Exhibit 7.1).

empowerment   Supporting and enabling a person to gain a sense of competence, relatedness, and autonomy. Empowerment leads to a more positive self-concept, increased motivation, and a heightened reliance on personal resources.

ethics   A set of principles that describe a system of moral behavior and rules of conduct toward others.

evaluation   The process of carefully and systematically appraising the status of performance indicators and studying the impact of independent variables (e.g., client characteristics, systems of support strategies, and/or organization characteristics) on dependent variables (e.g., personal outcomes and organization outputs). The three primary purposes of evaluation are to 1) provide information for data-based decision making and managing for results, 2) provide the data for continuous quality improvement, and 3) determine the significant predictors of personal outcomes and organization outputs.

evaluation capability   An organization or system's ability to assess personal outcomes and organization outputs that can be used for multiple purposes such as reporting, monitoring, evaluation, and continuous quality improvement.

evidence indicators   Measures of personal outcomes and organization outputs.

evidence-based practices   Practices that are based on current best evidence and used as the bases for clinical, managerial, and policy decisions. Current best evidence is information obtained from credible sources that used reliable and valid methods and is based on a clearly articulated and empirically supported theory or rationale. Within the text, evidence-based practices are approached from a systems perspective.

evidence-gathering strategies   Ways to gather evidence at the individual, organization, and societal levels. At the individual level, examples include randomized controlled trials, multiple baseline studies, and single-subject research designs. At the organization level, examples include experimental-control, quasi-experimental, multivariate, and qualitative research designs. At the societal level, examples include meta-analysis, experimental multivariate designs, and consumer surveys.

explicit knowledge   Empirically based information found in books, reports, research articles, and databases.

future consciousness   A way of thinking that allows people to appreciate and see the relevance of linking the past and future, engage in goal-directed thinking, and demonstrate growth and purpose through self-efficacy and self-responsibility.

high-performance teams   Horizontally structured work groups who focus on teamwork, synergy, raising the performance bar, focusing on "us" accountability, and promoting a learning culture. High-performance teams are organized around performing six primary functions: assessment; individual supports plan development, implementation, and monitoring; data gathering, processing, analysis, and reporting; outcomes evaluation; continuous quality improvement; and crisis management. They are characterized by being involved, informed, organized, accountable, and empowered.

human functioning   An umbrella term referring to all life activities of an individual. A multidimensional model of human functioning involves five dimensions (intellectual abilities, adaptive behavior, health, participation, and context) and a focus on the key role played by individualized supports.

human performance technology   Enhancing human functioning by reducing the mismatch between the person and his or her environment through the use of strategies related to organization systems, incentives, cognitive supports, tools, the physical environment, skills and knowledge acquisition, and building on inherent ability.

ID/DD   Intellectual and developmental disabilities.

individual supports plan (ISP)   The integration of assessed support needs with individualized support strategies based on a system of supports, support objectives, and desired personal outcomes.

individual supports plan (ISP) process   A logical, sequential, and transparent process for developing, implementing, monitoring, and evaluating the use of best practices and evidence-based practices to enhance personal outcomes.

innovation   Something new. The major ingredients of innovation are creativity and a learning culture.

intellectual disability   A disability characterized by significant limitations in both intellectual functioning and in adaptive behavior as expressed in conceptual, social, and practical adaptive skills. This disability originates before age 18.

intellectual functioning   A broader term than either intellectual abilities or intelligence. The term reflects an understanding that what is considered intellectual behavior is dependent on the other dimensions of human functioning: the adaptive behavior one exhibits, the person's mental and physical health, the opportunities to participate in major life activities, and the context within which people live their everyday lives.

interpretation guidelines   Guidelines used to evaluate the quality, robustness, and relevance of evidence.

ISP   see Individual support plan.

leadership functions   The critical roles and functions performed by an organization's leadership. Roles include mentoring and directing, coaching and instructing, inspiring and empowering, and collaborating and partnering. Functions involve: communicating a shared vision, encouraging and supporting the power of personal mastery, stressing a systems perspective that focuses on the major factors influencing a person's behavior, promoting a community life context; emphasizing the essential role of organizations as bridges to the community, monitoring and using personal outcomes and organization outputs, and ensuring the transfer of knowledge throughout the organization.

learning culture   An organization's commitment to growth and development, mentoring, integrating tacit and explicit knowledge, and encouraging learning and doing by all personnel.

long-term impacts   Benefits to the program participant that extend beyond the immediate effects of an intervention. Long-term impacts are typically reflected in an individual's socioeconomic position, health, and subjective well-being.

managerial decisions   Decisions about the strategies used by an organization to increase its effectiveness, efficiency, and sustainability.

managerial strategies   The strategies that are essential to implementing a performance-based evaluation and management system. These are leadership style, 21st century thinking styles, performance-based evaluation and management system, high-performance teams, and evidence-based practices.

mental models   Deeply ingrained assumptions, generalizations, and images used to understand the world. Mental models form the vision and culture of an organization.

monitoring   At the organization level, monitoring is an oversight and interactive process that has four primary purposes: 1) to demonstrate compliance with the organization's policies and practices, 2) to ensure that the input, process, and outcome/output service delivery components are in place and functioning as anticipated, 3) to provide benchmarks for self-comparisons, standards for evaluating current organization performance, and goals that direct quality improvement efforts, and 4) to ensure the precision, accuracy, and integrity of the information that is used for reporting, monitoring, evaluation, and continuous quality improvement. The monitoring of performance indicators is the basis for performance management. At the individual level, monitoring ensures that the individual supports plan is developed on the basis of personal goals and assessed support needs and employs a system of supports to enhance personal outcomes.

networking   Partnering among private companies, nonprofit organizations, and public entities to achieve a common goal. Governance by network represents the confluence of four trends: third-party government, joined-up government, the digital revolution, and consumer demands.

open system   A way of thinking in which organizations view themselves as bridges to the community and use the resources of the community including generic agencies, social networks, and natural supports.

operationalize   To define a construct on the basis of how it is observed and measured.

organization outputs   Organization-referenced products that result from the resources a program uses to achieve its goals and the actions implemented by an organization to produce these outputs. Organization outputs are assessed via a broader class of performance indicators that include personal outcomes, effort and efficiency indicators, staff-related measures, program options, and network indicators (see Table 3.4 and Exhibit 3.2).

organization services   Services provided or procured for an organization's clientele; which include community living alternatives, employment and education options, community-based activities, transportation, and professional activities.

paradigm   The constellation of beliefs and techniques that reflect an approach to an issue and provide a pattern or example. Currently, there are four major paradigms: That affect ID/DD organizations quality-of-life concept, the ecological model of disability, a system of supports, and the reform movement. Each of these has emerged in response to doubts and difficulties with previous approaches and the social, political, and economic changes that have occurred during the later part of the 20th century and the first decade of the 21st century.

performance-based evaluation and management system   A systematic approach to measuring performance-related indicesv and using that information for performance evaluation, performance management, and continuous quality improvement. A performance-based evaluation and management system is based on three performance-related indices: those related to the organization's outputs, effectiveness, and efficiency.

performance-related indices   Measures of organization outputs from the perspectives of the customer, the organization's growth, the organization's financial processes, and the organization's internal processes.

personal outcomes   The benefits derived by program recipients that are the result, direct or indirect, of program activities, services, and supports. Within the text, personal outcomes are related to quality-of-life domains and measurable indicators associated with each domain.

policy decisions   Decisions regarding strategies for enhancing an organization's effectiveness, efficiency, and sustainability.

program logic model   A graphic model that articulates the operative relationships among a program's inputs, processes, and outcomes/outputs. A program logic model: 1) identifies critical indicators to monitor, evaluate, and use for multiple purposes, 2) specifies the core processes that can become the targets for quality improvement, 3) clarifies for stakeholders the sequence of events from inputs through short-term effects and long-term impacts, and 4) provides a fuller understanding of the factors that affect an organization's performance. The components of the prototypic program logic model used in the text are targeted individuals, provider system, contextual variables, individual support strategies, organization services, personal outcomes, organization outputs, and long-term impacts.

quality assurance   A monitoring and evaluation process that guarantees basic assurances in the areas of health, safety, and continuity. Increasingly, quality assurance is based on a conceptualization and measurement framework that includes personal outcomes and organization outputs.

quality improvement strategy   A systematic approach to enhancing an organization's effectiveness and efficiency. The four components involved in developing a quality improvement plan are specifying targeted areas, measurable goals, and specific quality improvement strategies; providing a rationale for why the strategies employed will logically enhance the targeted area(s) and, thus, facilitate goal achievement; identifying the responsibility center, role of leadership, and empirically based evidence to determine the effectiveness of the strategy; and stating the values that will govern the process.

quality management   Management strategies that focus on organizational performance indicators and valued personal outcomes.

quality of life   A multidimensional phenomenon composed of core domains influenced by personal characteristics and environmental factors. These core domains are the same for all people, although they may vary individually in relative value and importance. Assessment of quality-of-life domains is based on culturally sensitive indicators.

quality-of-life domains   The set of factors that constitute personal well-being. The set represents the range over which the quality-of-life concept extends and, thus, defines a life of quality.

quality-of-life indicators   Quality of life–related perceptions, behaviors, and conditions that give an indication of the person's well-being. The assessment of quality-of-life indicators provides measures of personal outcomes.

redefined intellectual and developmental disability (ID/DD) organization   An organization characterized by being community based, horizontally structured, support coordinators, evidence-based practitioners, knowledge producers, and quality improvement oriented.

redefining   Transforming and/or changing an organization so that it is more effective, efficient, and sustainable. Redefining involves the eight change strategies discussed in the text.

reliability   The measurement consistency of a test, assessment instrument, or assessment process.

reporting   Describing key variables associated with an organization's service delivery system and giving an account of measurable personal outcomes and organization outputs. The major purpose of reporting is to communicate descriptive information to multiple stakeholders.

resource allocation   How the various resources (e.g., time, money, expertise, experience, technology) are used within an organization to produce enhanced personal outcomes and organization outputs.

right-to-left thinking   A two-phase process: 1) identifying components of quality services and supports and/or desired personal outcomes and 2) asking what needs to be in place for these phenomena to occur.

service delivery framework   Systems-level conceptual and measurement framework used by jurisdictions to implement public policy. Two frameworks are increasingly being used:

The World Health Organization's (WHO) [2001] International Classification of Functioning, Disability, and Health model of disability, and the concept of quality of life. Either framework is implemented through the supports paradigm.

short-term effects   Changes in personal outcomes that result from an organization's services and supports. Short-term effects result either directly or indirectly from the resources a program uses to achieve its goals.

support needs   A psychological construct referring to the pattern and intensity of supports necessary for a person to participate in activities linked with normative human functioning. Support needs are assessed in reference to major life activity areas and to the individual's exceptional medical and/or behavioral support needs.

support objectives   Provision-oriented objectives related to the procurement or provision of a needed support. Support objectives, which are distinct from behavioral objectives that focus on client behavior and/or achievement, focus on the activities of support staff who provide or procure the specific support.

supports   Resources and strategies that aim to promote the development, education, interests, and personal well-being of a person and enhance his or her functioning. Services are one type of support provided by professionals and agencies.

sustainability   To keep up, prolong, and nourish. Sustainability reflects the organization's ability to adapt and change and, thus, provide a range of sound service delivery opportunities and practices.

sustainability index   A measure of the organization's strengths and limitations in reference to its effectiveness and efficiency. An organization's sustainability index is obtained by summing the effectiveness and efficiency indices obtained on the Organization Effectiveness and Efficiency Indices Scale (Exhibit 7.1). The sustainability index can be interpreted from the perspective of the customer, the organization's growth, the organization's financial processes, or the organization's internal processes.

synthesis   The integration of information from multiple sources to improve the precision, accuracy, and validity of a decision or practice. Synthesis involves the critical thinking skills of analysis, evaluation, and interpretation.

system of supports   An approach to the provision of individualized supports. The system is based on a standardized assessment of the pattern and intensity of support needs and involves the implementation of individualized support strategies that include policies and practices, cognitive supports (assistive and information technology), skill acquisition strategies, environmental accommodation, incentives, prosthetics, positive behavior supports, natural supports, professional services, and organization- and system-level policies. A system of supports model aligns the supports provided to the person's assessed support needs and provides a structure for the organization to enhance human performance elements that are interdependent and cumulative. A system of supports provides three essential functions in a redefined organization: 1) it organizes potential support strategies into a system through which individualized supports can be planned and implemented according to the individual's assessed support needs; 2) it provides a framework for coordinating the procurement and application of individualized supports across the sources of support; and 3) it provides a framework for evaluating the impact of individualized supports on the individual's functioning level and personal outcomes.

systems approach   Integrating into one's thinking and actions the three systems that affect human functioning: the individual, the organization, and society.

systems change   Changes in how an organization or system provides services and supports. Systems change is typically monitored on the basis of trends in measured performance indicators.

systems thinking   Focusing on the multiple factors that affect human functioning and organization performance. Systems thinking reflects the critical role played by the micro-, meso-, and macrosystems and employs the critical thinking skills of distinctions, perspectives, and relationships.

tacit knowledge   The wisdom that comes from personal experience. Tacit knowledge refers to the skills, information, and ways of working that people acquire and includes feelings about values, norms, and expectations. Tacit knowledge is sometimes referred to as intuition.

technology   Instruments or strategies used to enhance personal outcomes and organization outputs. In reference to personal outcomes, assistive and information technology are used in providing a system of supports to reduce the discrepancy between a person's capabilities and his or her environmental demands. In reference to organization outputs, information technology is used to implement a performance-based management system to collect, upload, analyze, download, and summarize personal outcomes and organization outputs.

thinking errors   Faulty reasoning that negatively affects one's clinical, managerial, or policy decisions.

validity   The ability of a test, assessment instrument, or assessment process to measure what it was designed to measure.

values   Properties of an entity or phenomenon that are desirable, important, and of worth. Values form the basis of mental models. Values-based policies include dignity, equality, empowerment, self-direction, nondiscrimination, and inclusion.

wisdom   An evolving process of learning and transformation that allows one to understand the challenges facing him or her and to see how everything is interconnected. Wisdom allows people to understand and explain what is important, ethical, and meaningful.

Index

Tables, exhibits, and figures are indicated by *t, e,* and *f,* respectively.